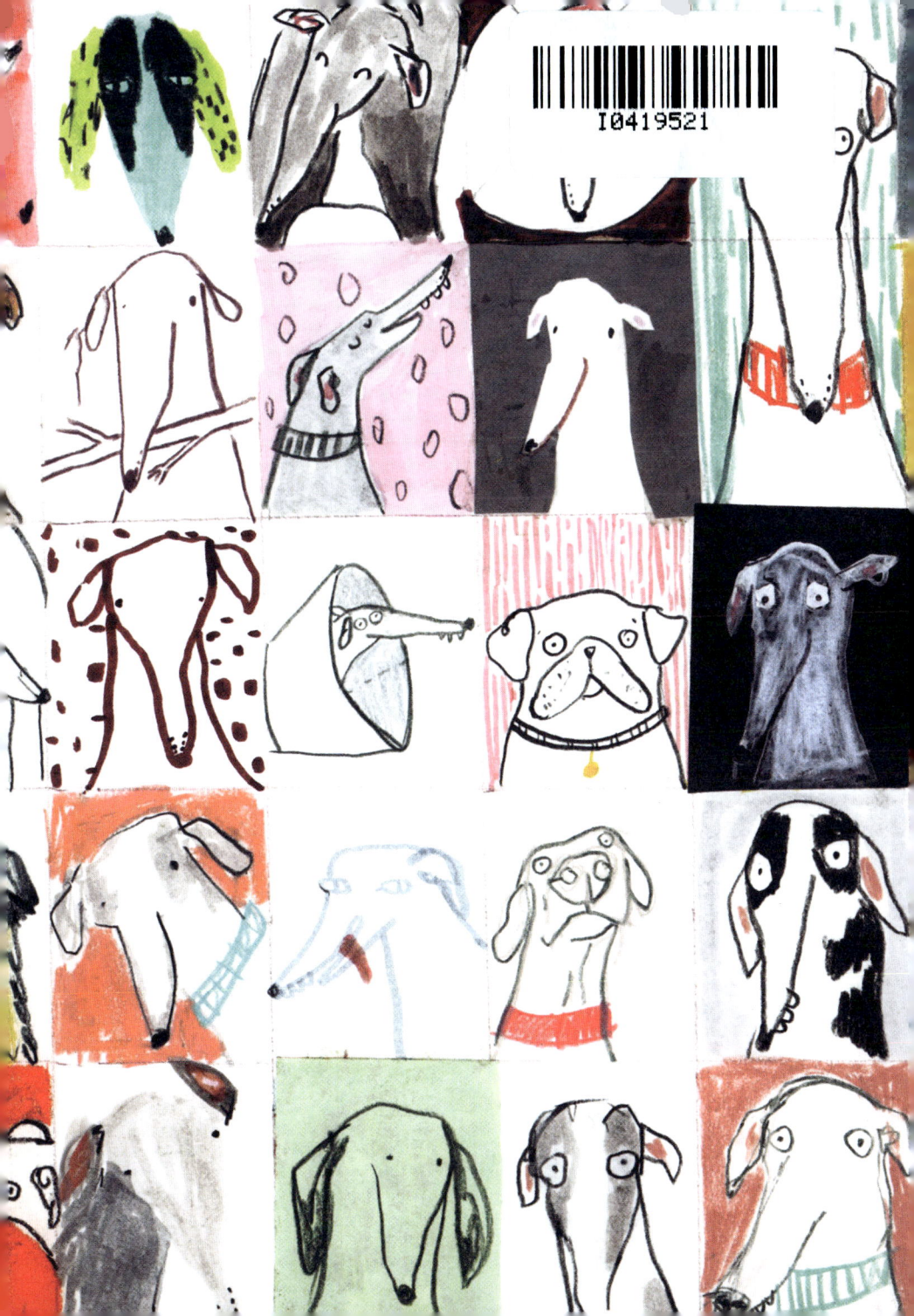

TELL YOUR DOG I LOVE THEM

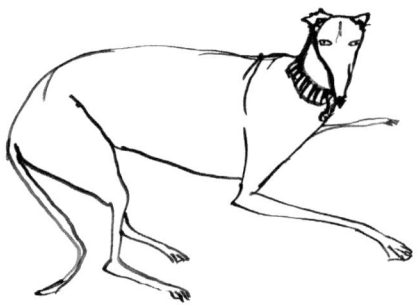

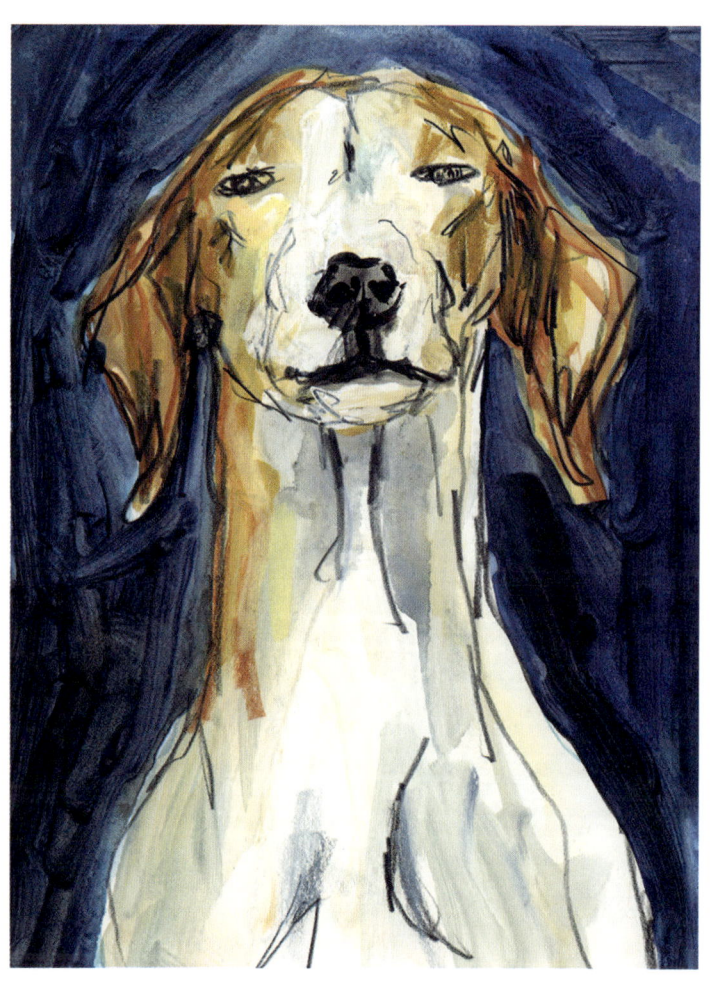

TELL YOUR DOG
I LOVE THEM

Harriet Lowther

F
FRANCES
LINCOLN

INTRODUCTION

I remember my grandad's dog, Sinbad. I think he was a smooth-haired Collie. I would put the hoop he loved so much around my ankle and let him drag me around the house squealing. I hope it was as fun for him as it was for me.

The first dog of our own was called Pepper, a Welsh Springer Spaniel whom I took my first steps with. I recall pestering my mum to let us have two more dogs, which we would call 'Salt' and 'And'. Pepper was a wonderful dog, and she adapted incredibly well after losing her sight due to diabetes. We moved from the Isle of Man to England, and she coped brilliantly, only walking into something once before figuring out where everything was. She was great, and I think about her a lot.

It's hard not to love dogs, especially after growing up with them. When I became an adult (which I still refuse to accept most days), I longed for a dog of my own. Working in a band took me overseas for weeks at a time, so there was never a good time to bring a dog into our family. As some sort of not-at-all-like-having-a-dog-of-my-own 'compromise', I began to draw dogs while travelling. Using a gnarly biro, I scrawled dogs on the backs of boarding passes and itineraries while waiting at airports and hotels. These drawings were ropey, created without intent or an expectation to make anything 'good'. It was just nice to make something, anything. Little did I know, this was the start of Made By Harriet.

As the years passed and we were at home more often, I kept my eyes peeled for rescue dogs needing a home. I'd already fallen in love with sighthounds; they'd become a firm favourite in my early drawings. I frequently visited local greyhound rescue centres, and although I was not at all looking for a puppy, it felt a little serendipitous when Doughnut popped up after being abandoned at three days old with his mum and seven siblings.

I imagined life with a dog who went everywhere with me. I imagined life with a dog who loved all other dogs. I imagined life with a dog who was desperate for my love and affection, just as I would be for theirs. In reality, Doughnut is none of those things. He's a guardian dog, part Anatolian Shepherd. And while he will accompany us to places, he doesn't love it. And that's okay. He doesn't cuddle on the sofa or sleep on the bed, or demand love and affection, and that's also okay. We connect in so many other ways. He is reactive, so walks involve lots of doubling back and darting behind parked cars, which doesn't make for the most fun outing, but that's okay too. He is wonderful and unique and I love him all the more for it.

As time went on, my drawings progressed. I'm reluctant to use the word 'improved', as there is so much onus put on art and creativity being 'good' or 'bad'. As a result, we can quickly disregard and devalue our own creations. Having the desire to create is precious, and it is all too easy to deem something as 'not good enough'. I'm telling you that if it warms your heart, keep making, keep creating and keep putting it out there. I've learnt so much more from every single 'bad' drawing than I ever will from something classed as 'good'.

In the past, I have taken on briefs which resulted in me changing how I make drawings. I've also turned down work that didn't feel right or authentic. It's taken me a long time to reach a point where I know how to create work which makes my heart sing. When Frances Lincoln reached out to me and pitched a book of my work, without a set brief or theme, or trying to change who I am and how I work, it was the perfect partnership. This book shows you my raw, unfiltered, unstructured work, exactly how I make it. I hope you love this little book, as much as I love dogs.

Harriet x

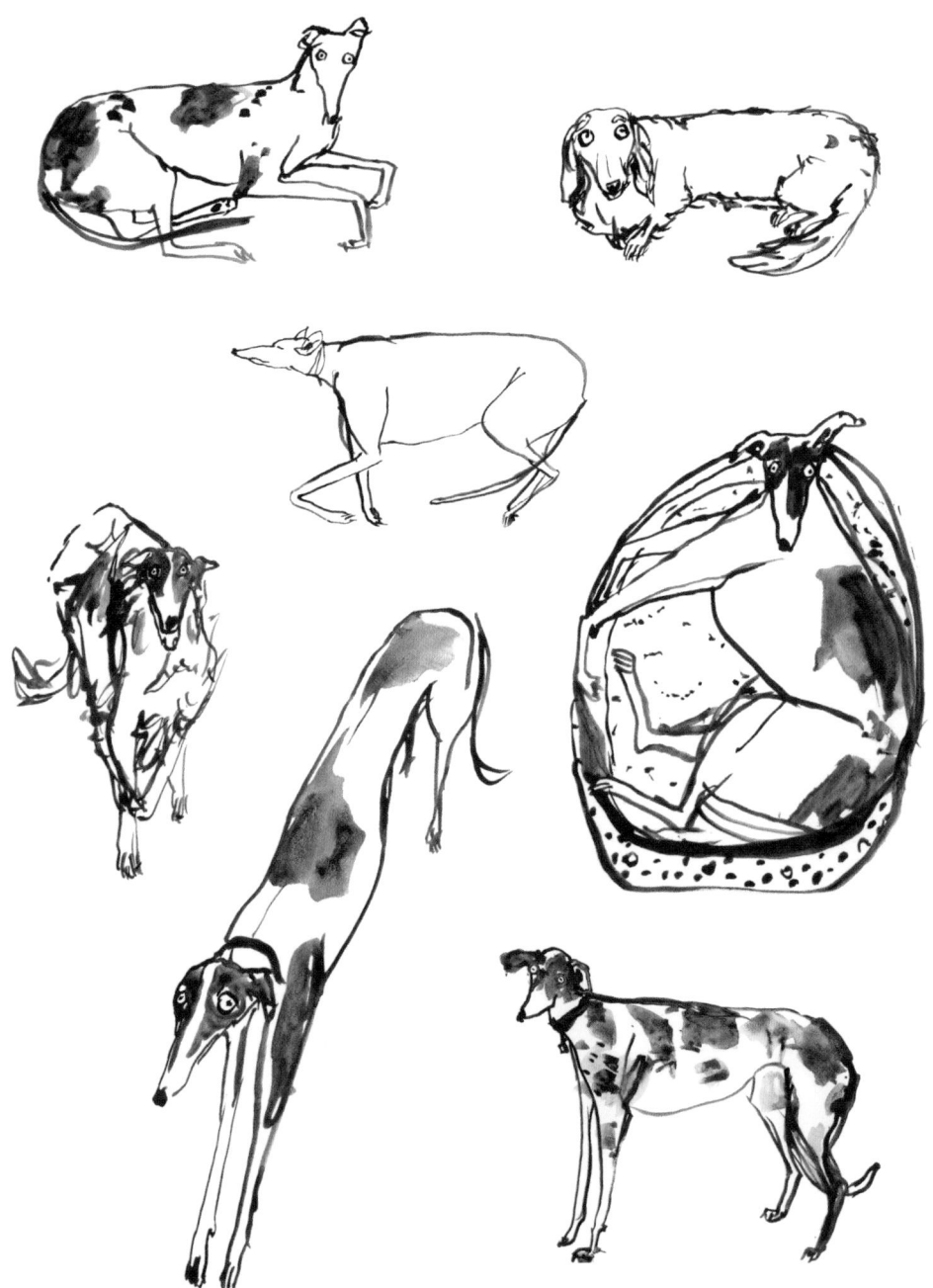

6

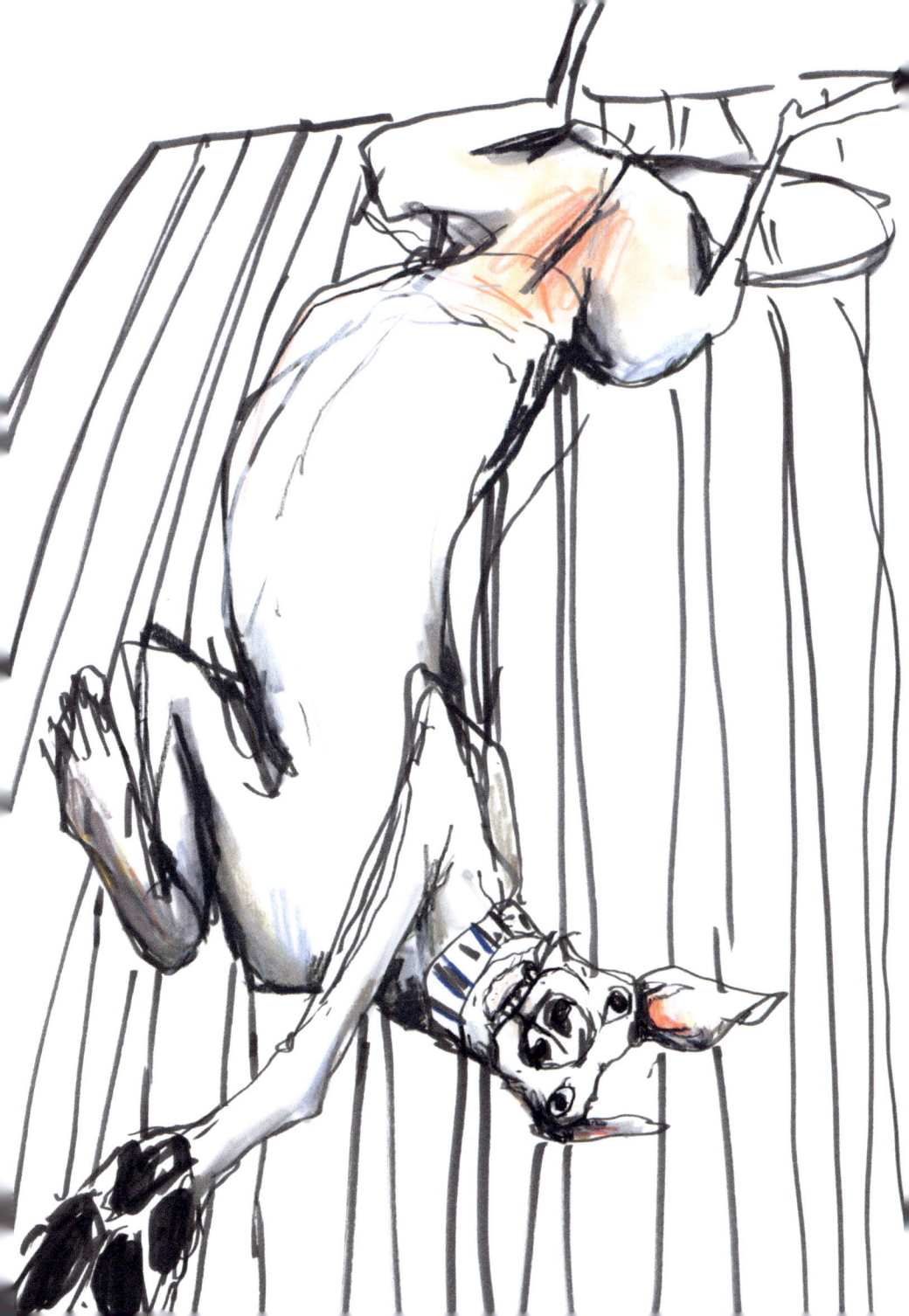

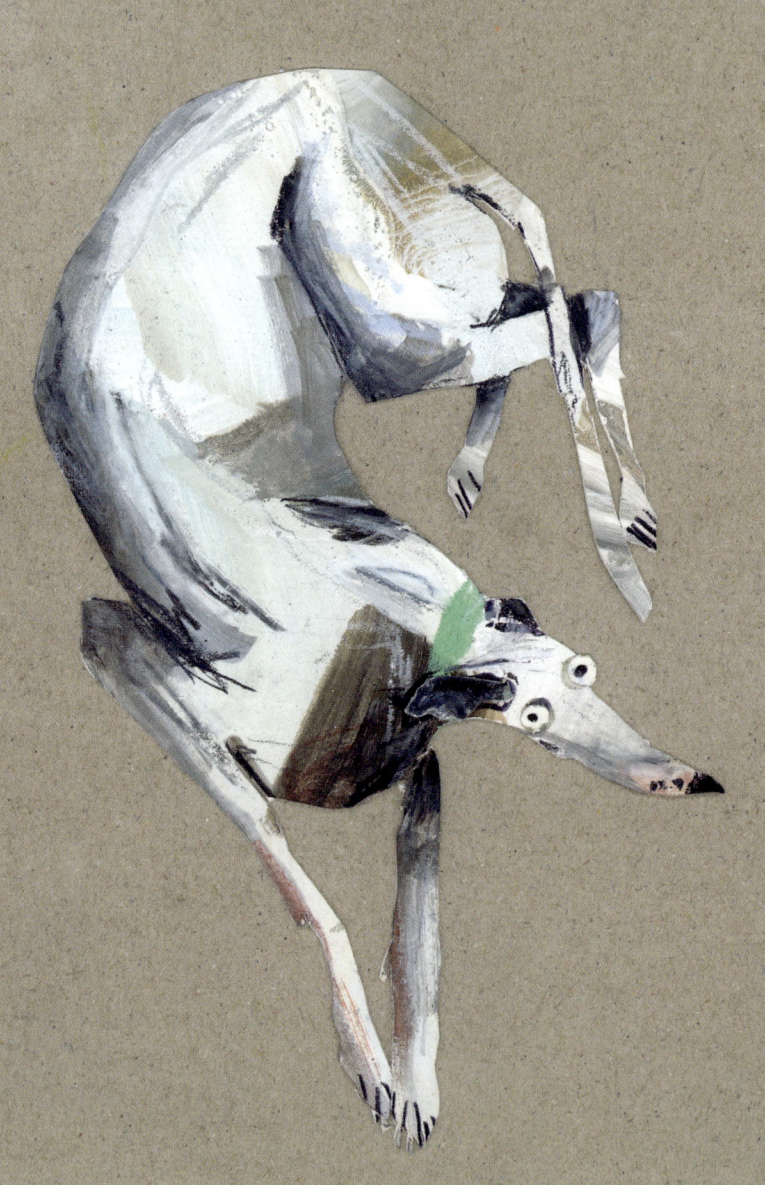

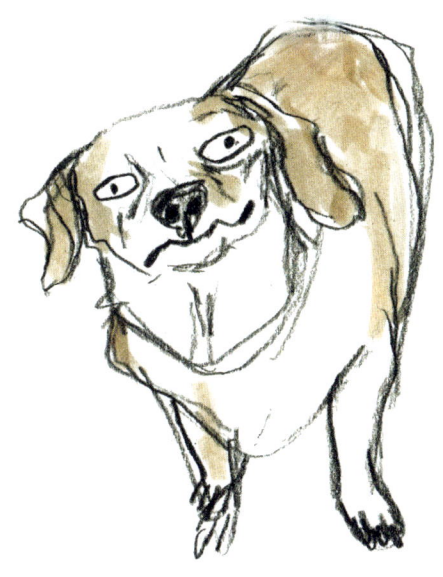

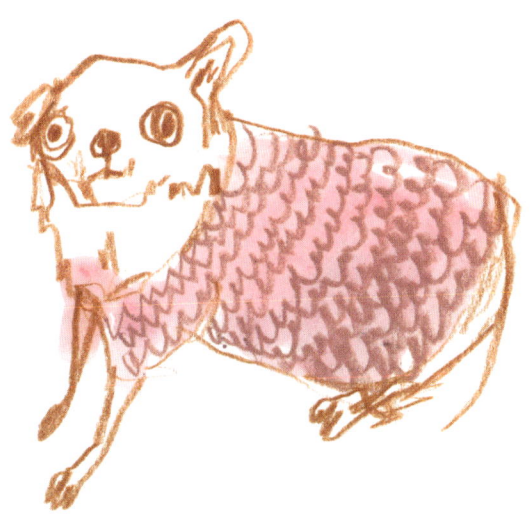

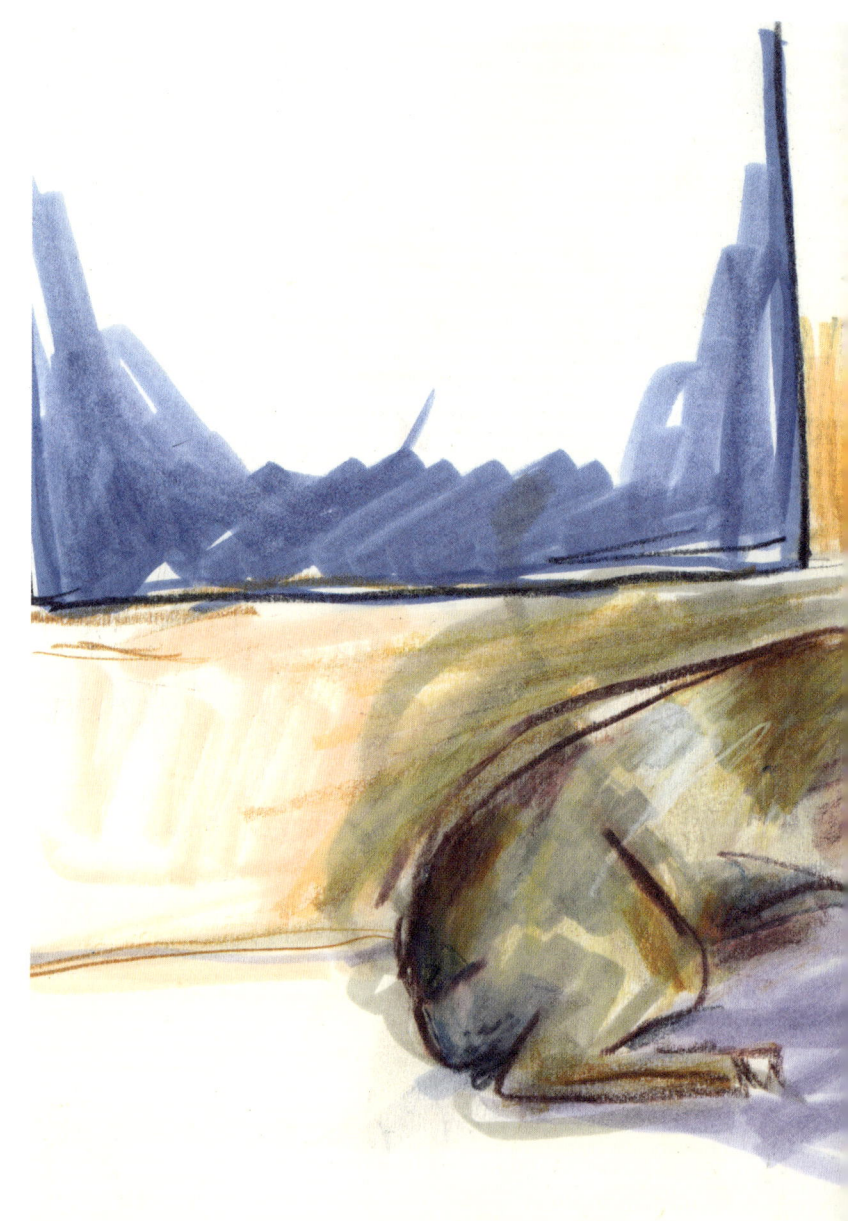

You have been gone for

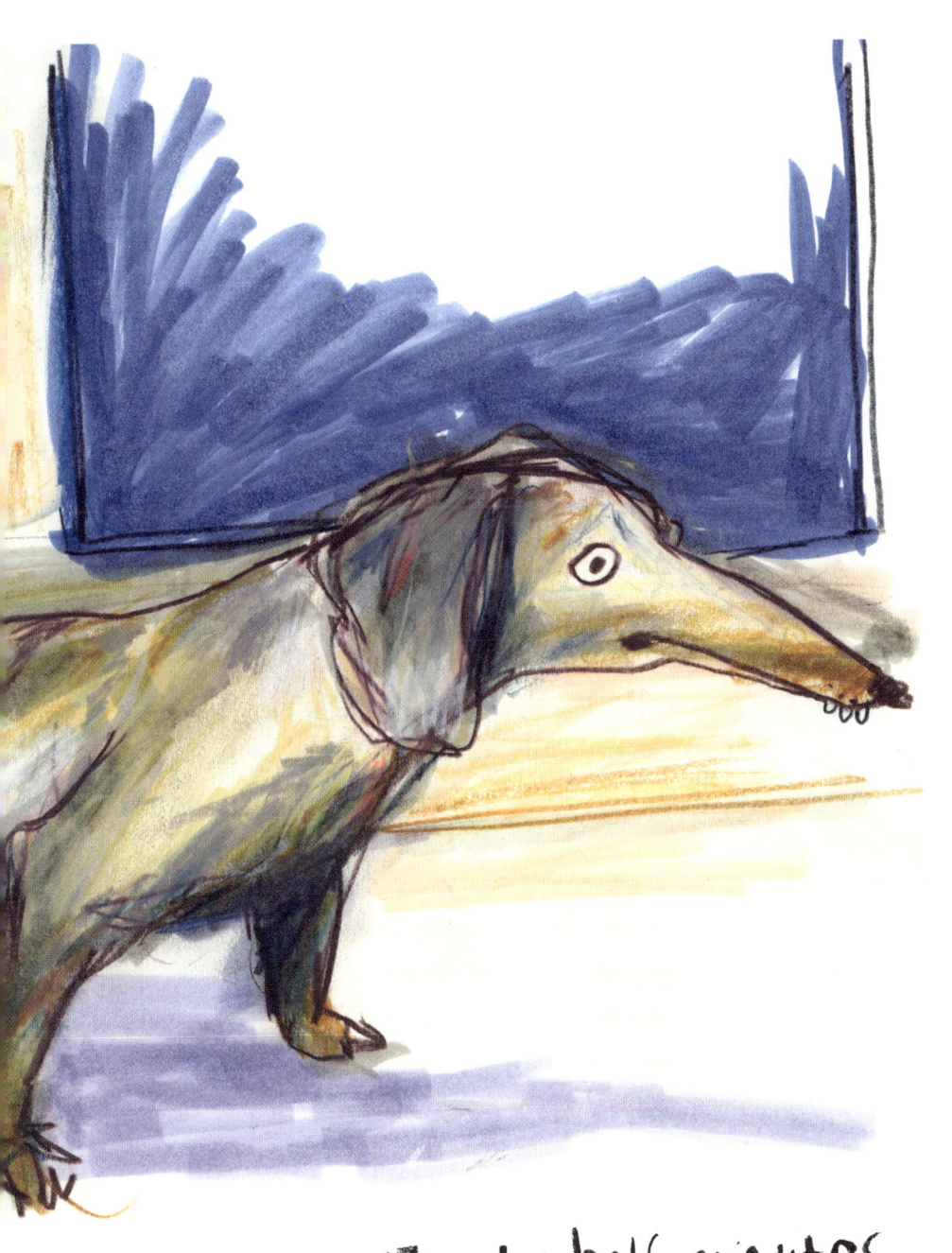

13 and a half minutes

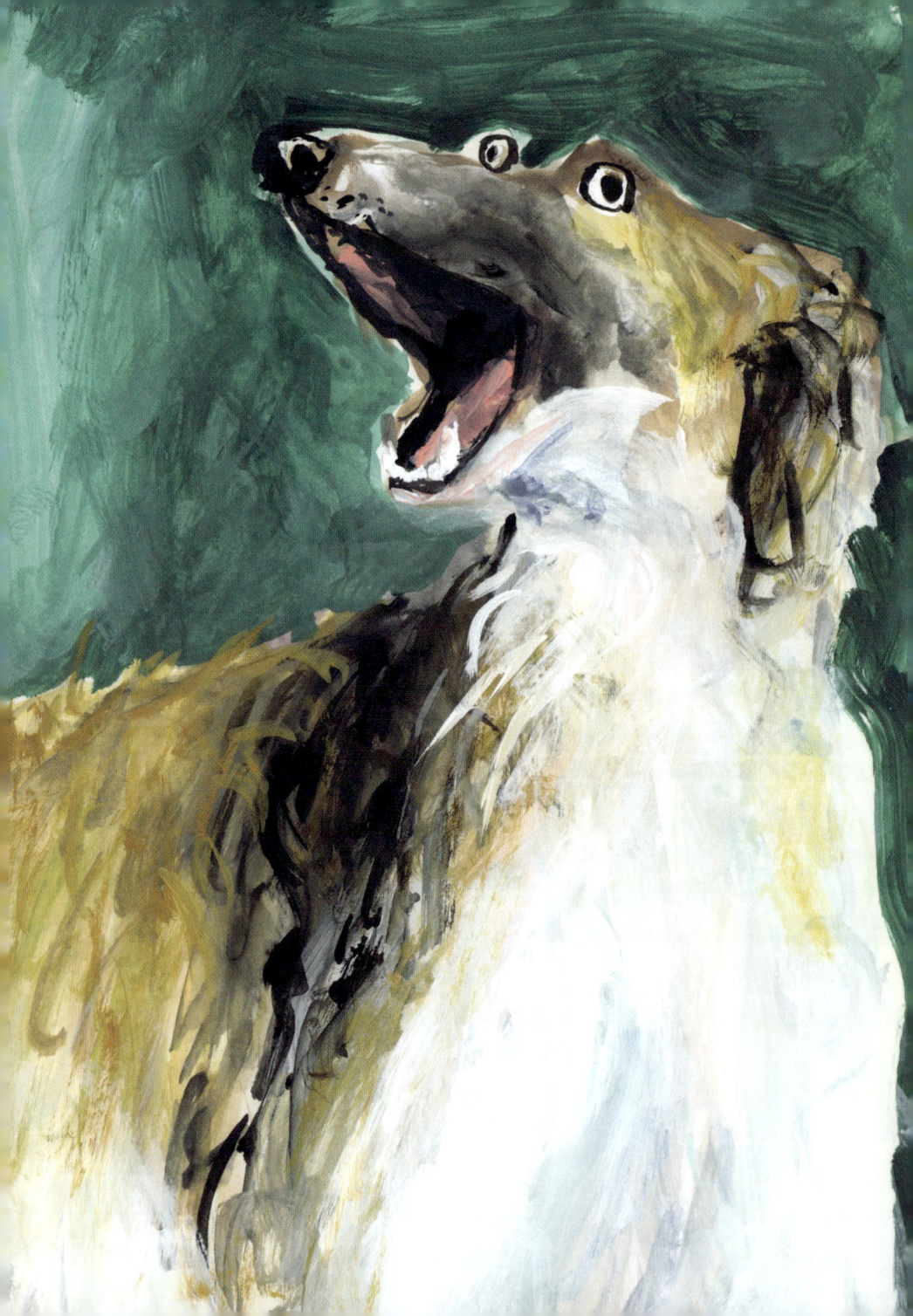

Ooh! me! me! I've got it!
I'm getting it!
Let me get it

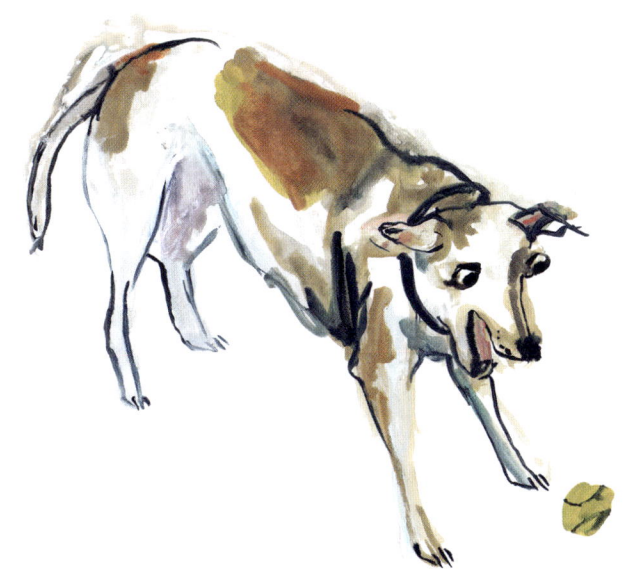

Mine.

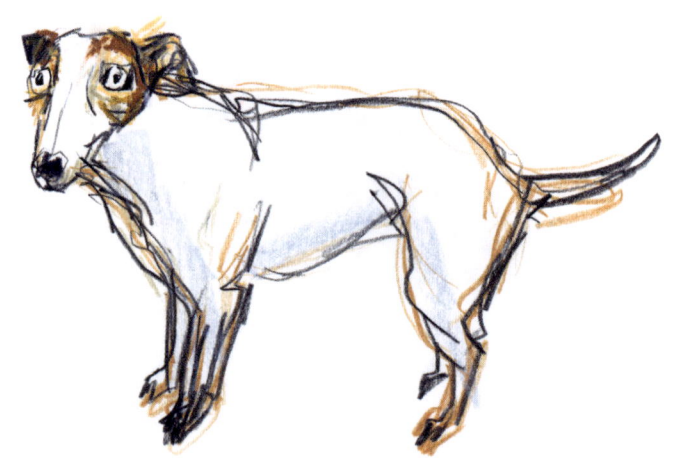

ANXIOUS

14

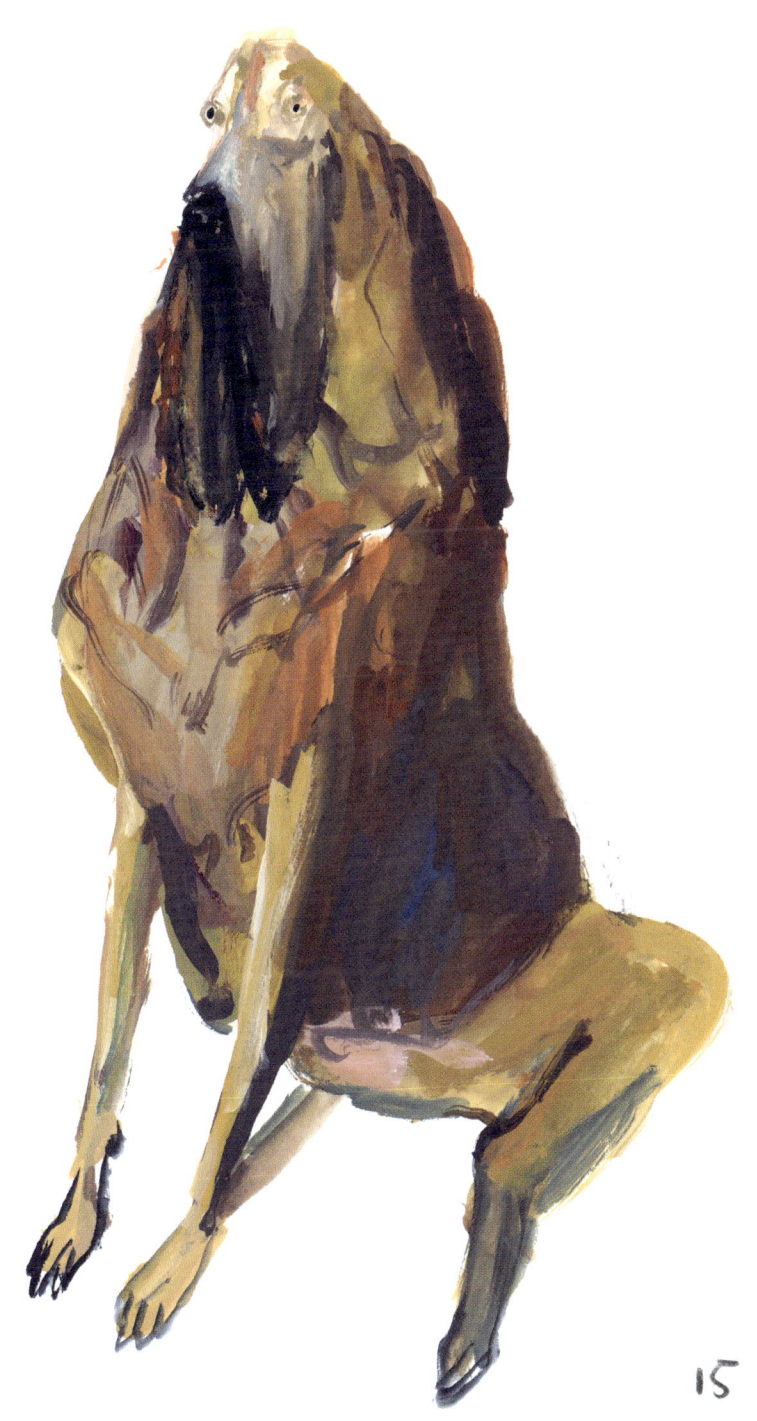

15

I like you

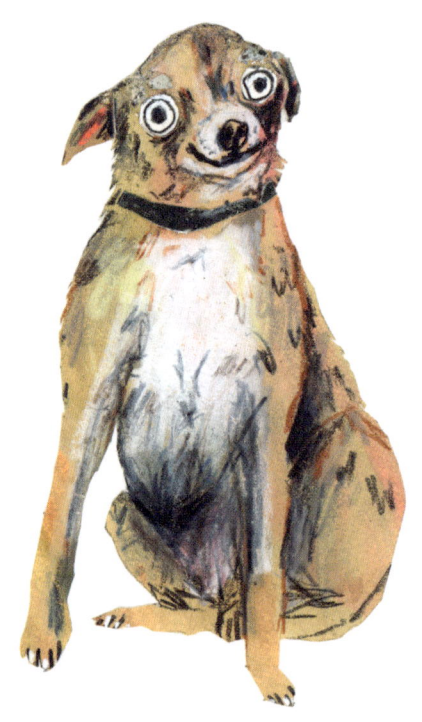

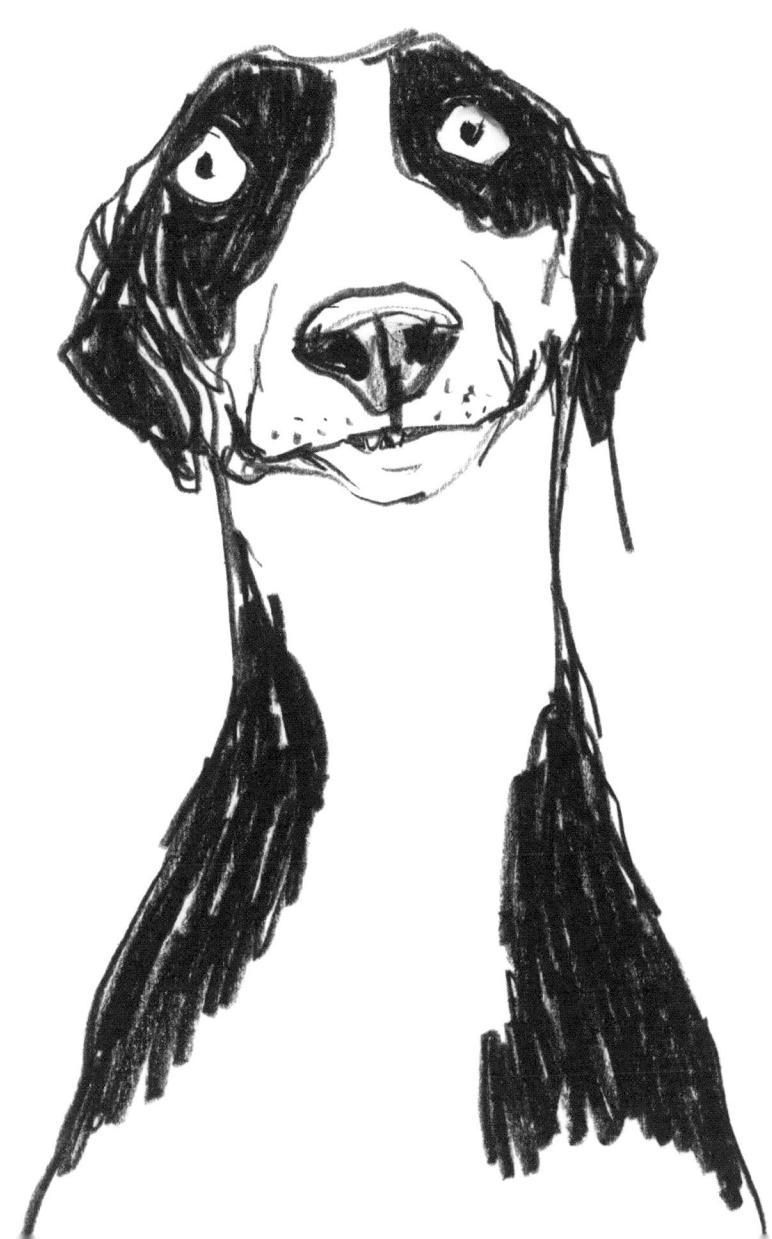

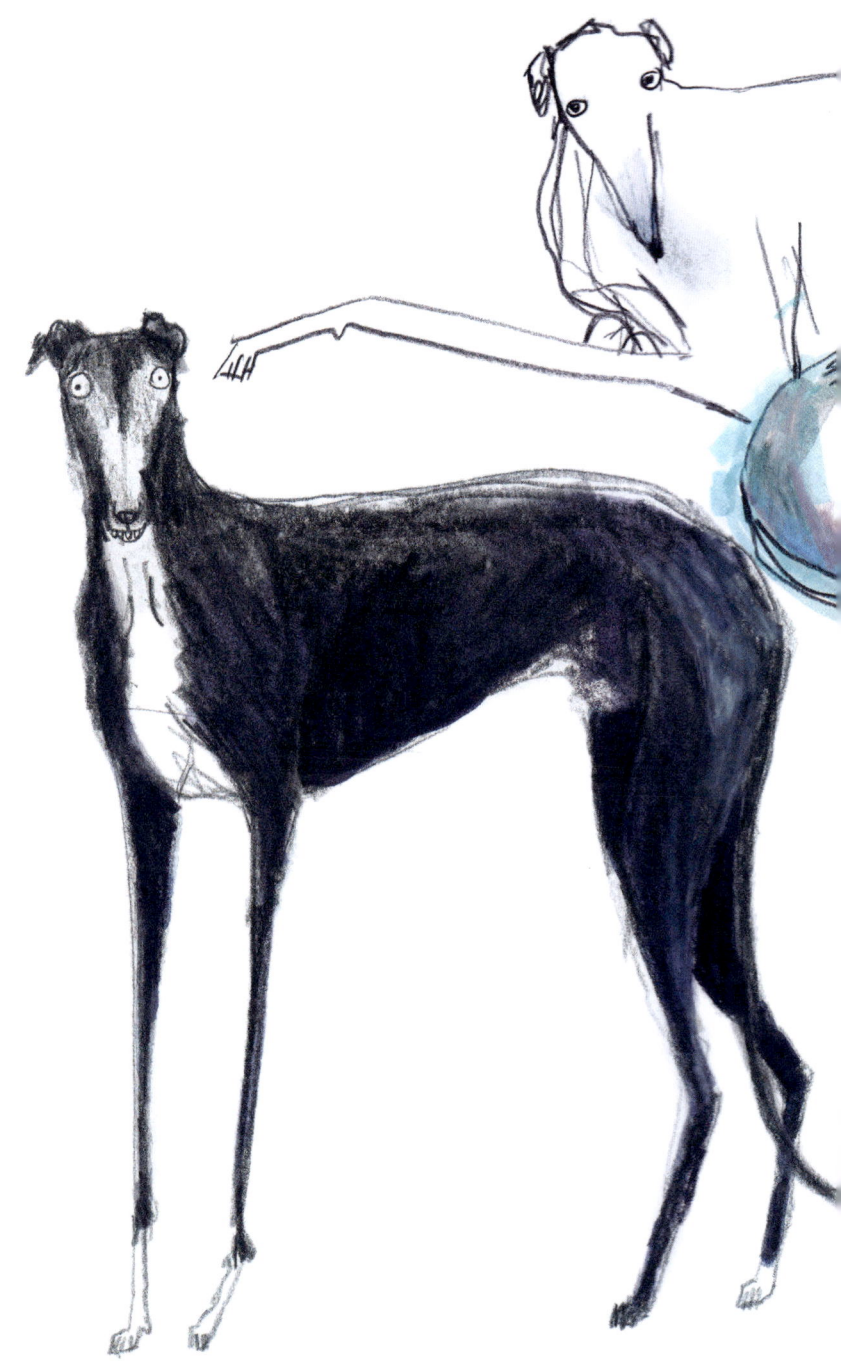

18

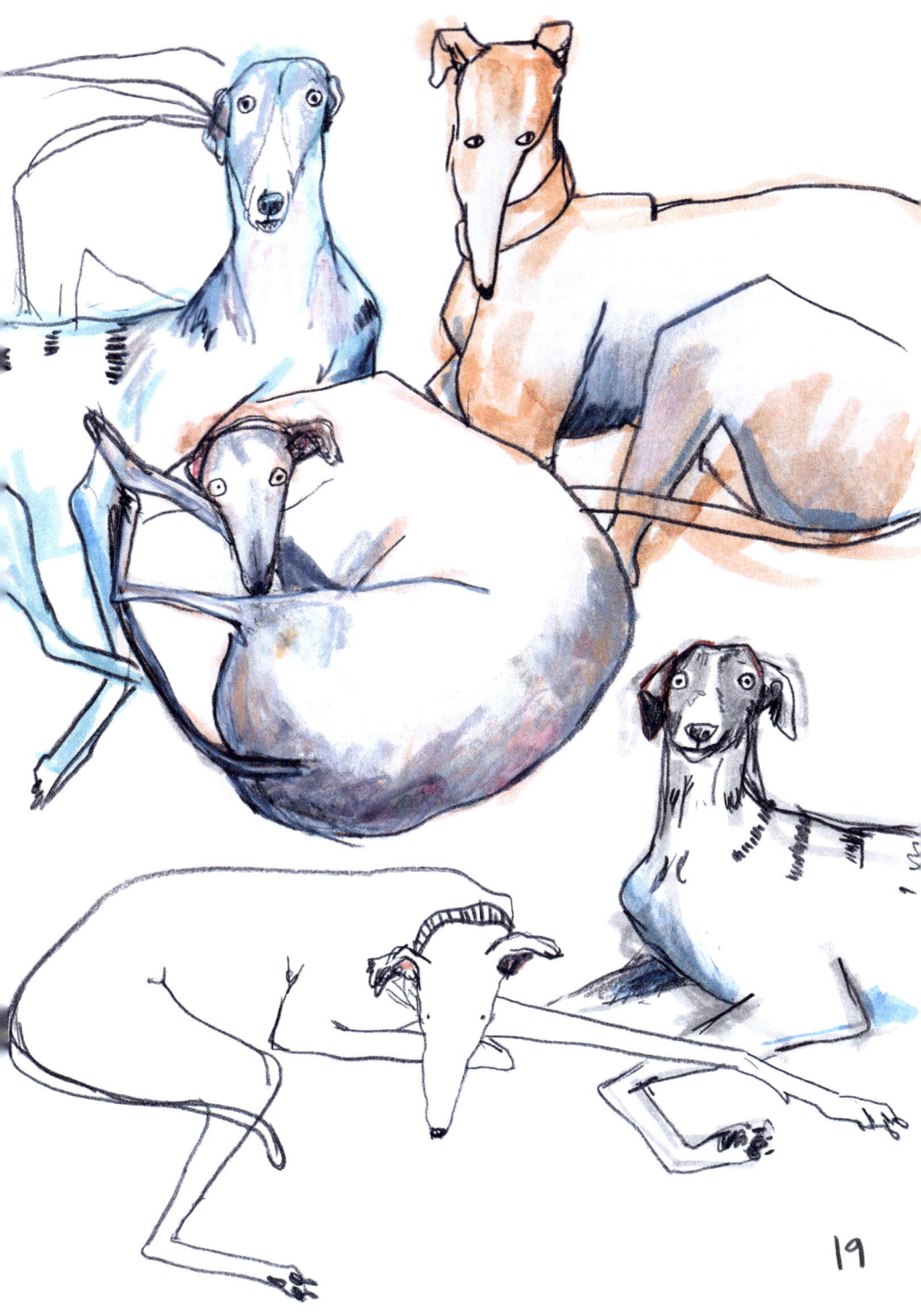

19

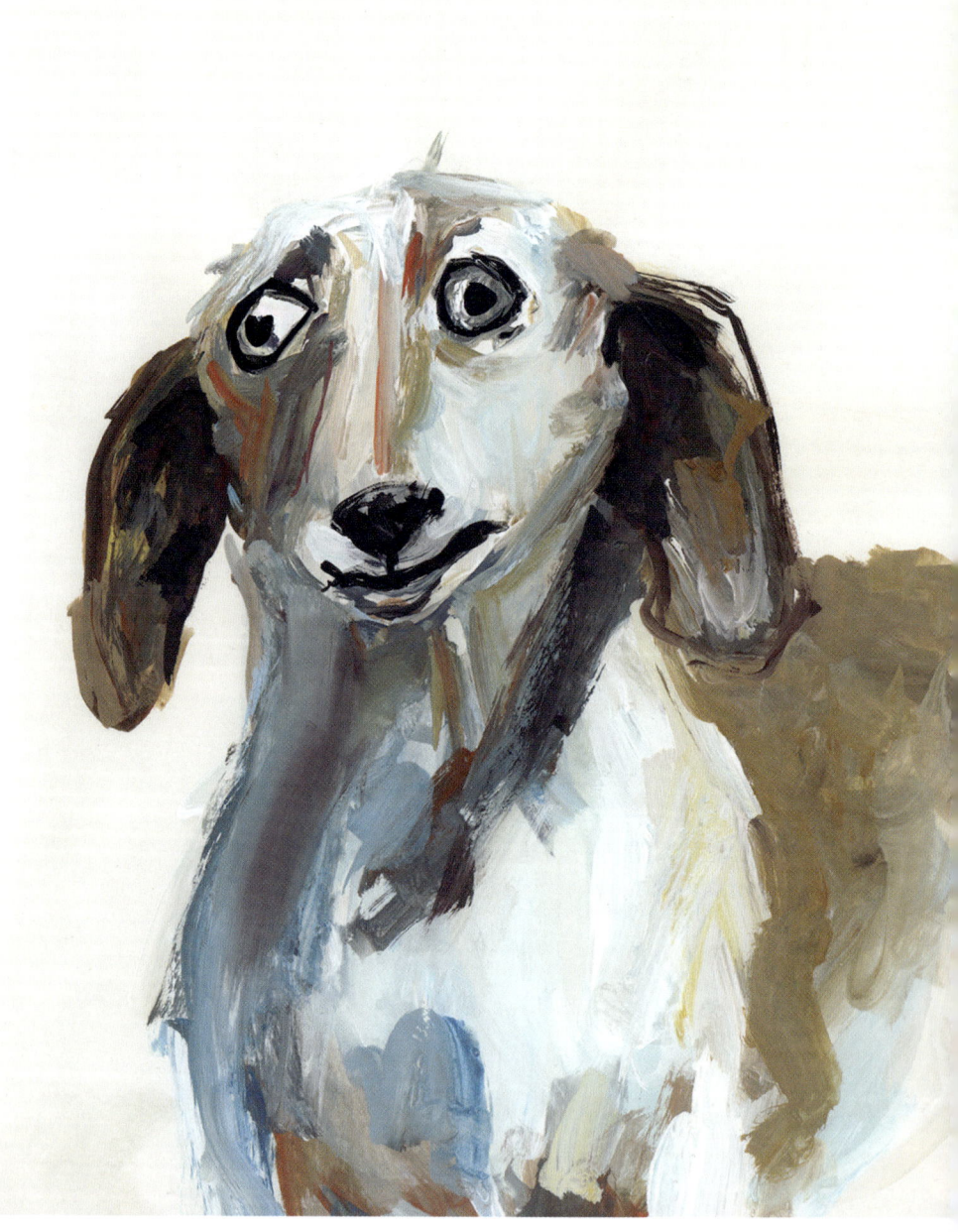

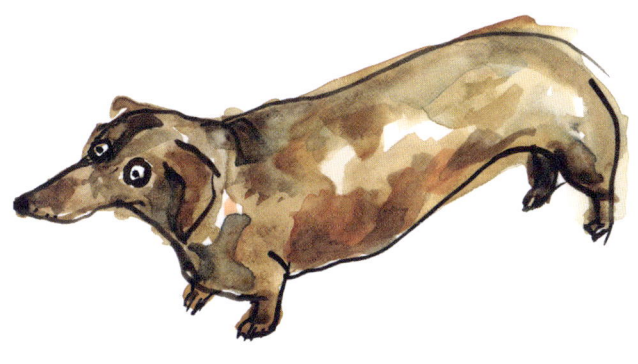

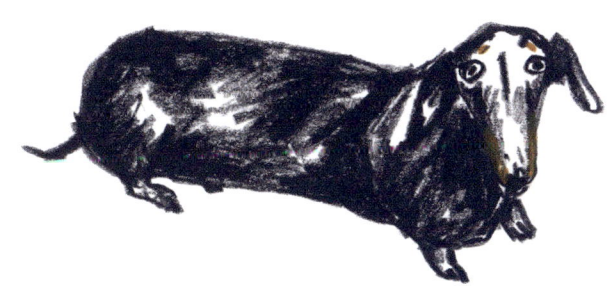

two sausages

21

FLOOF

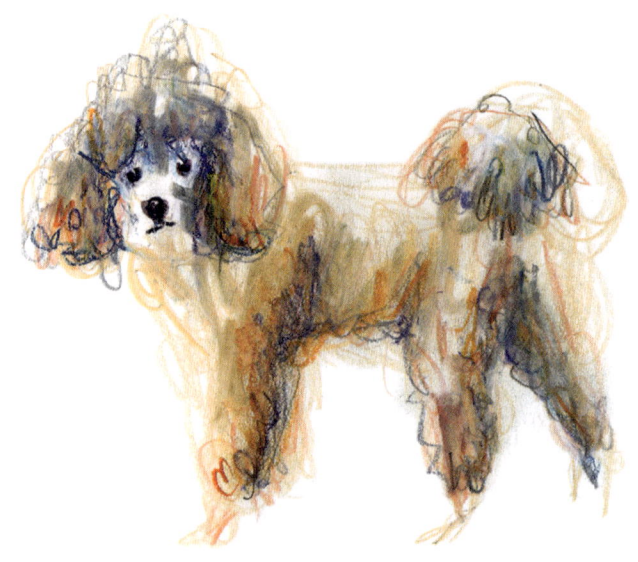

SO MUCH FLOOF.

22

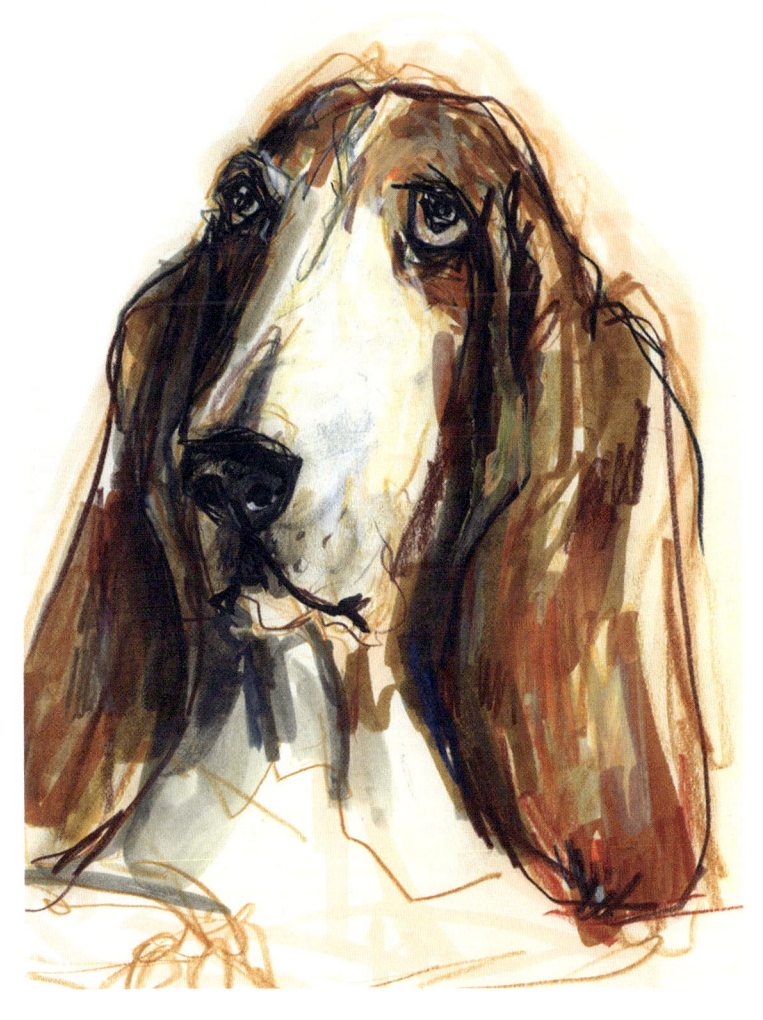

23

I do
<u>not</u>
like
bathtime.

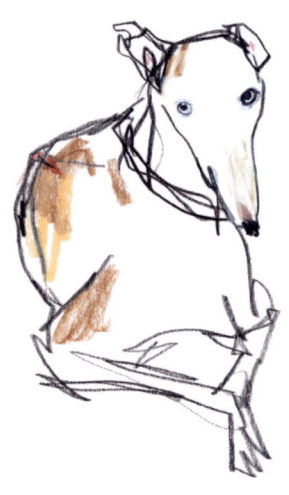

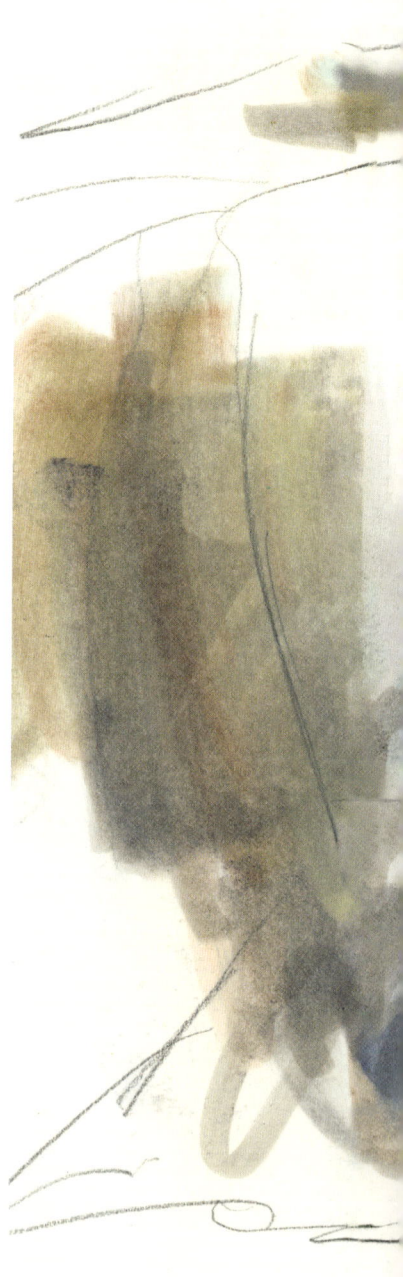

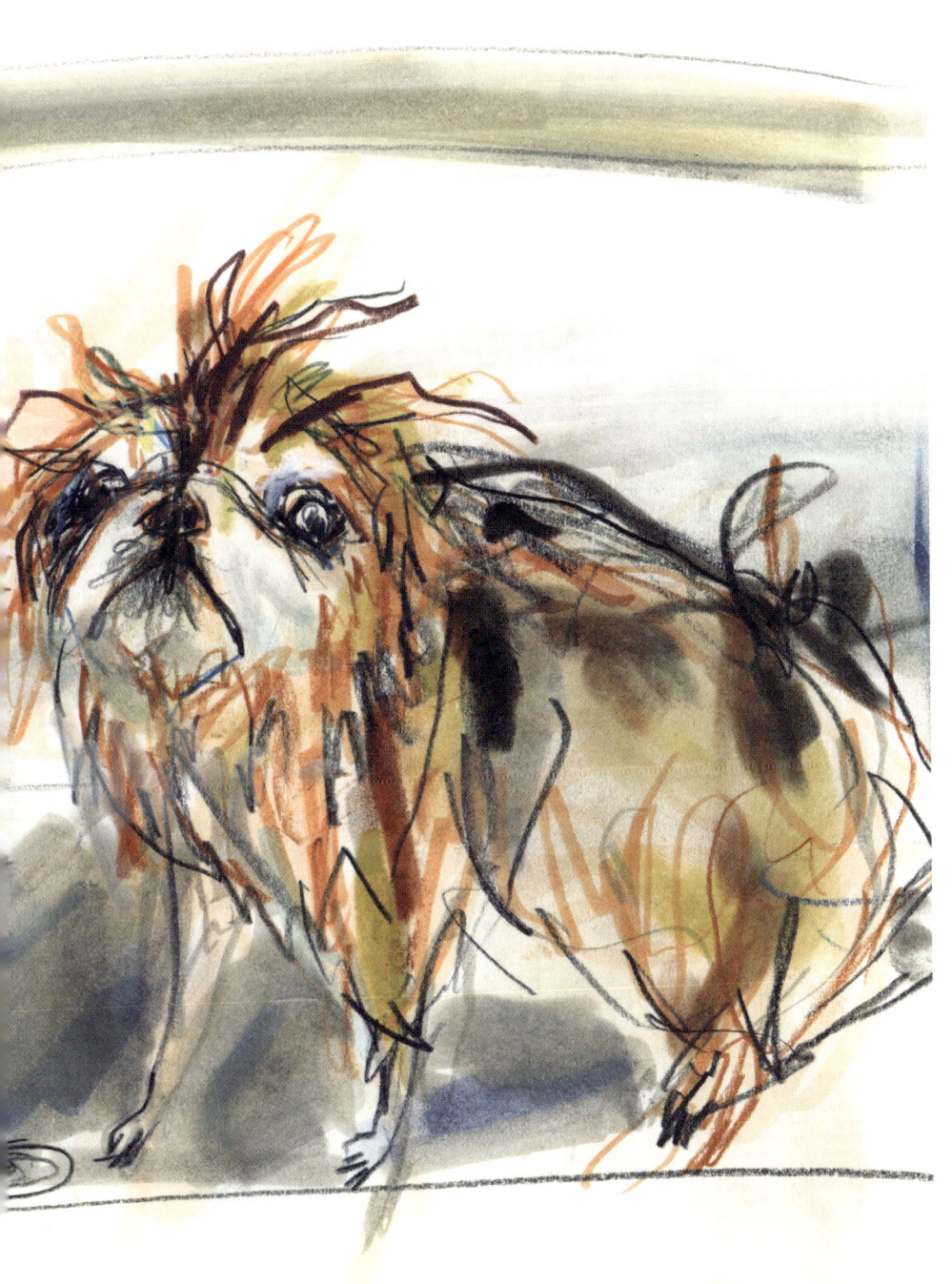

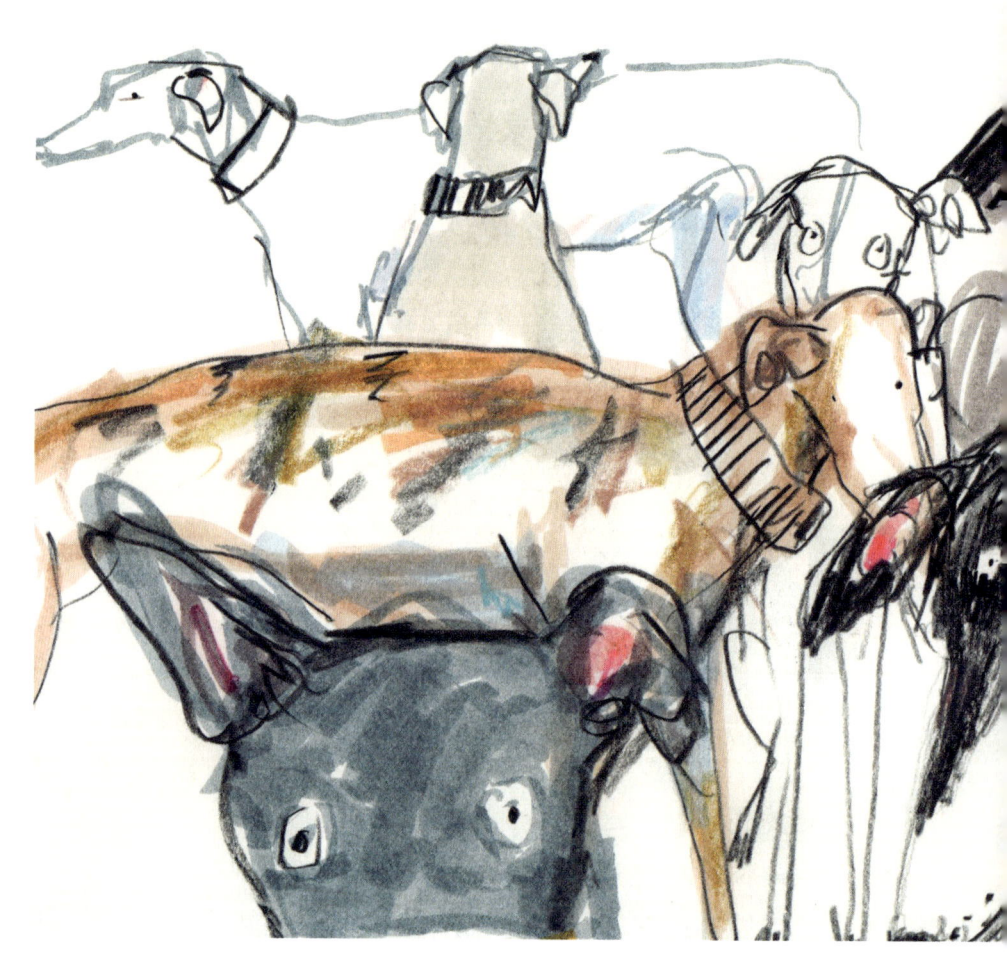

Existential

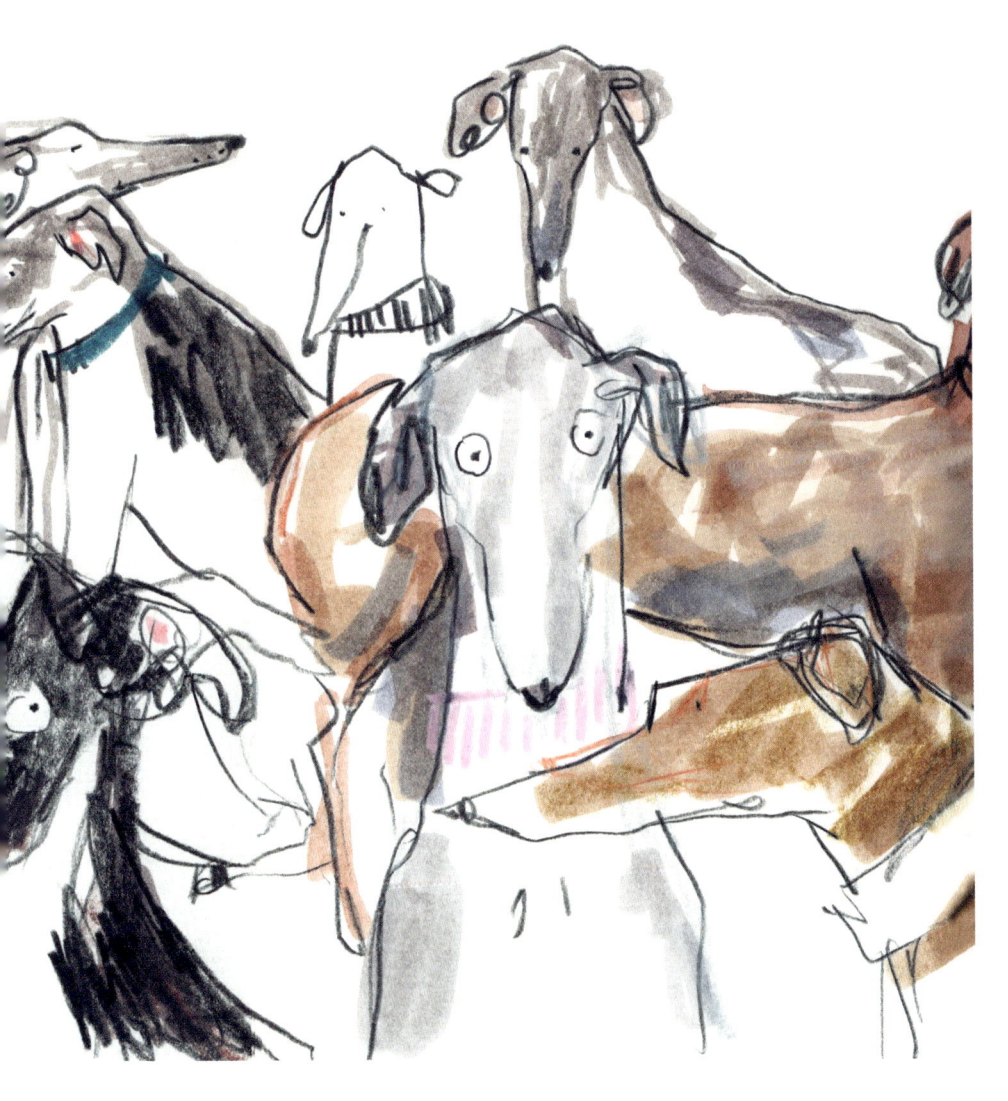

crisis

come CLOSER

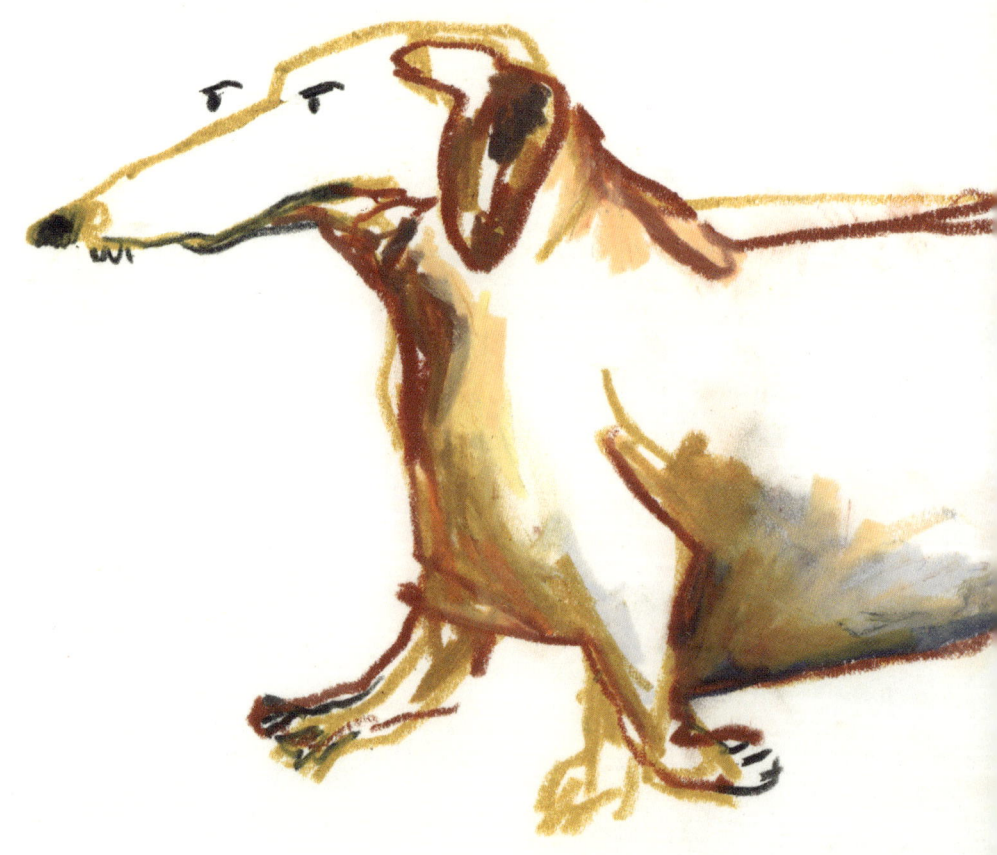

SO I CAN

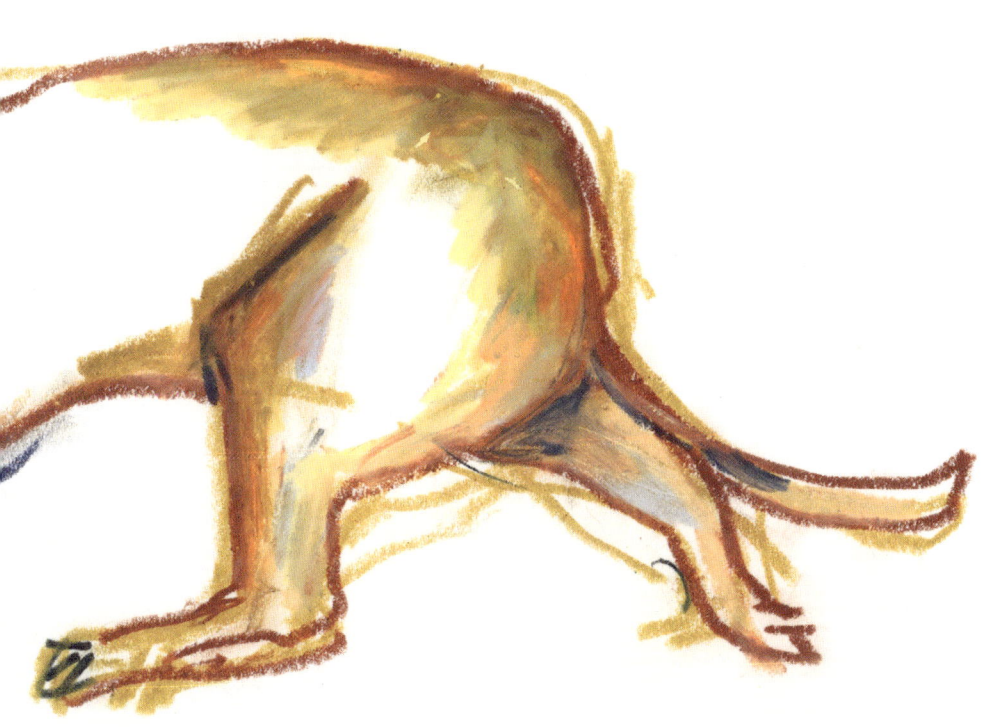

SMELL YOU

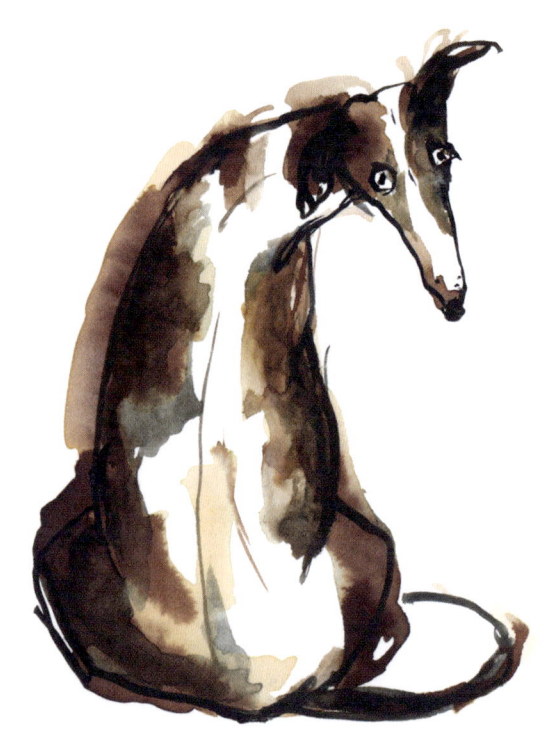

Can I help you?

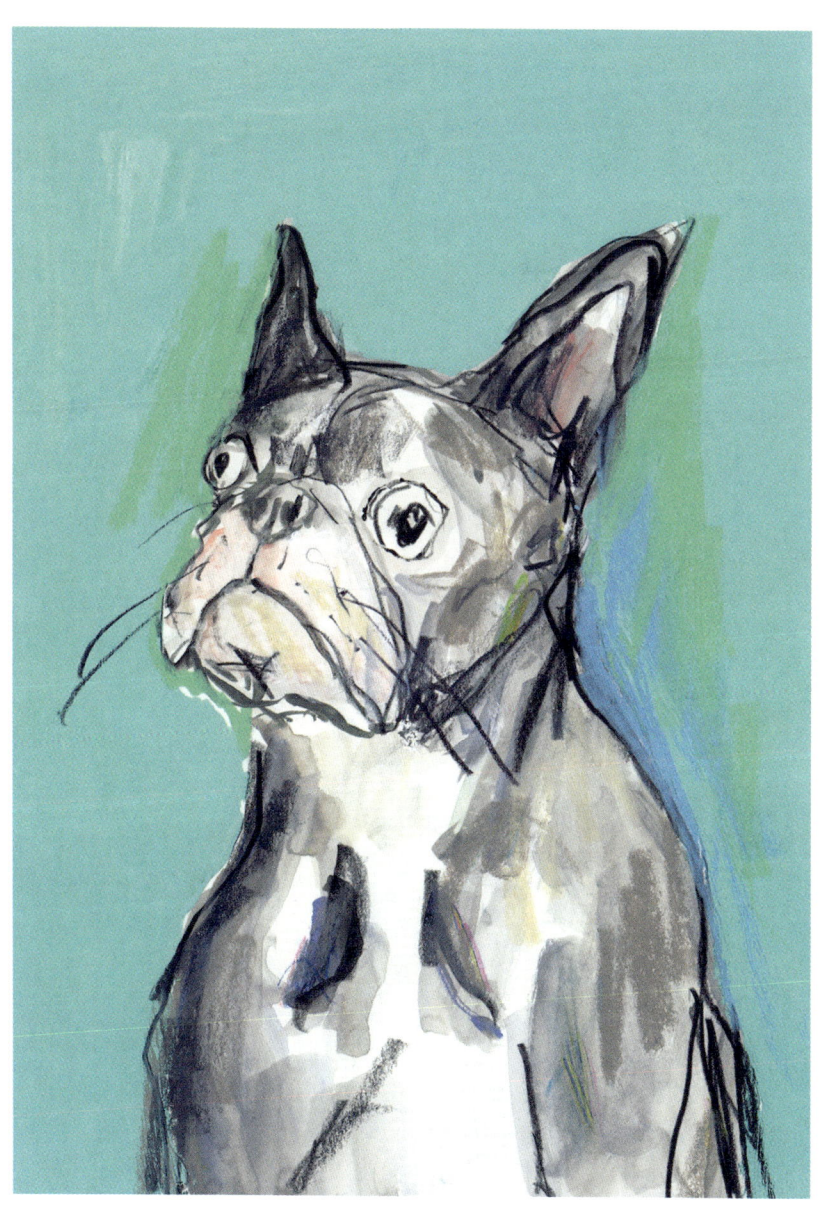

31

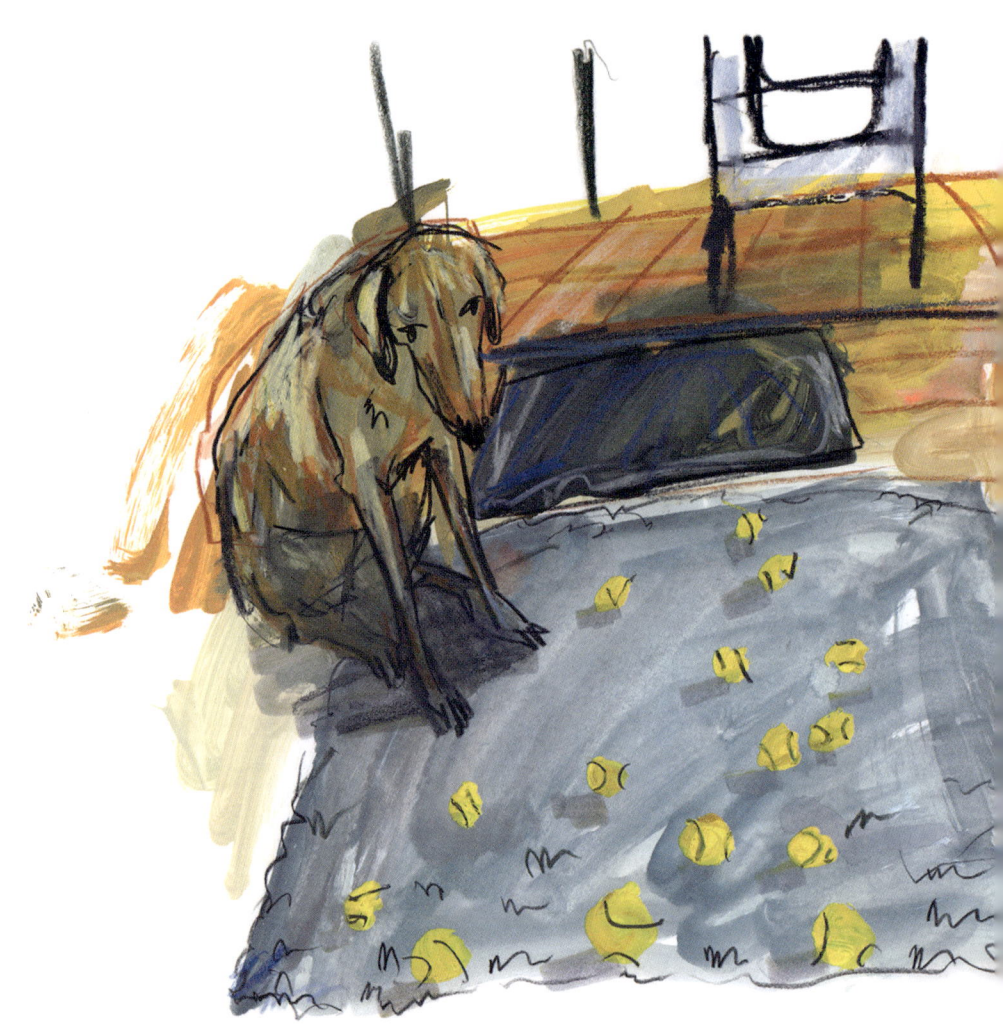

choices

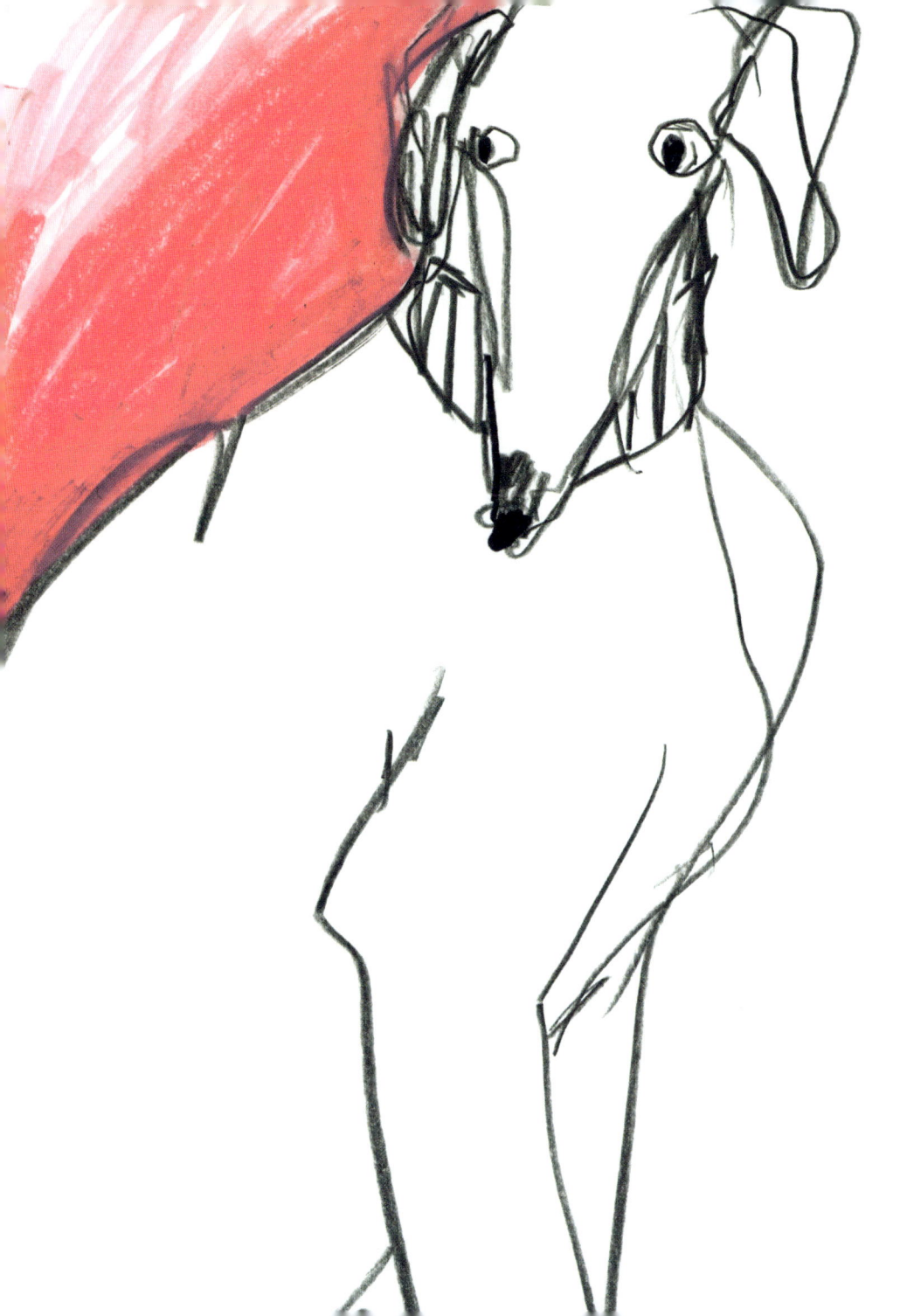

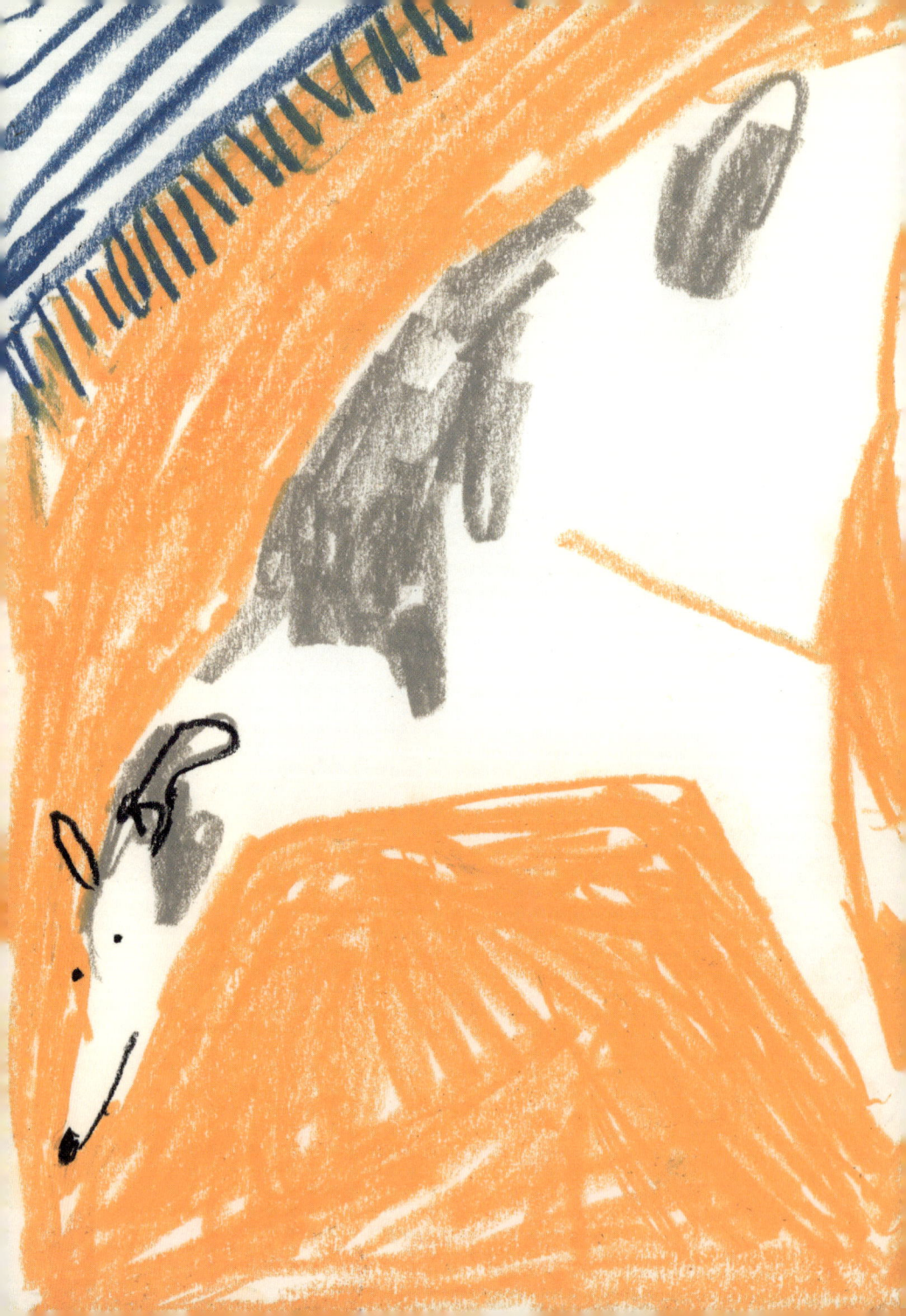

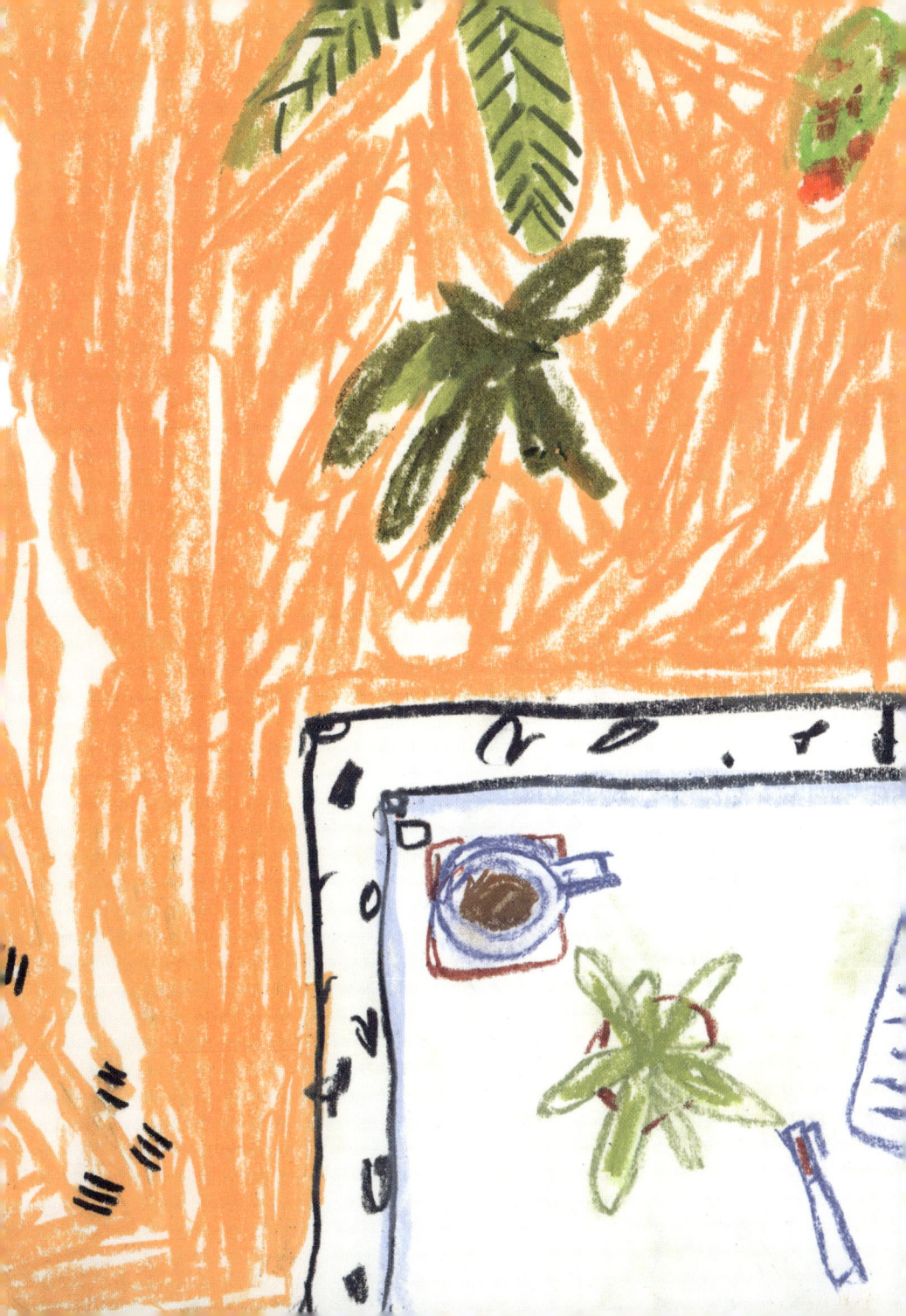

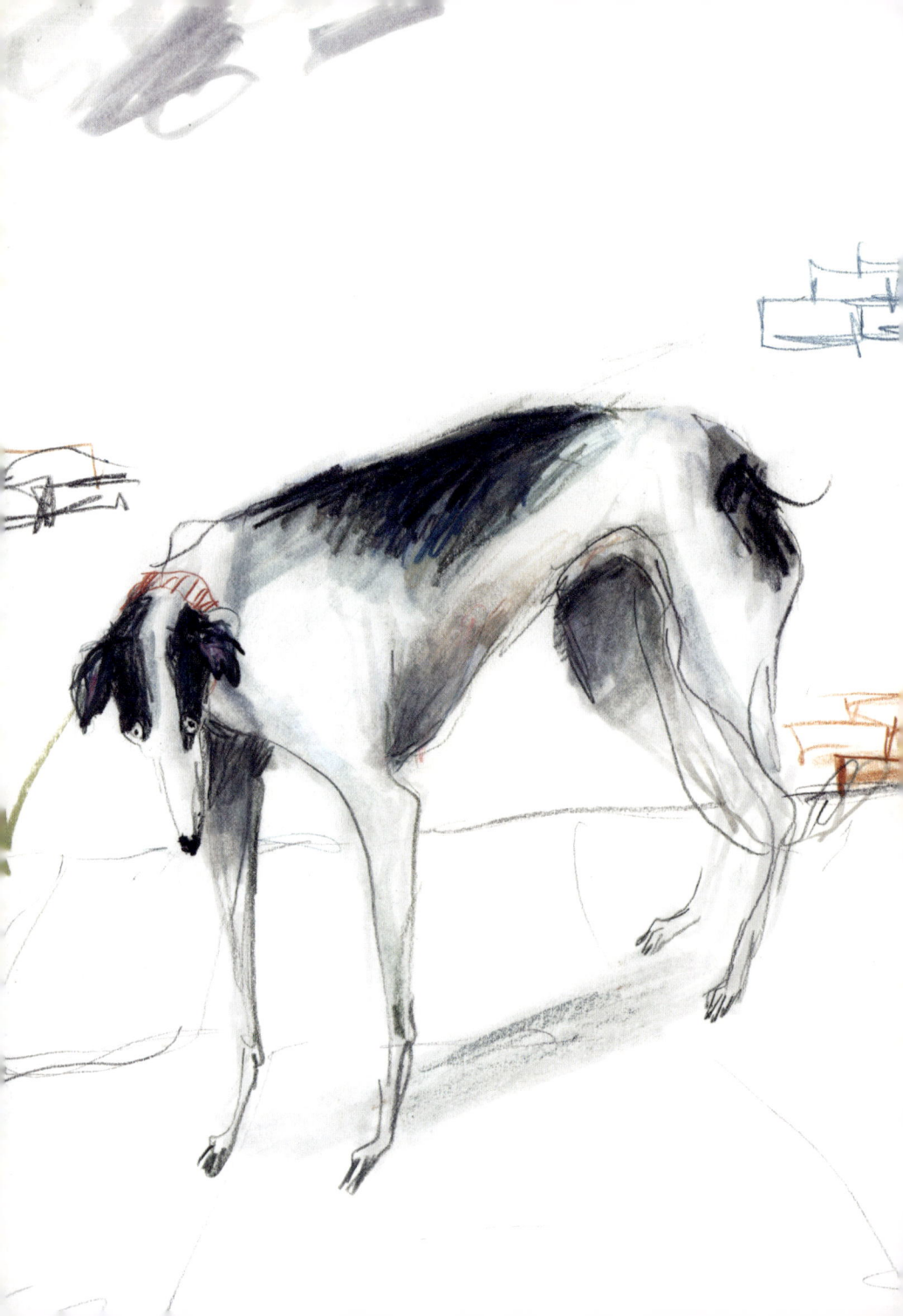

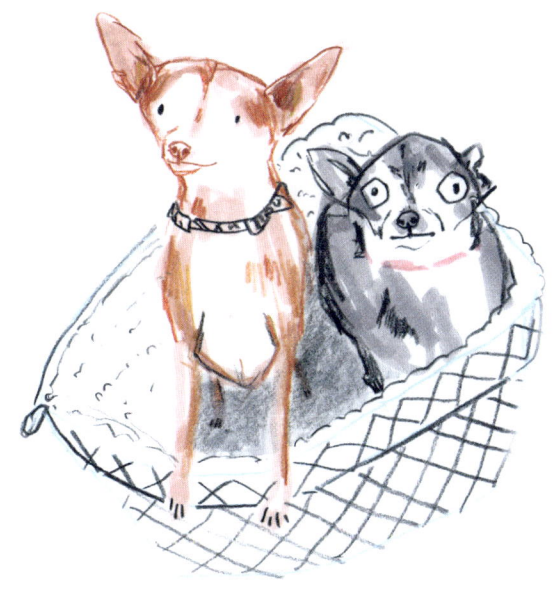

COMPACT
BUNDLE

REST

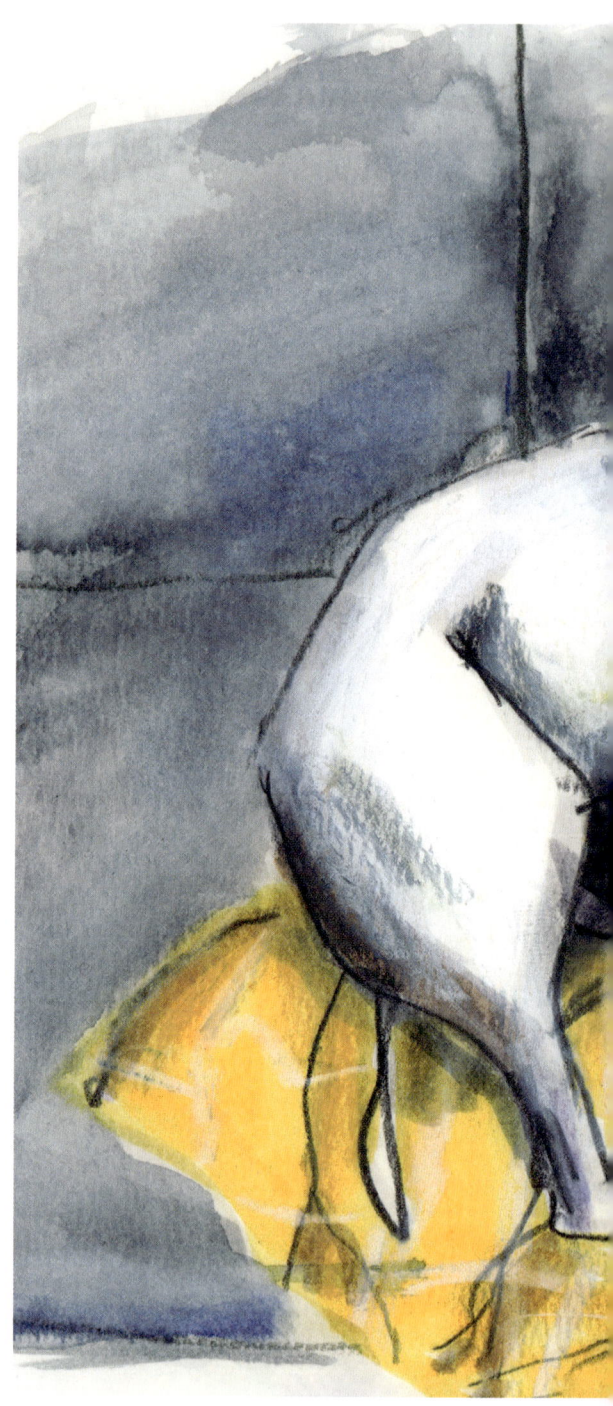

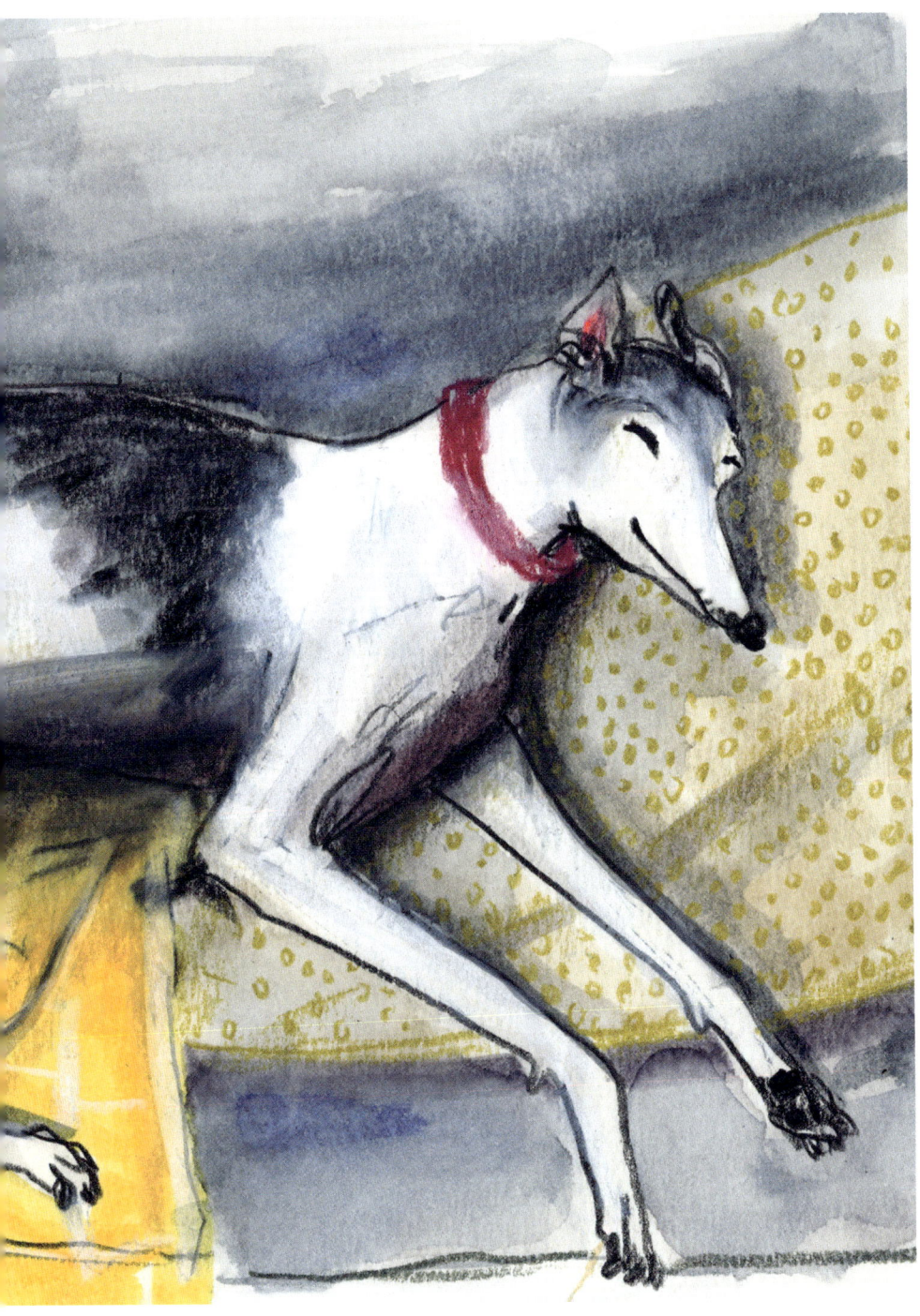

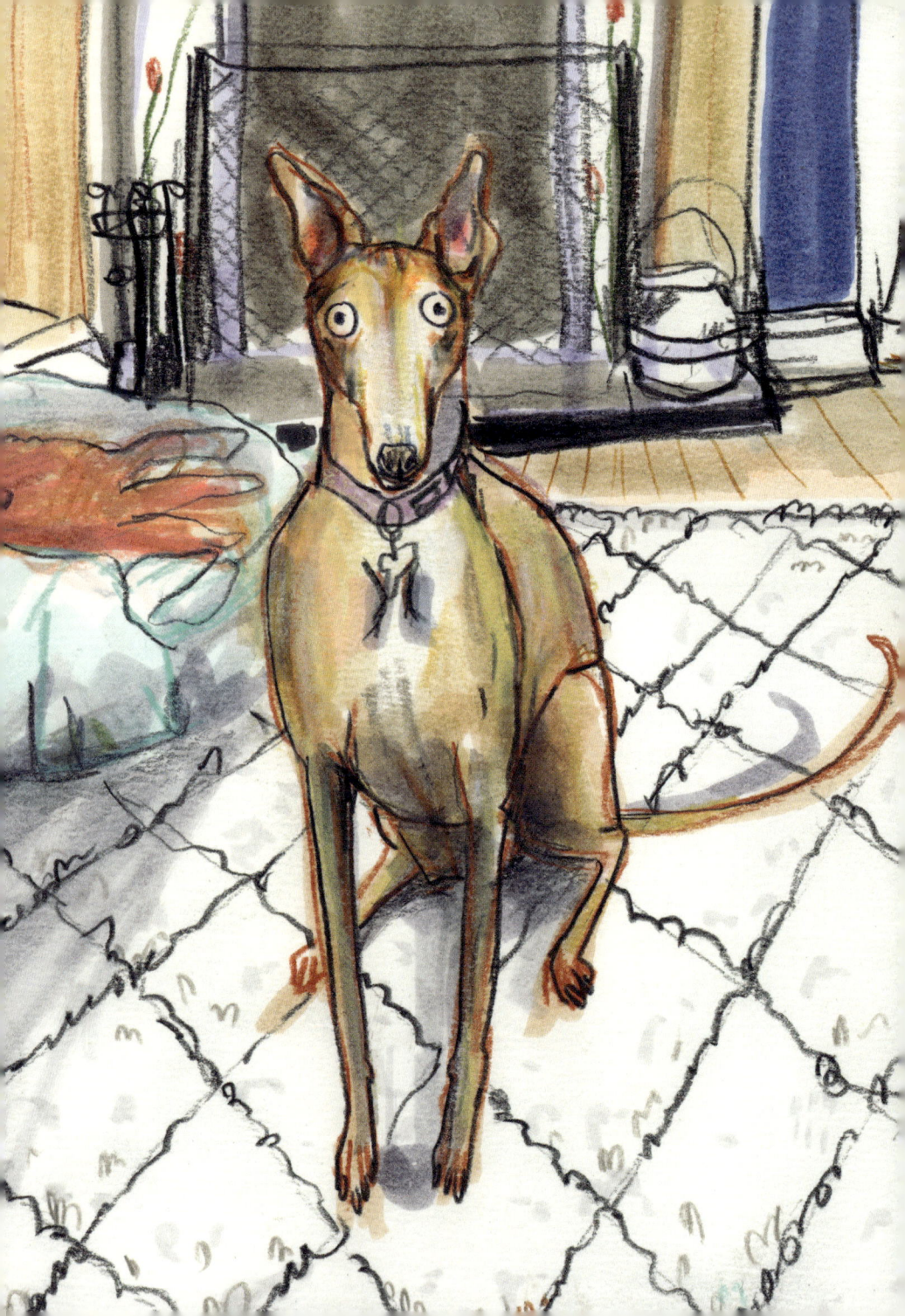

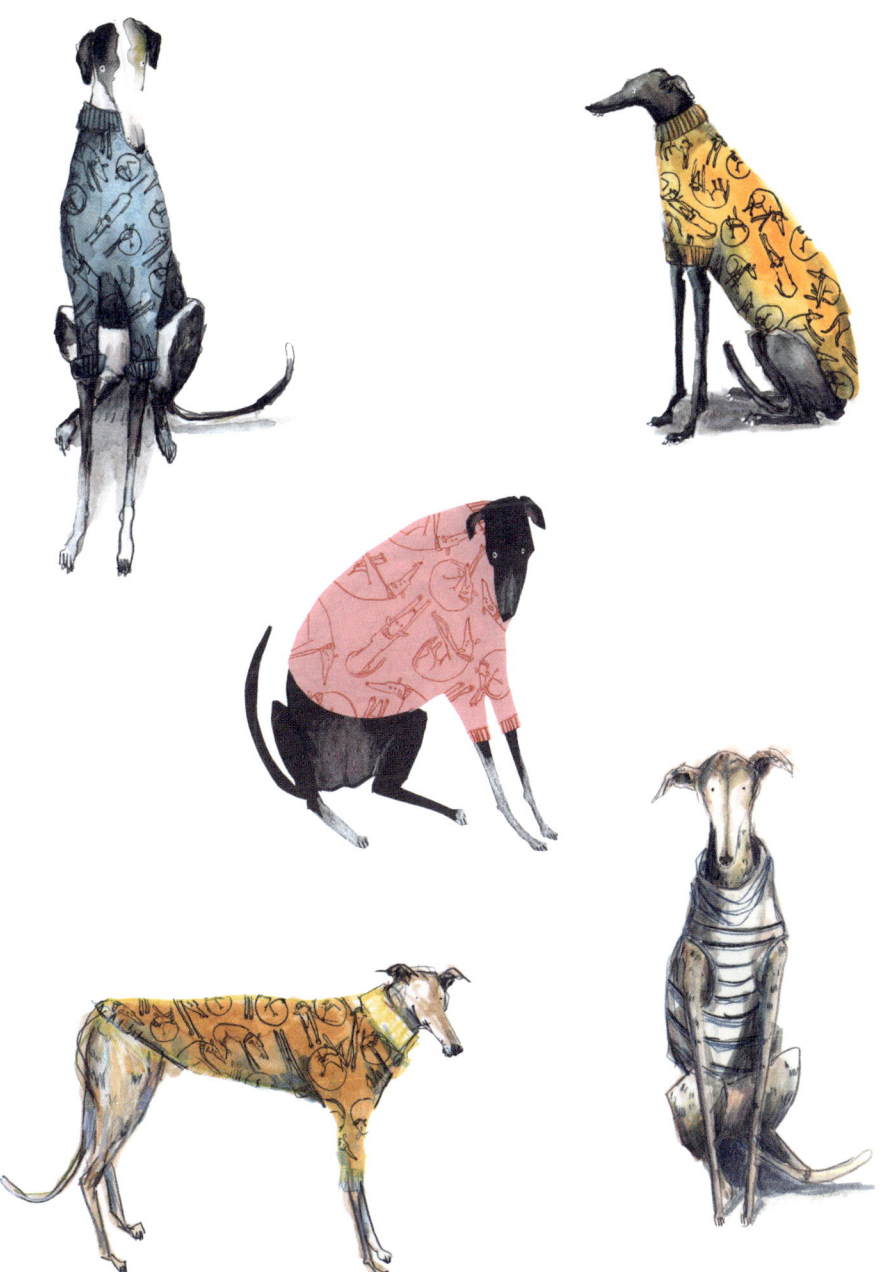

41

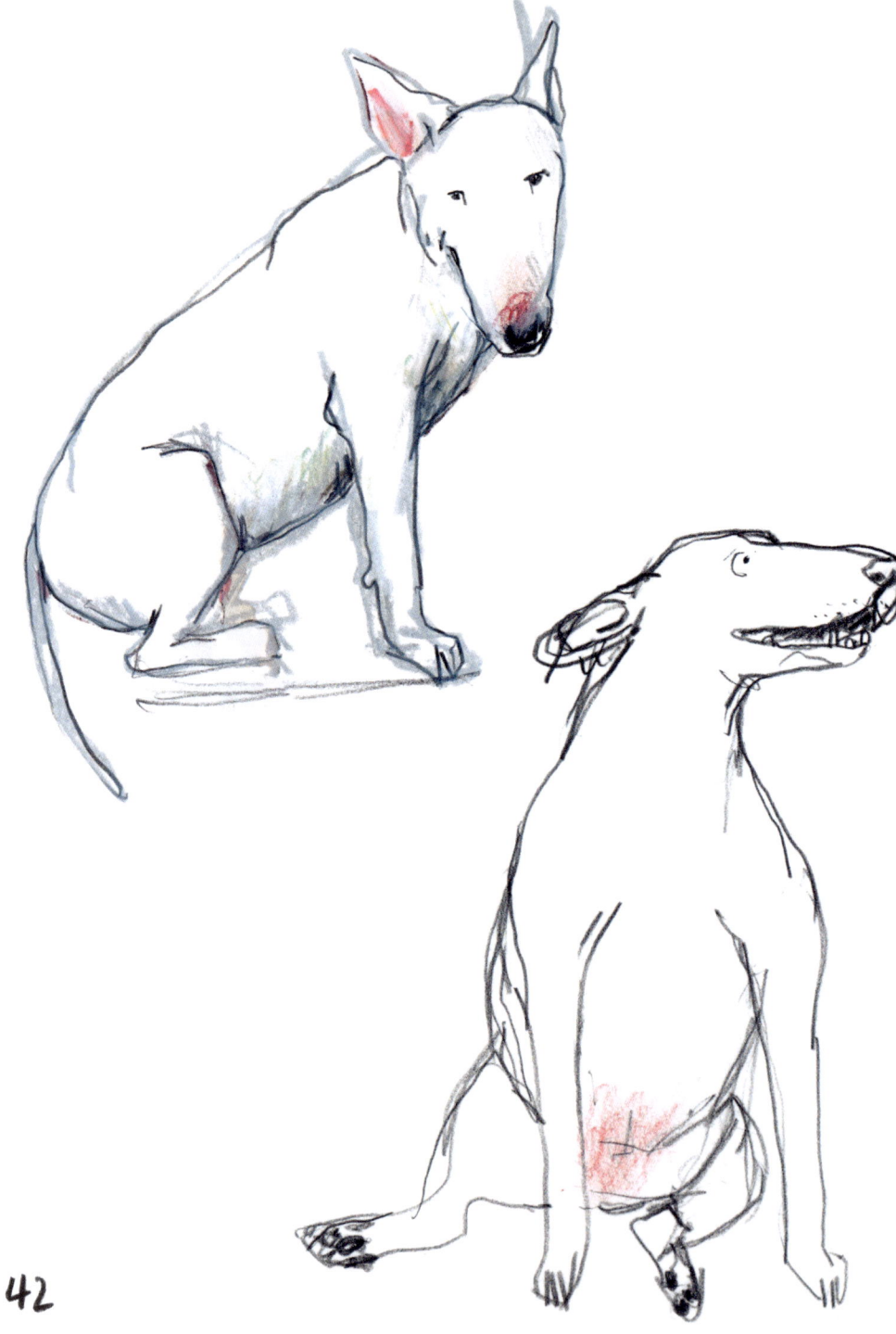

42

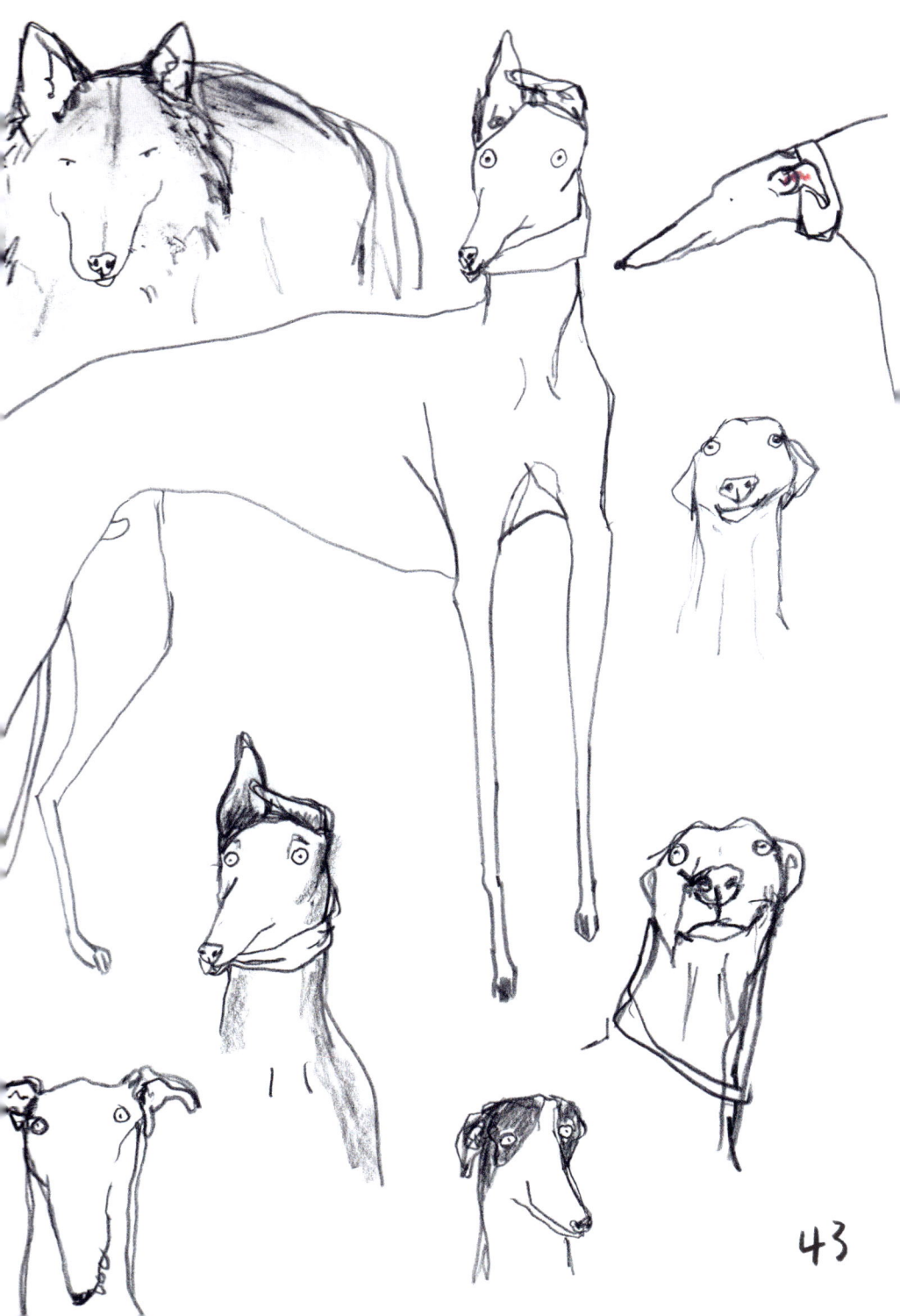

43

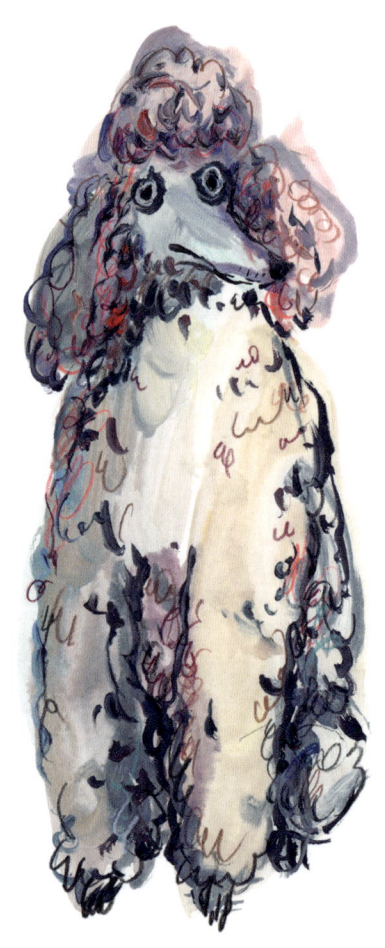

44

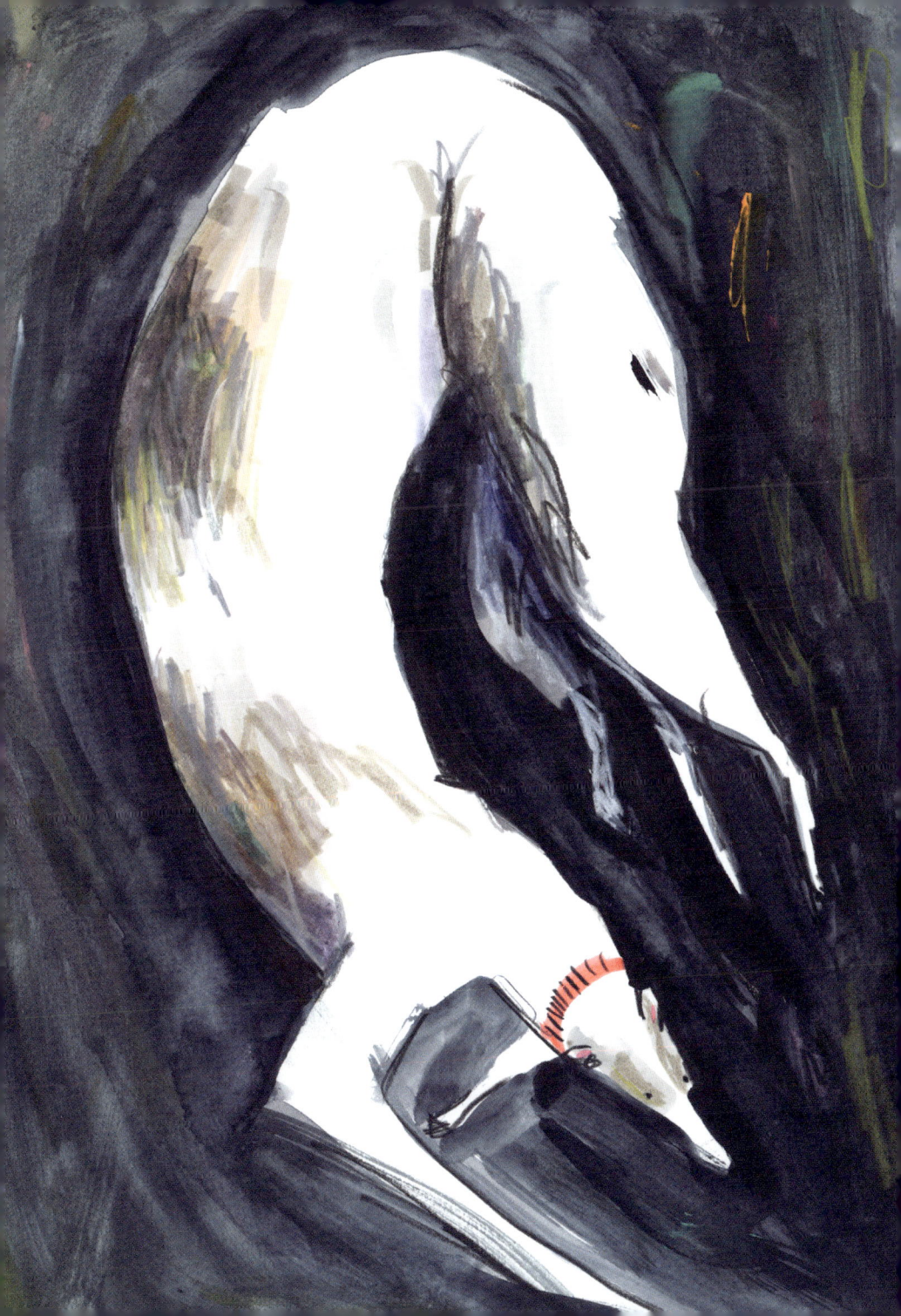

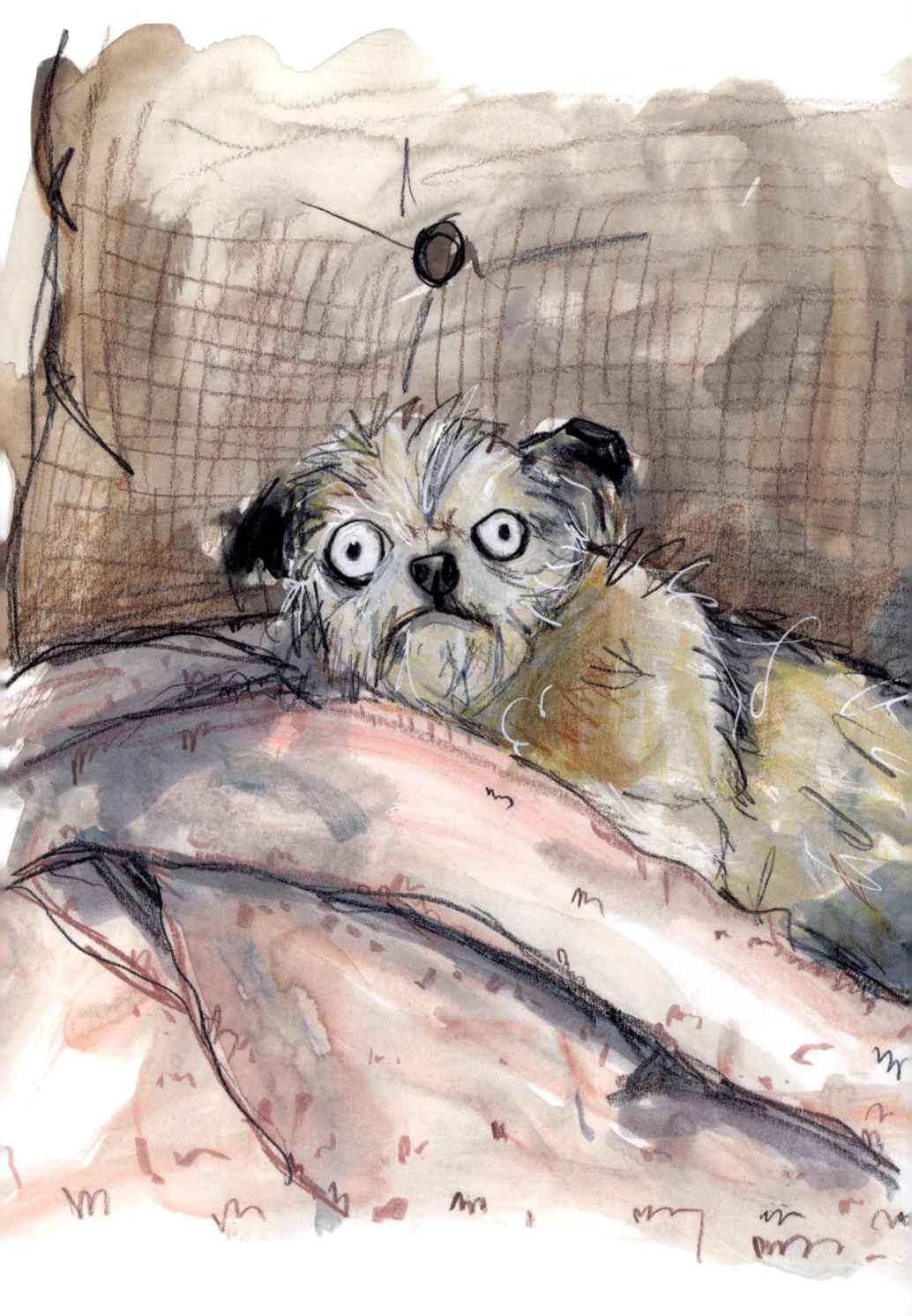

HE HEARD THE SOUND OF
A CHEESE WRAPPER.

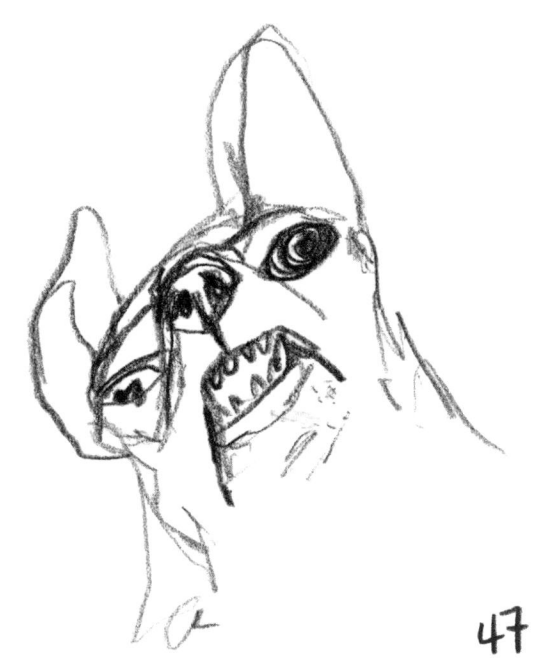

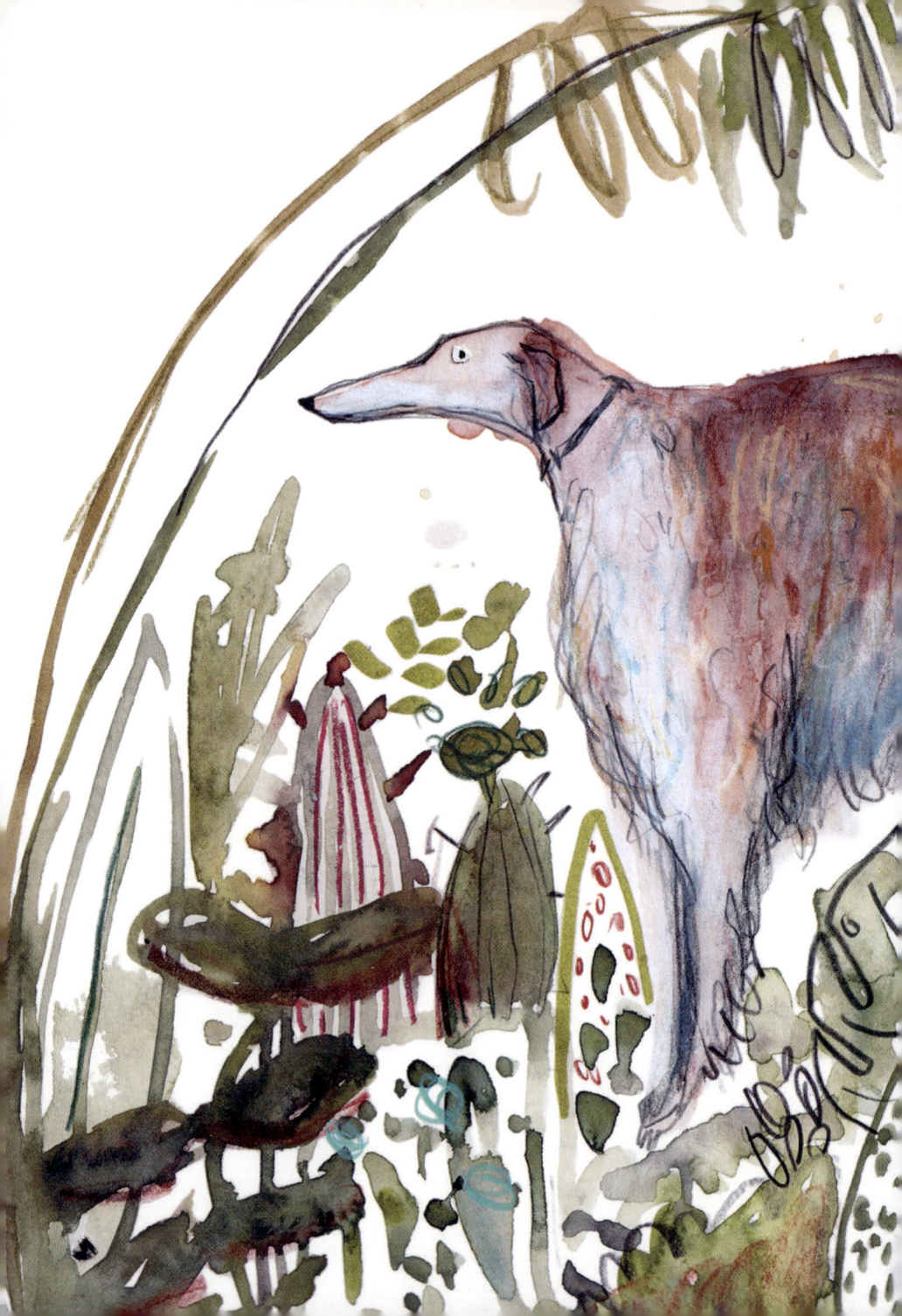

I WOULD RATHER
BE AT HOME

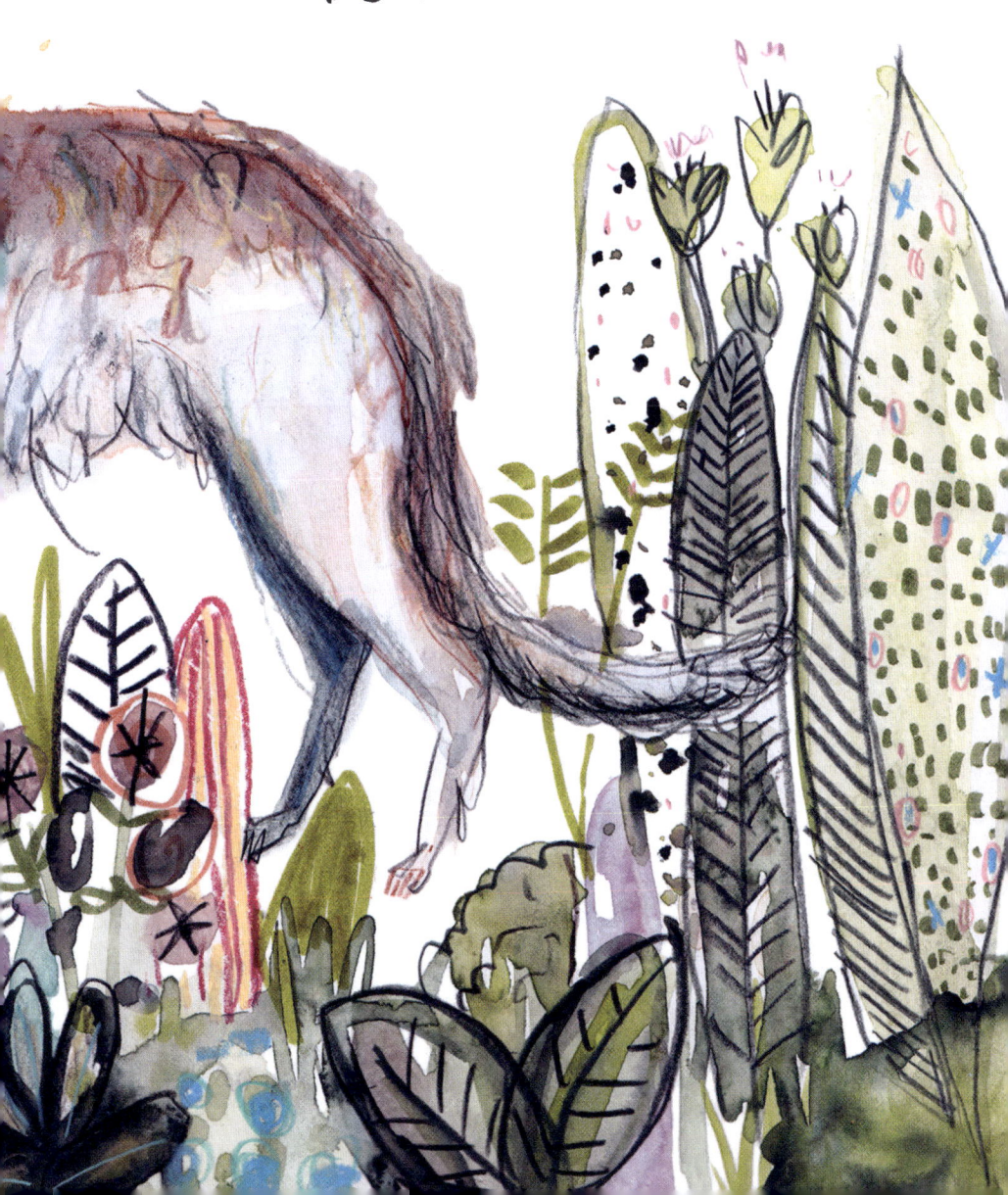

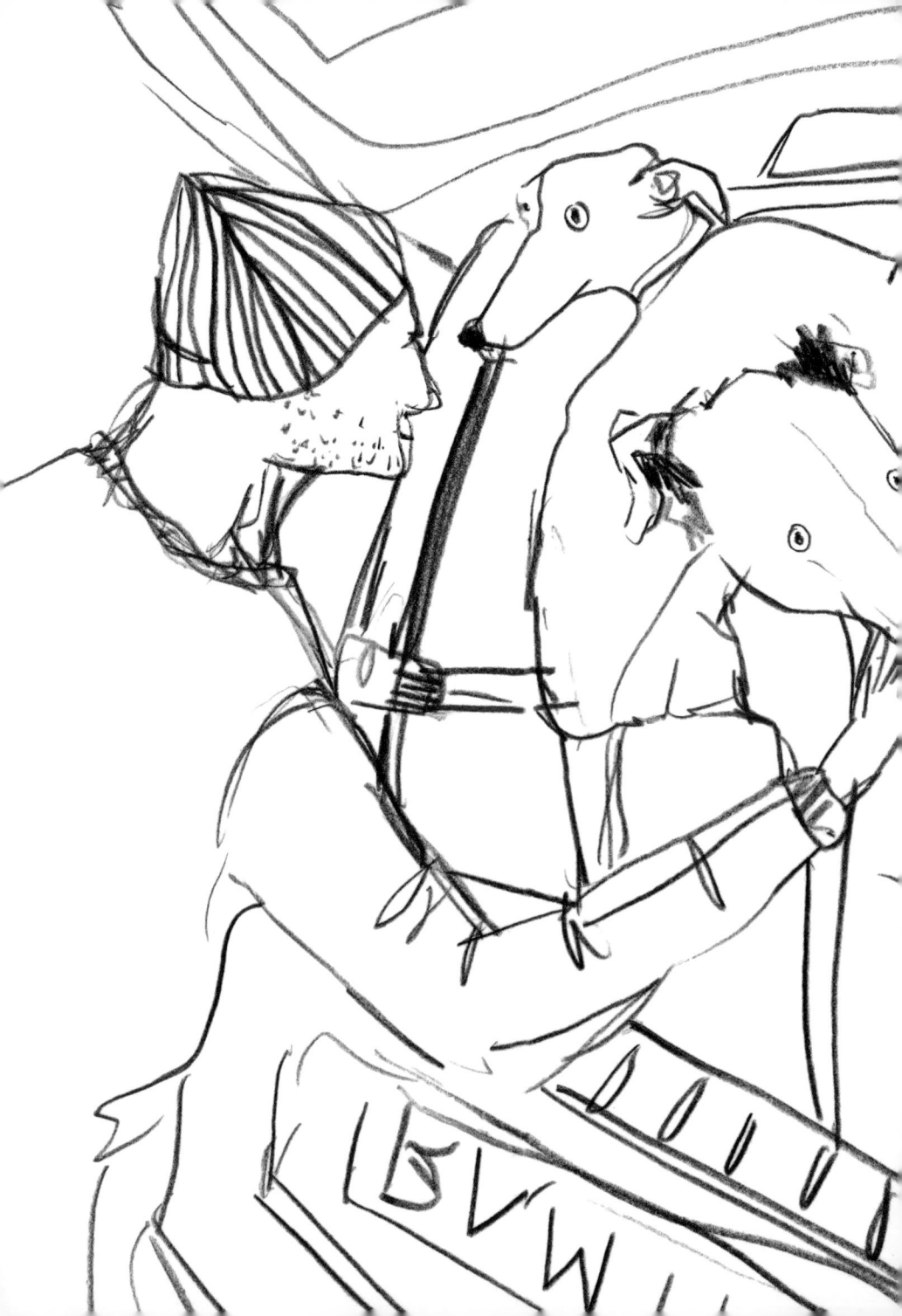

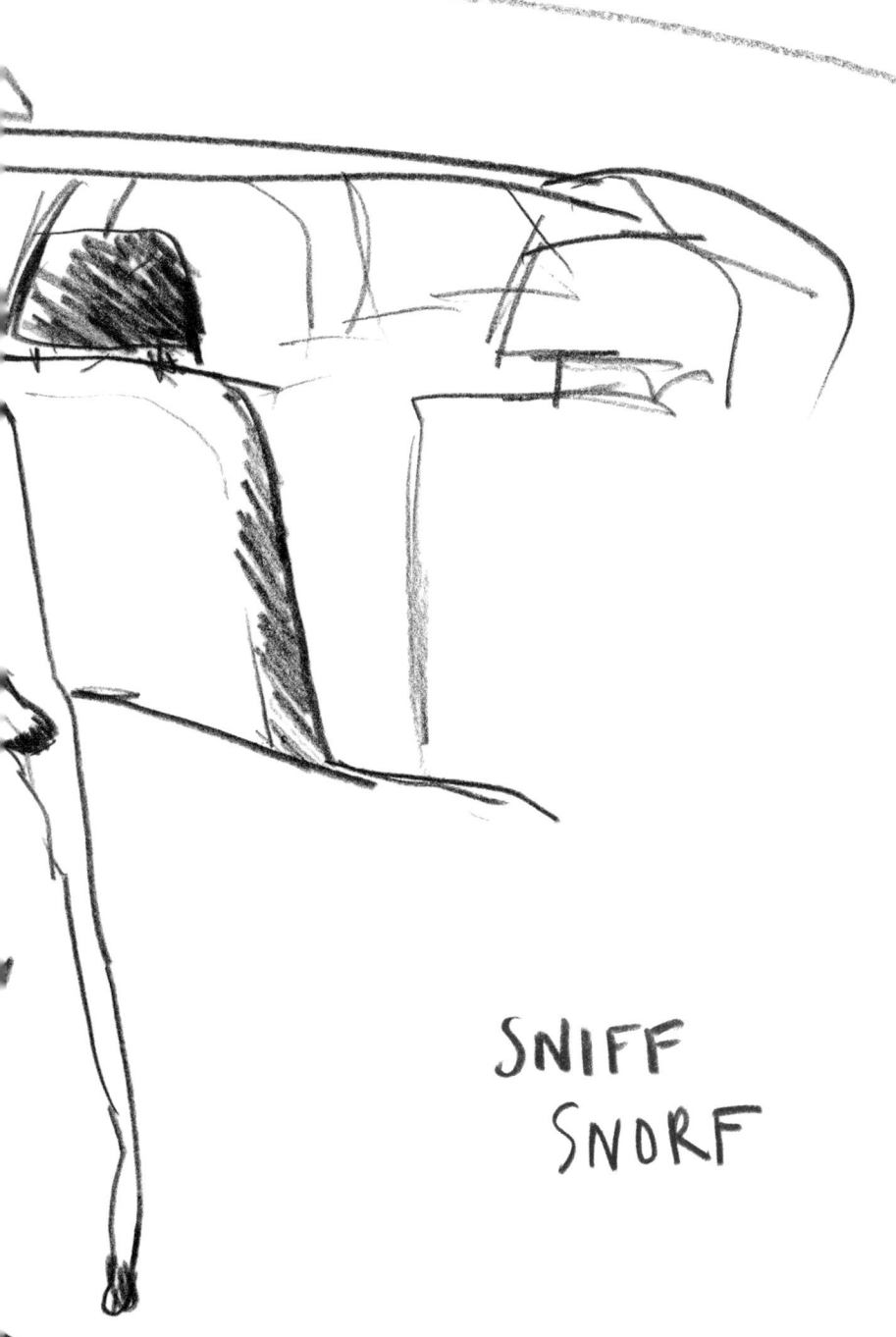

SNIFF
SNORF

51

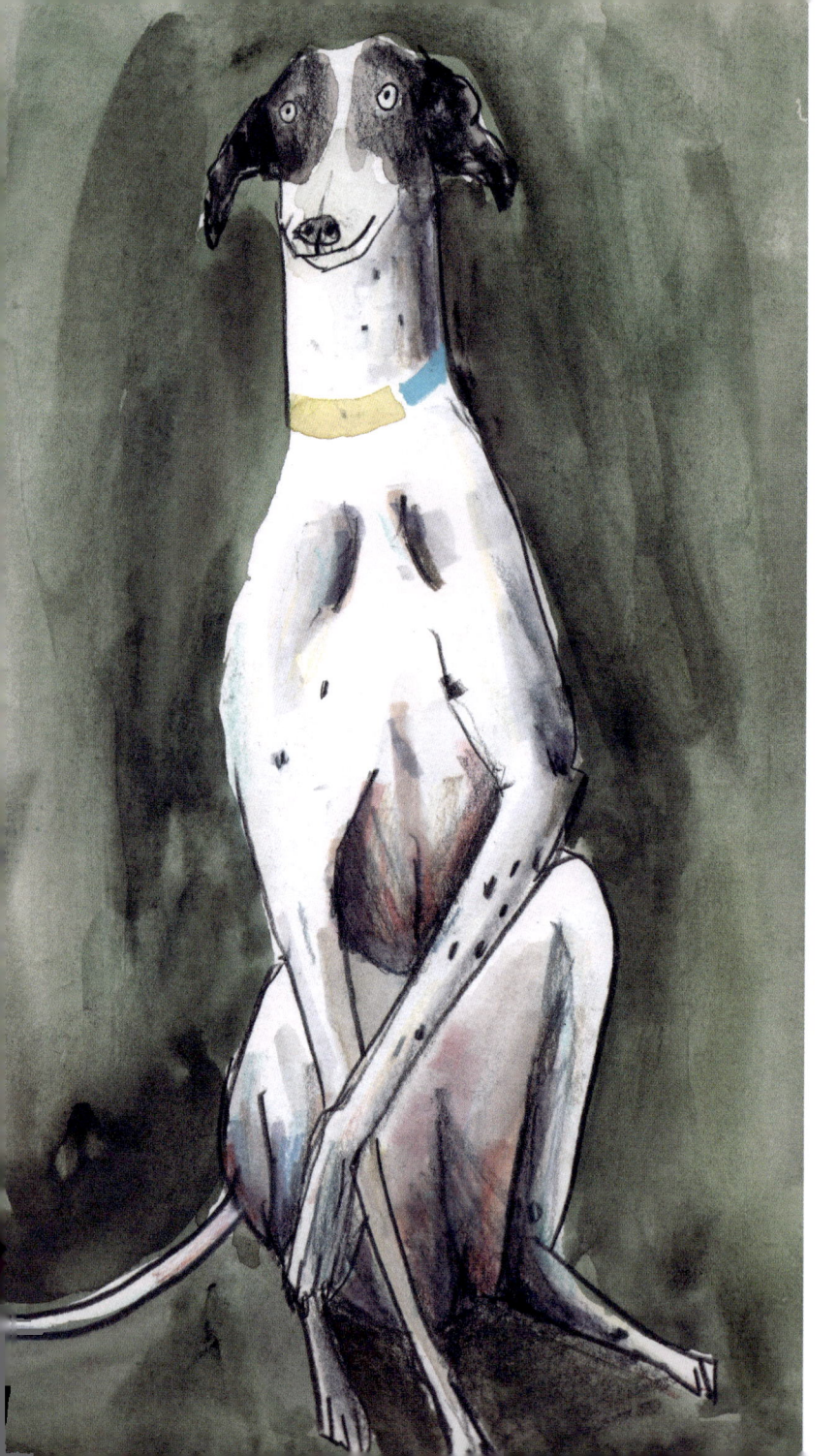

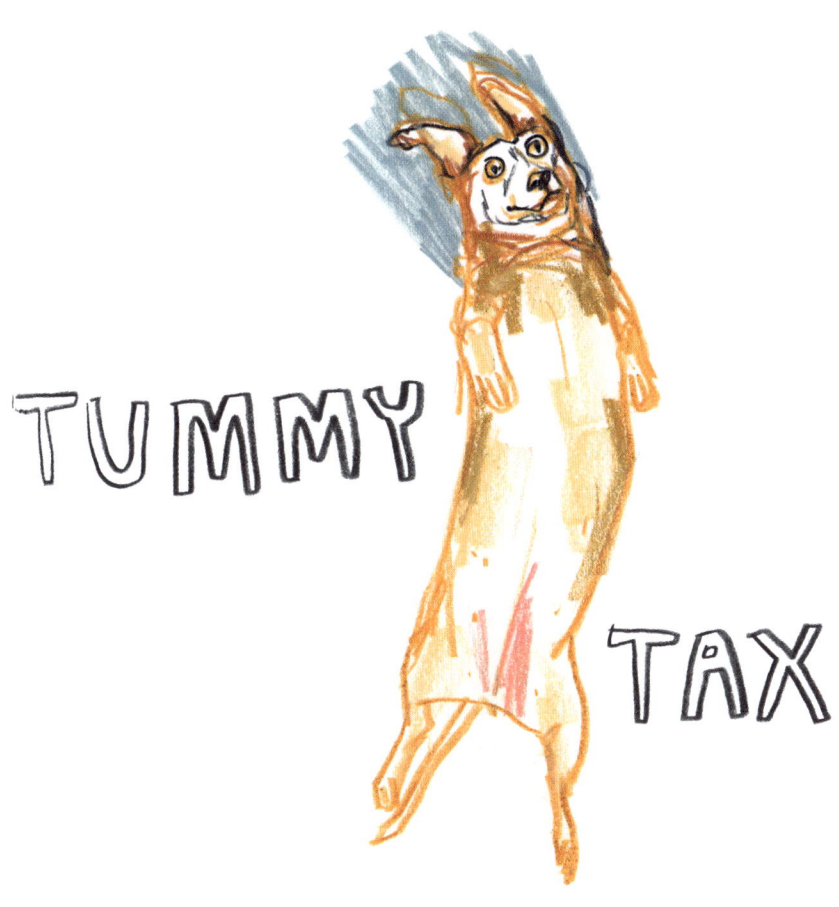

TUMMY

TAX

53

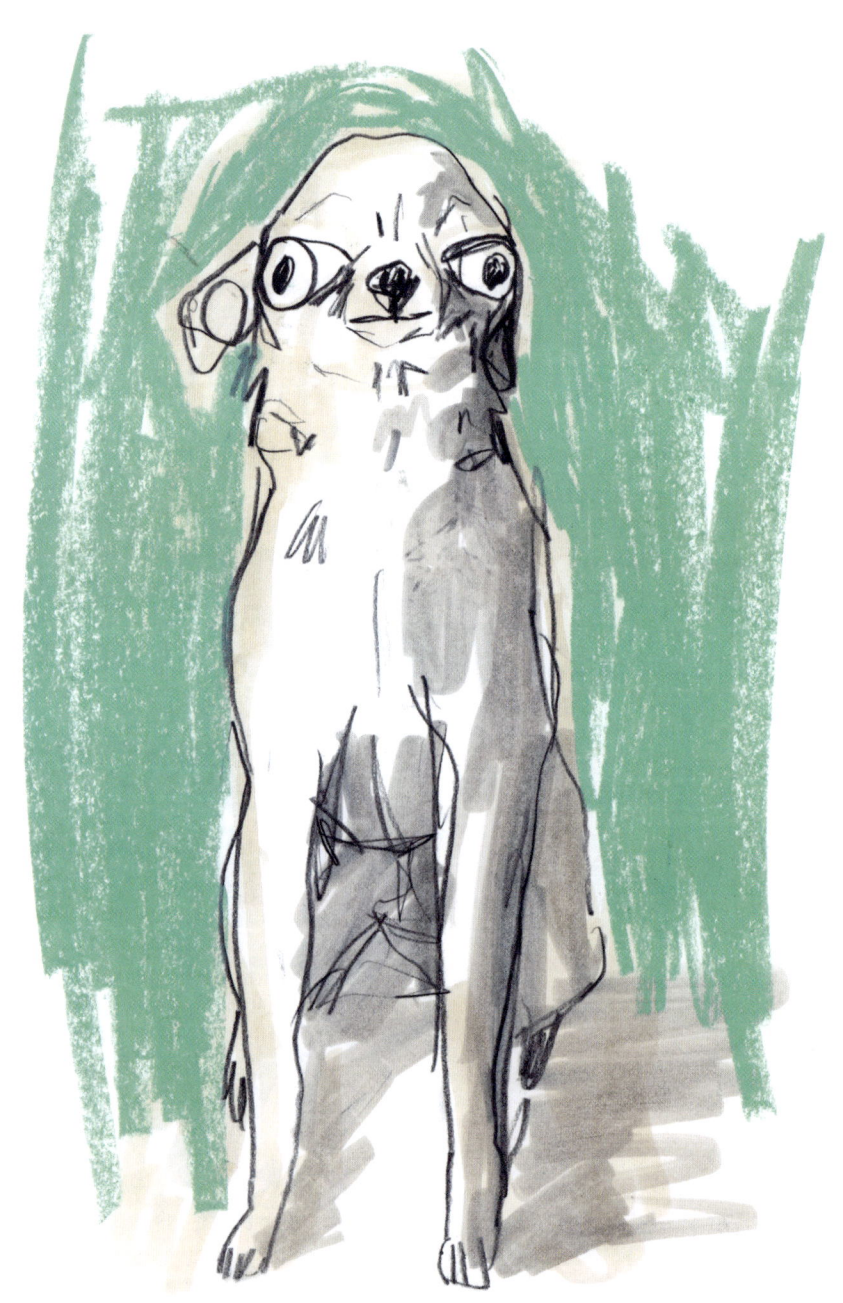

54

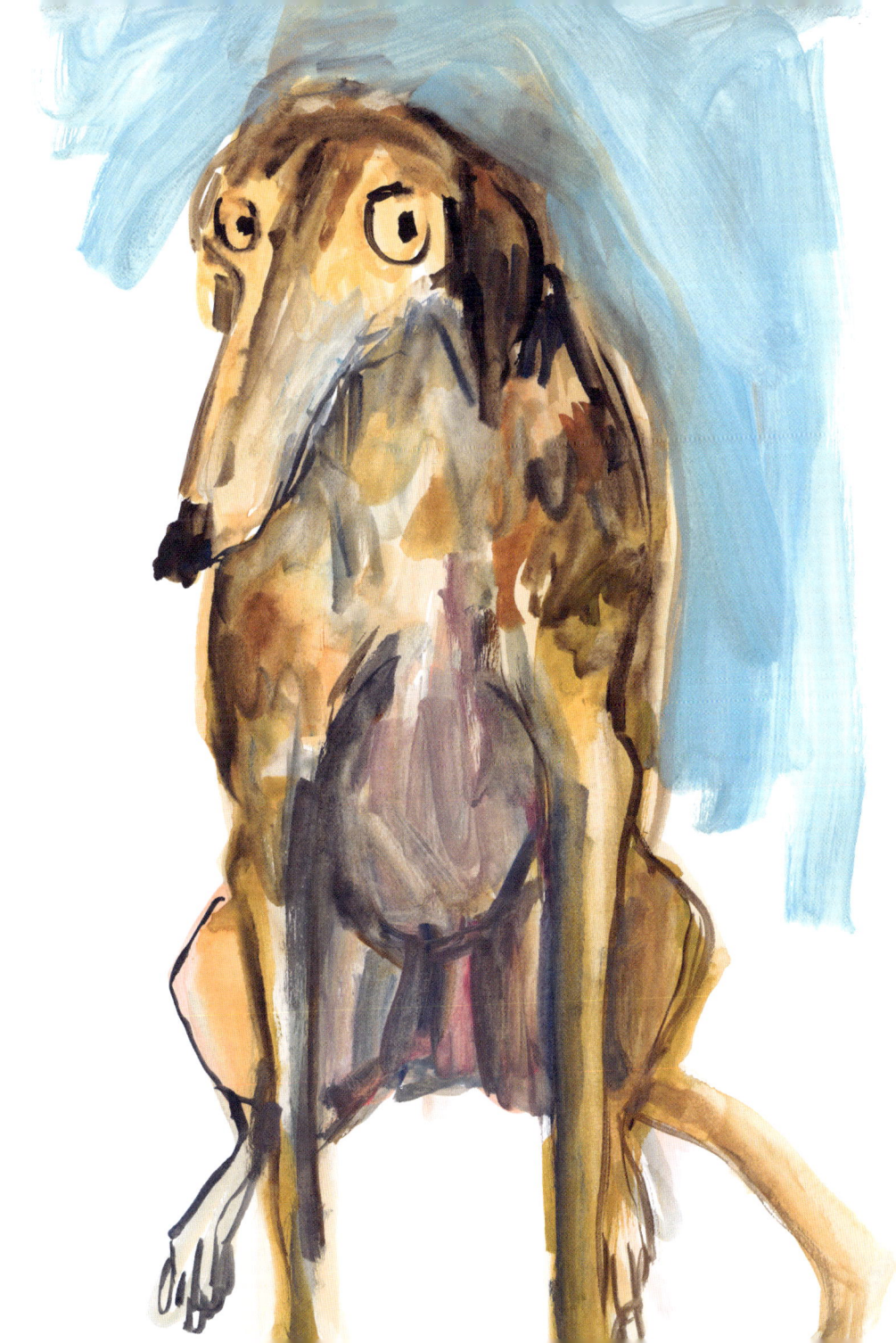

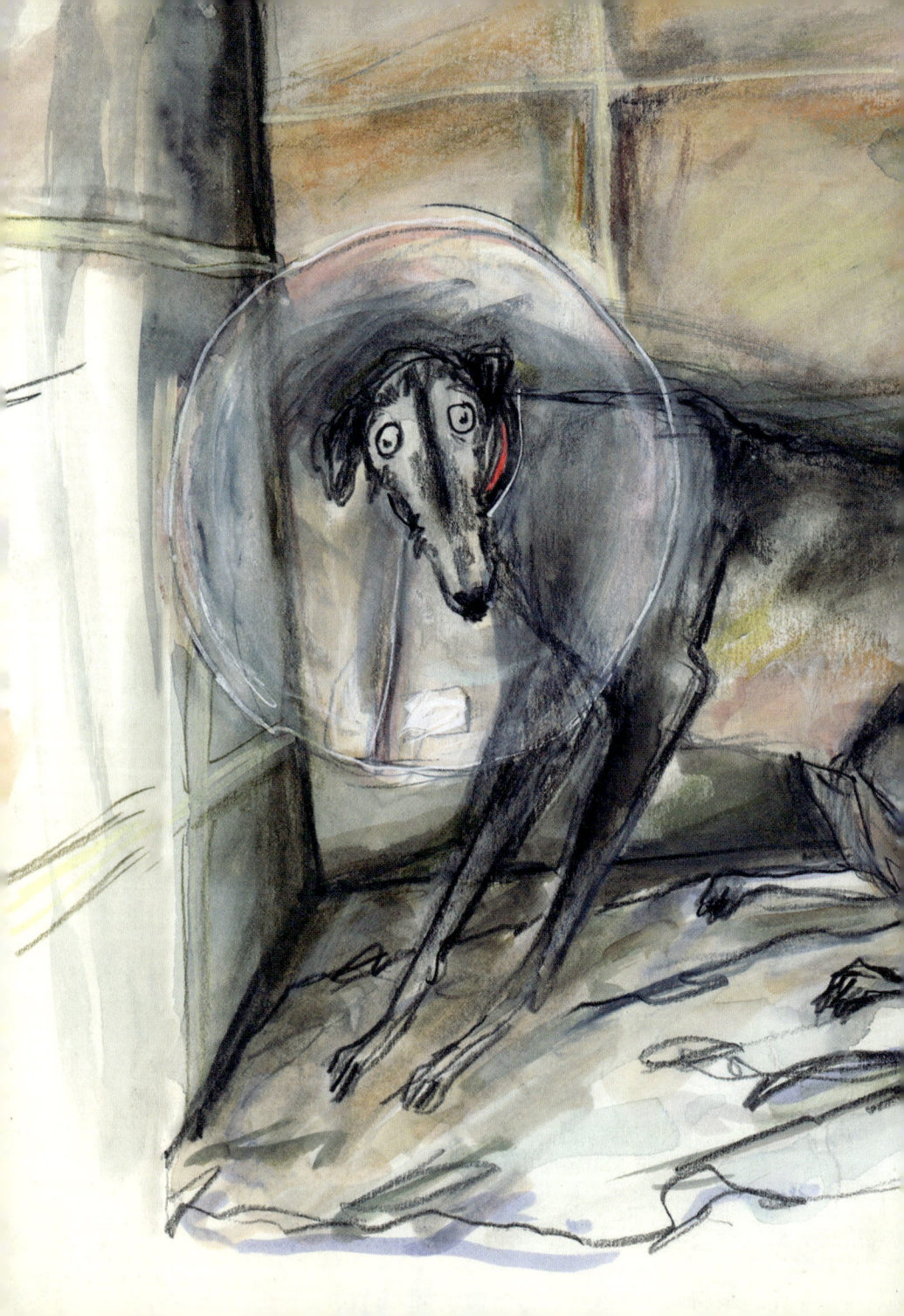

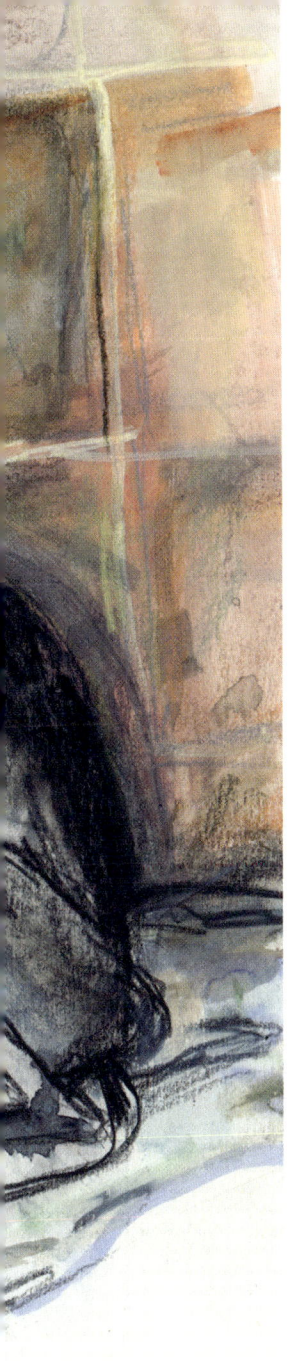

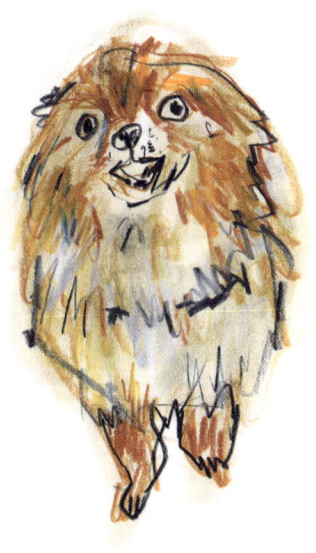

57

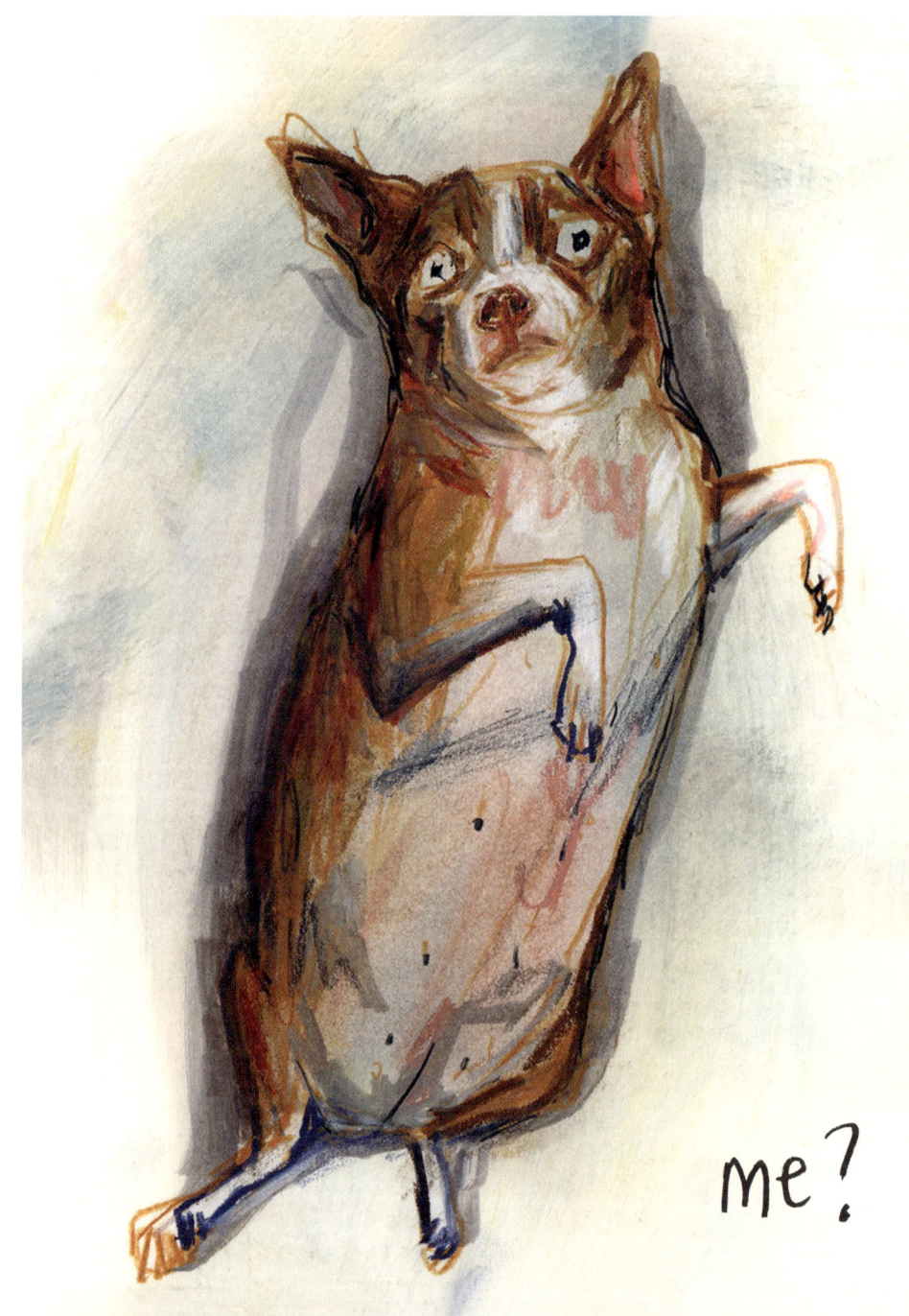

me?

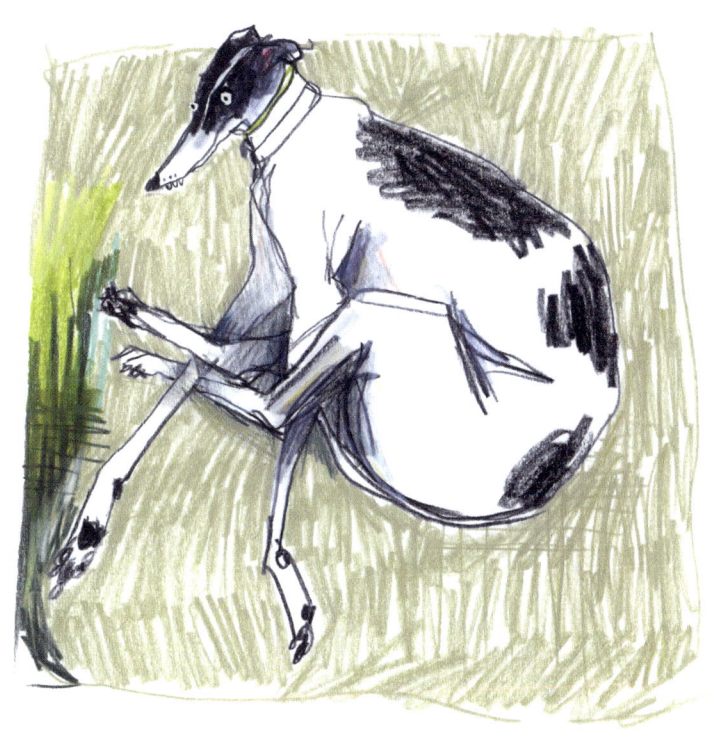

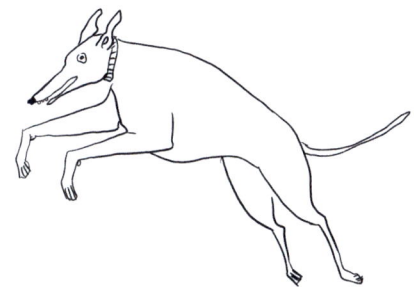

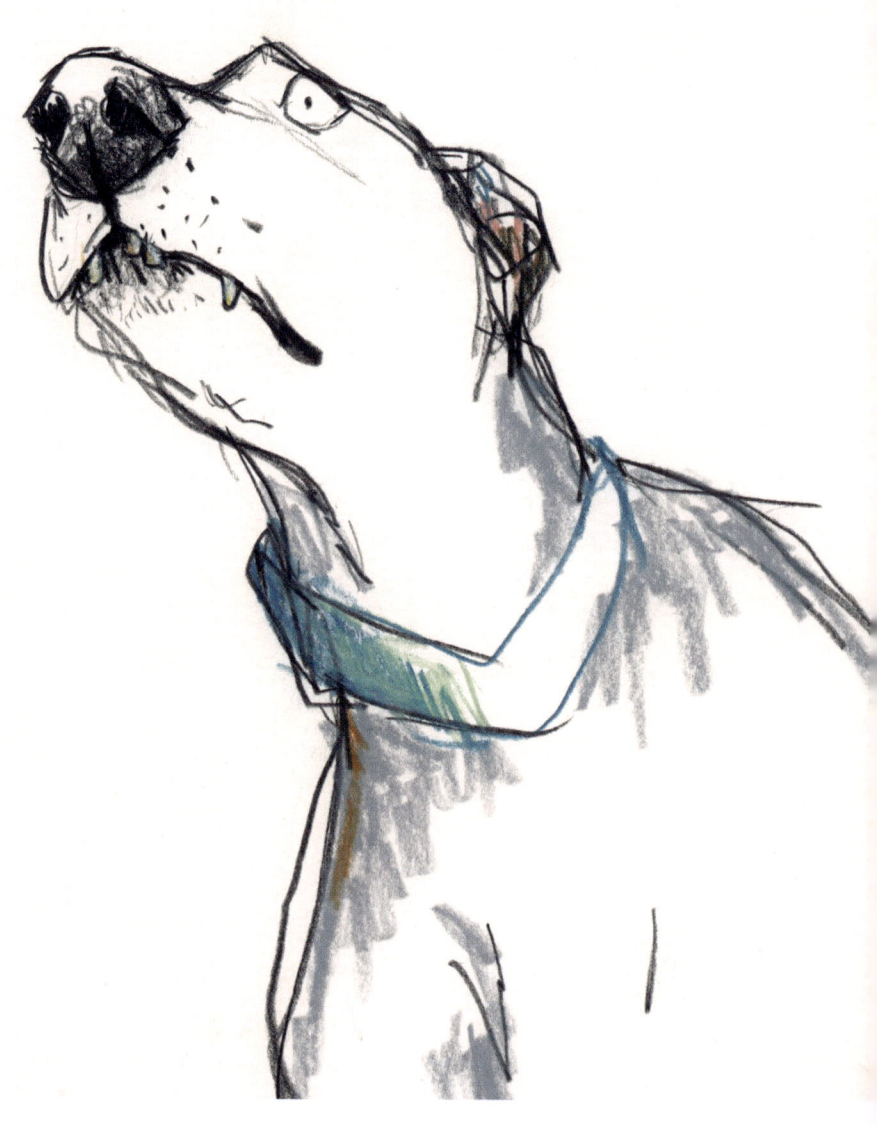

So smol.
So mighty.

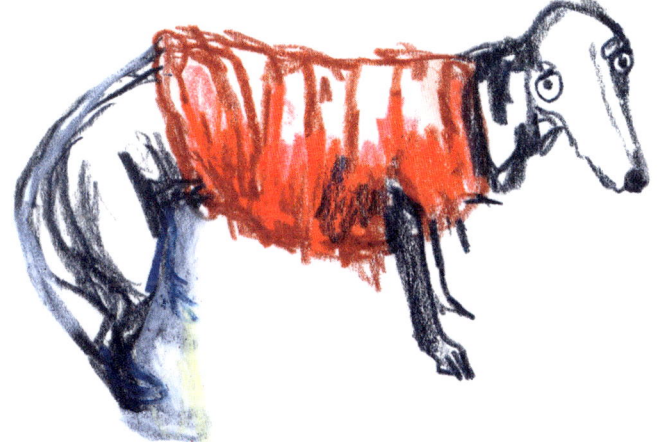

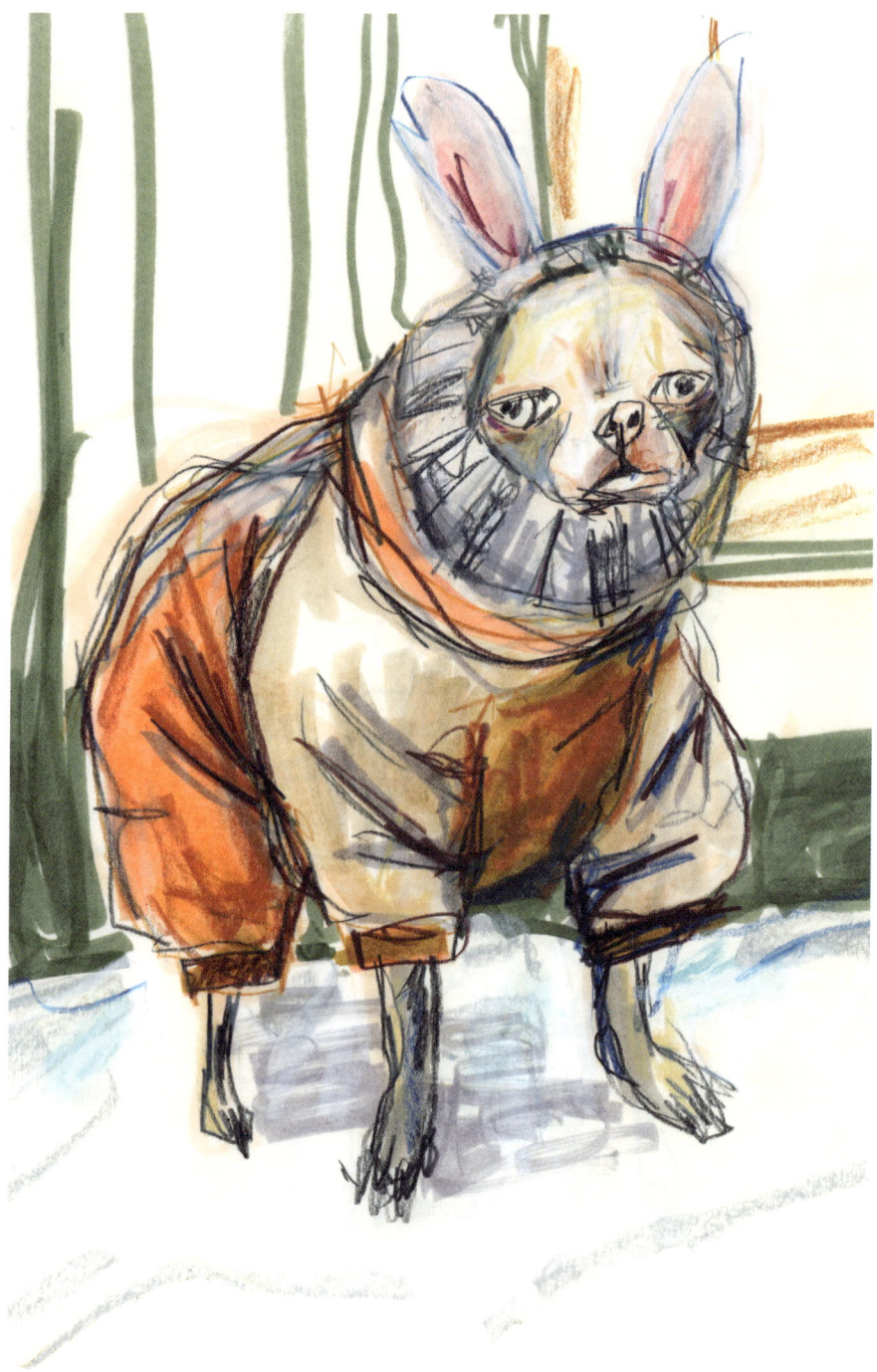

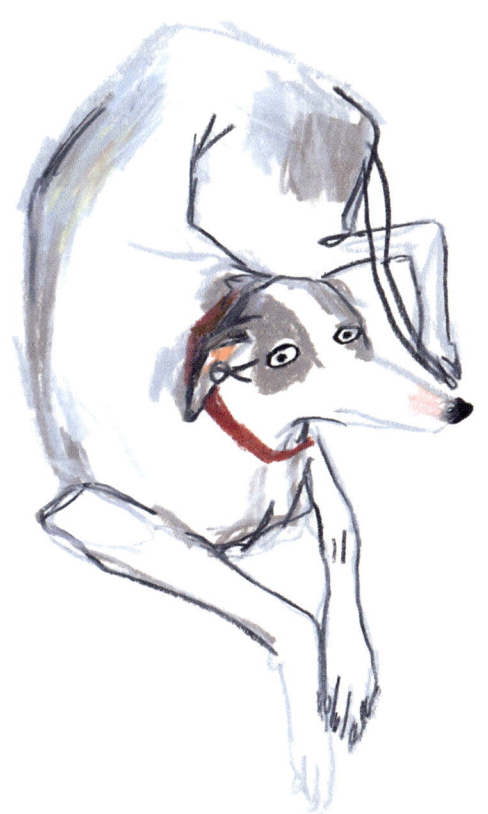

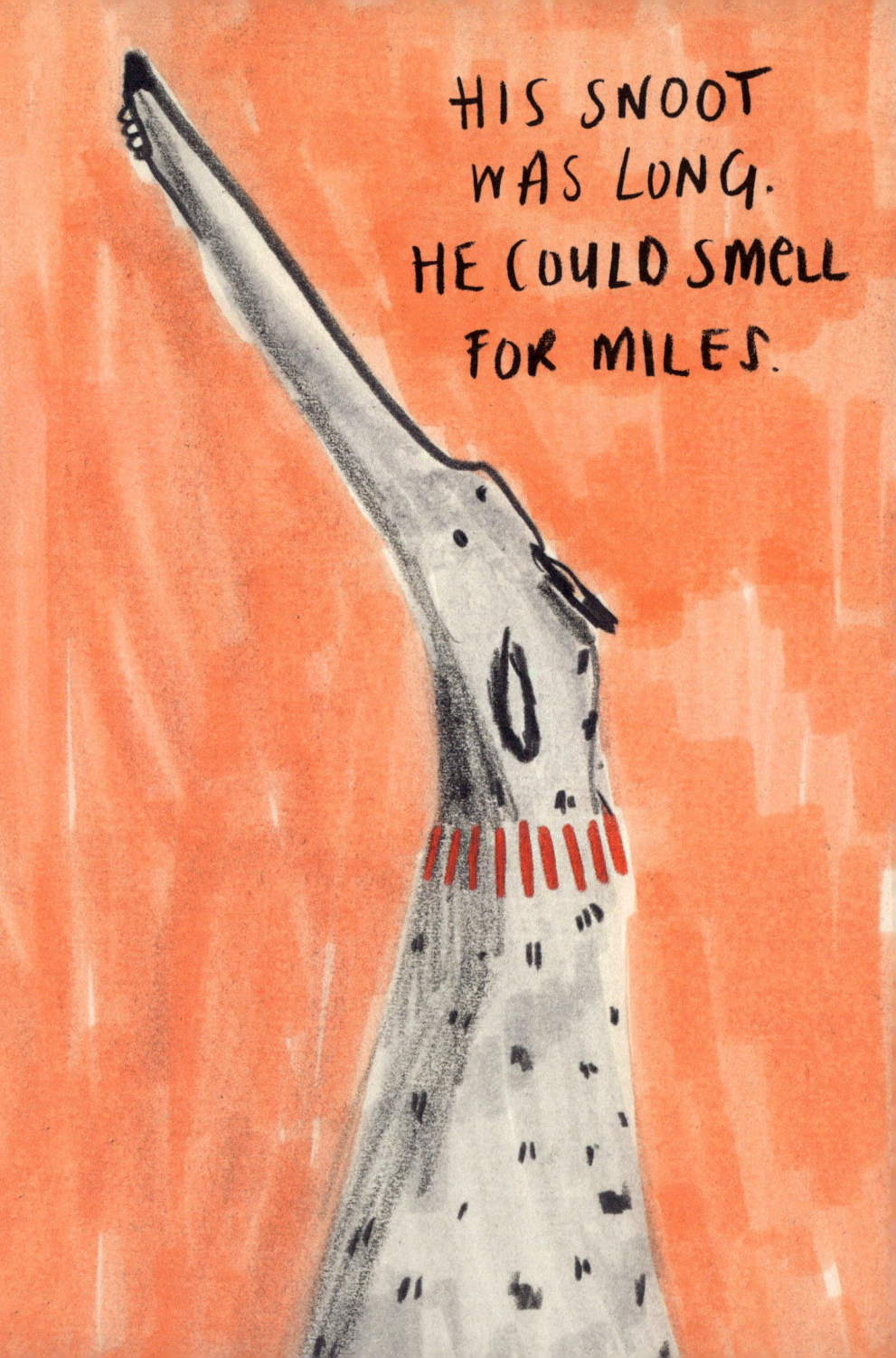

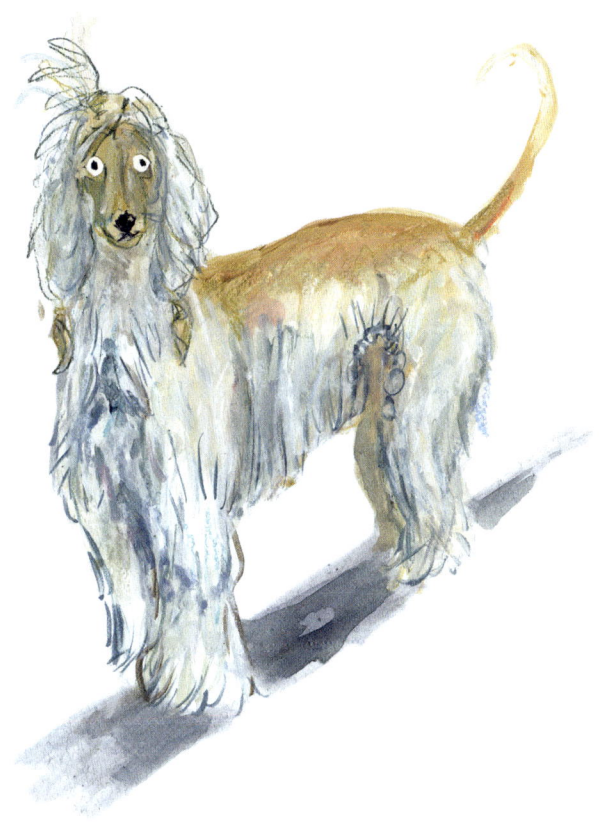

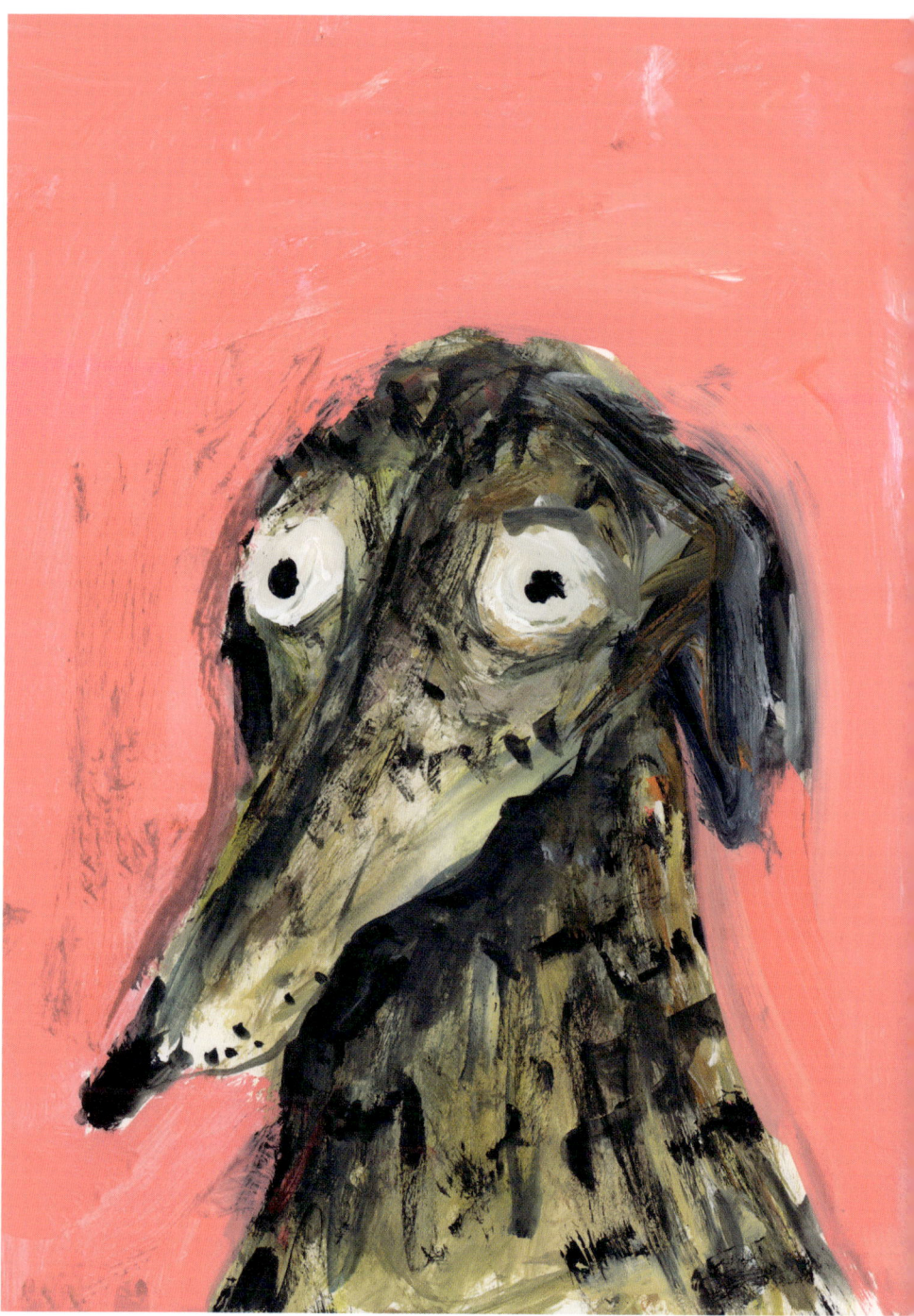

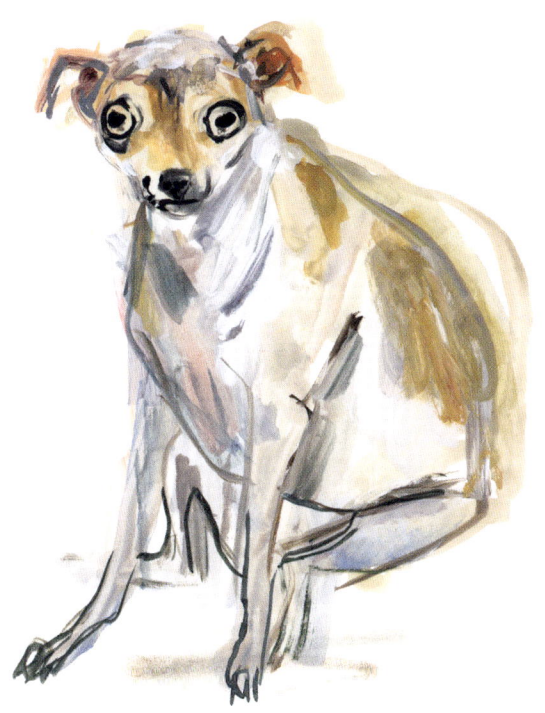

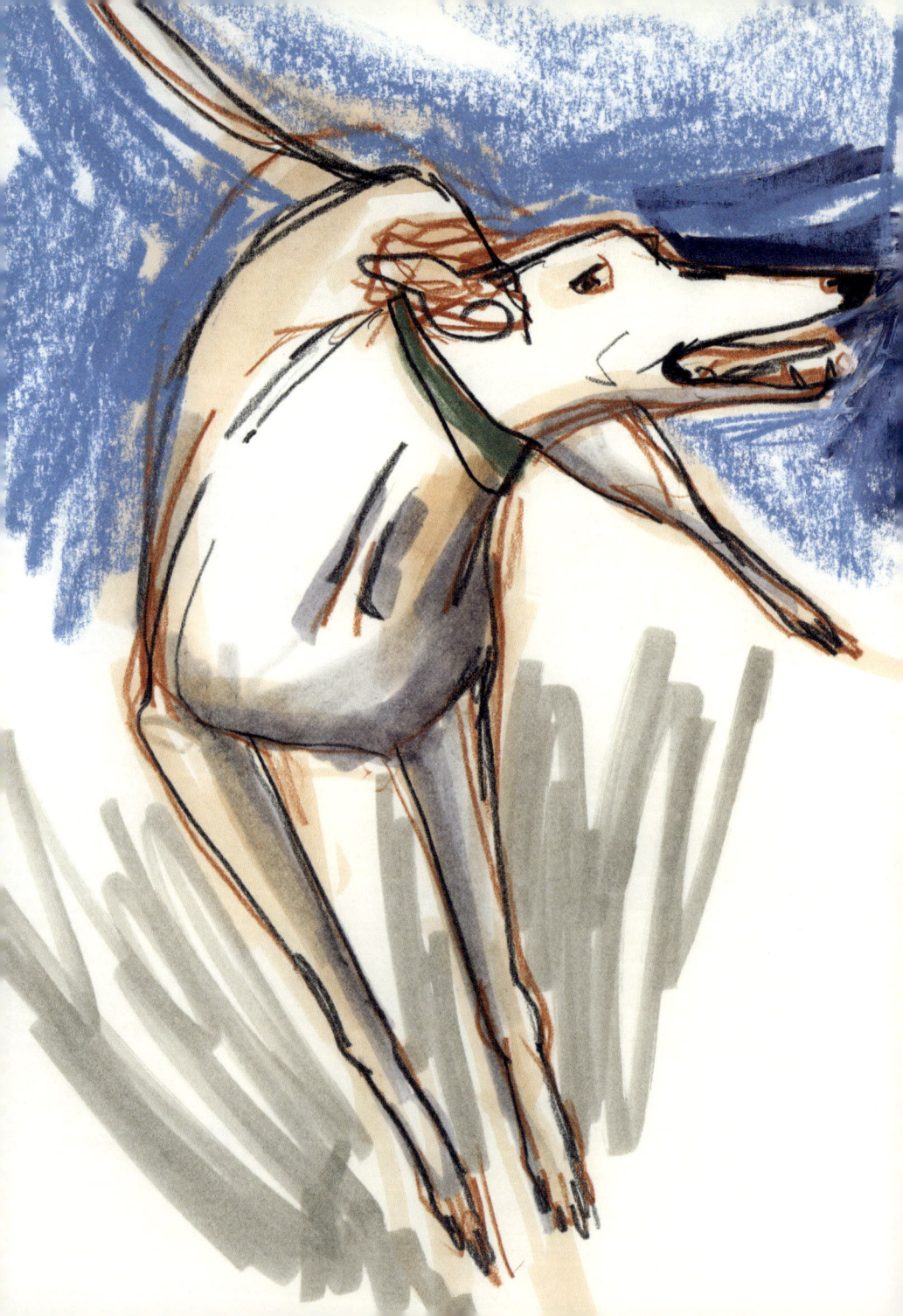

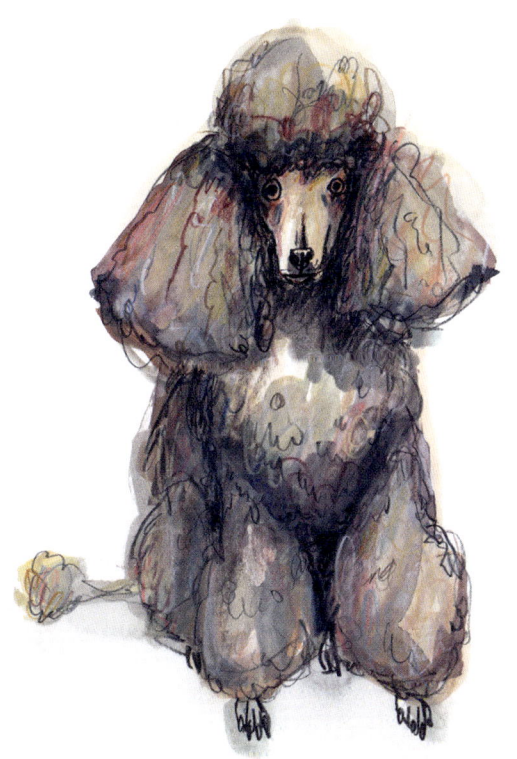
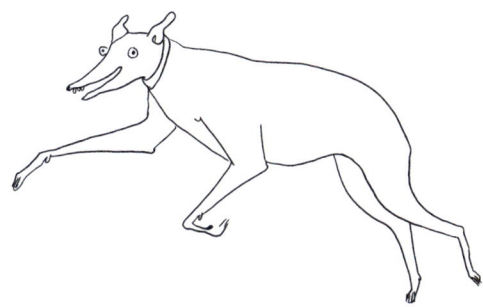

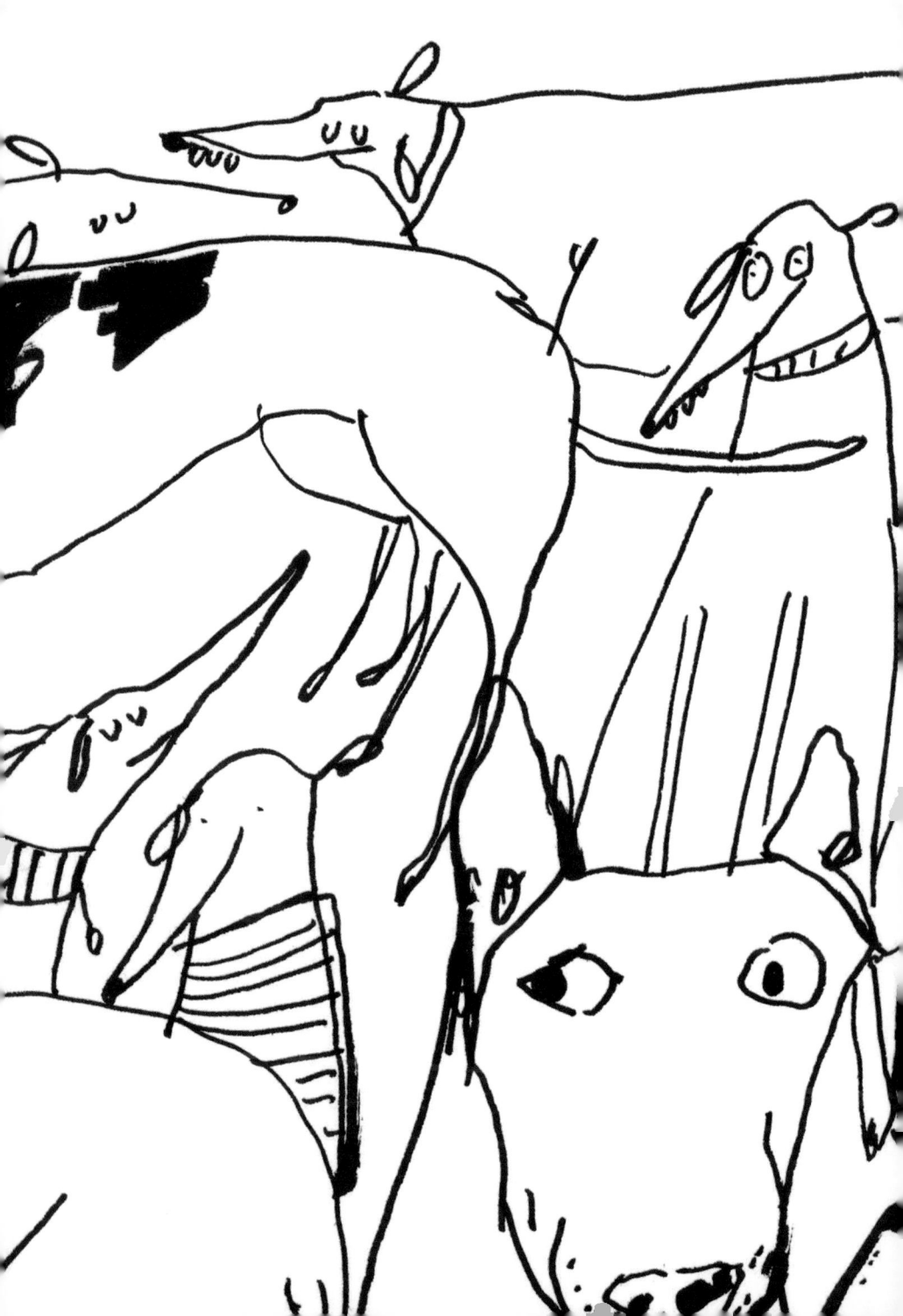

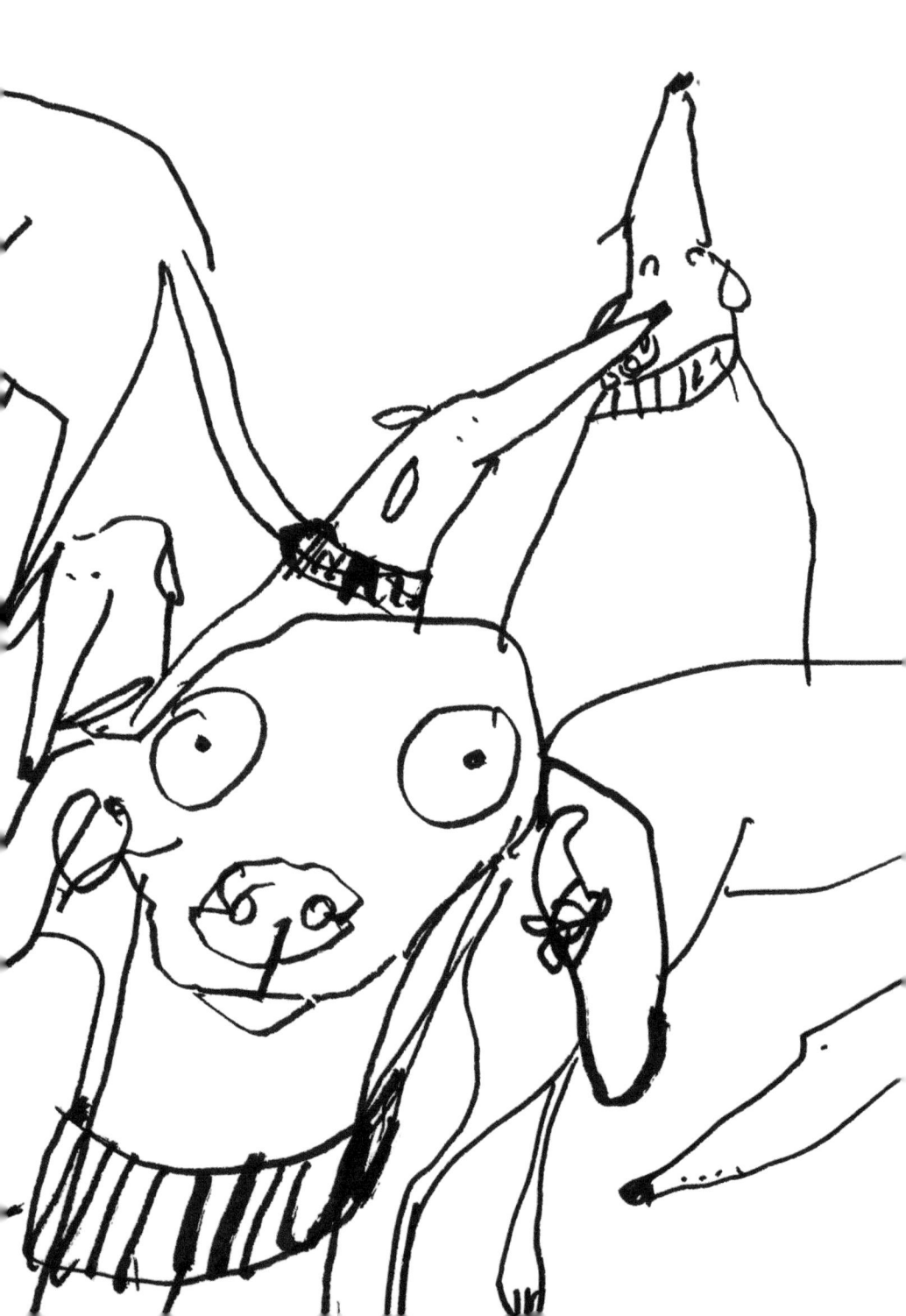

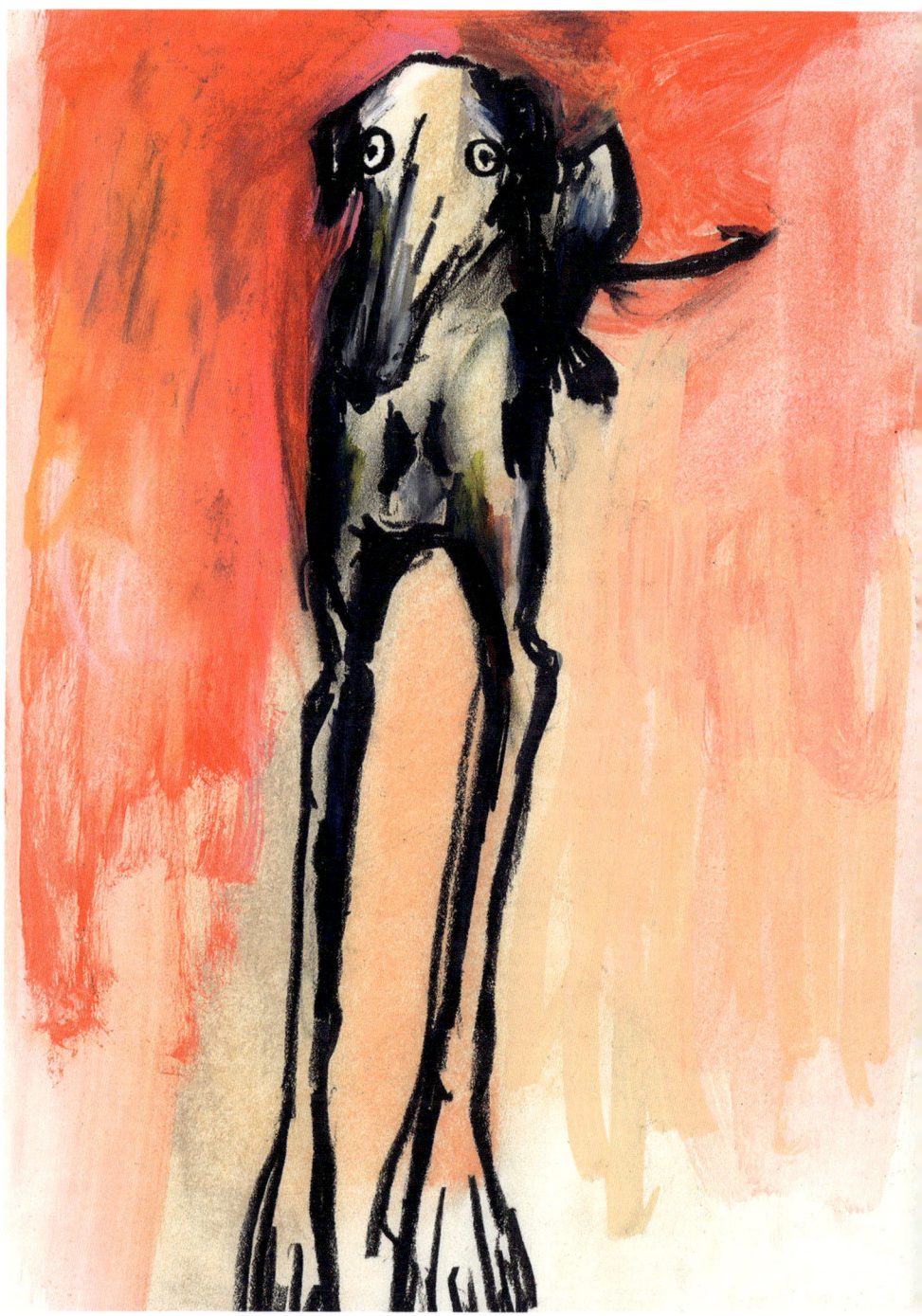

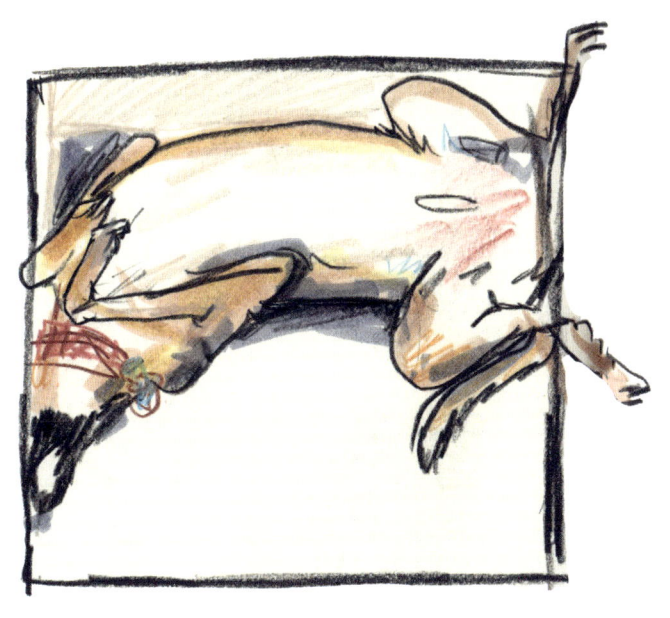

So elegant,
even in slumber.

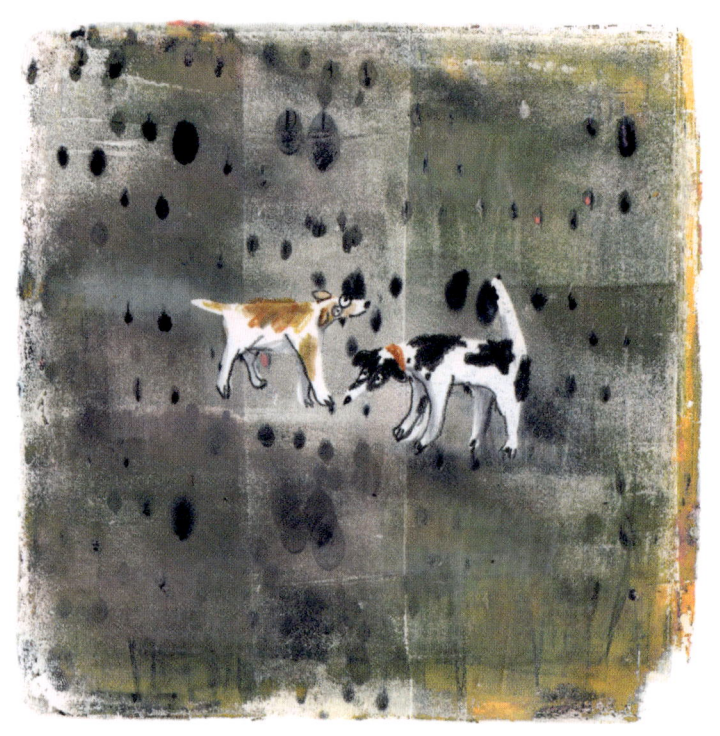

74

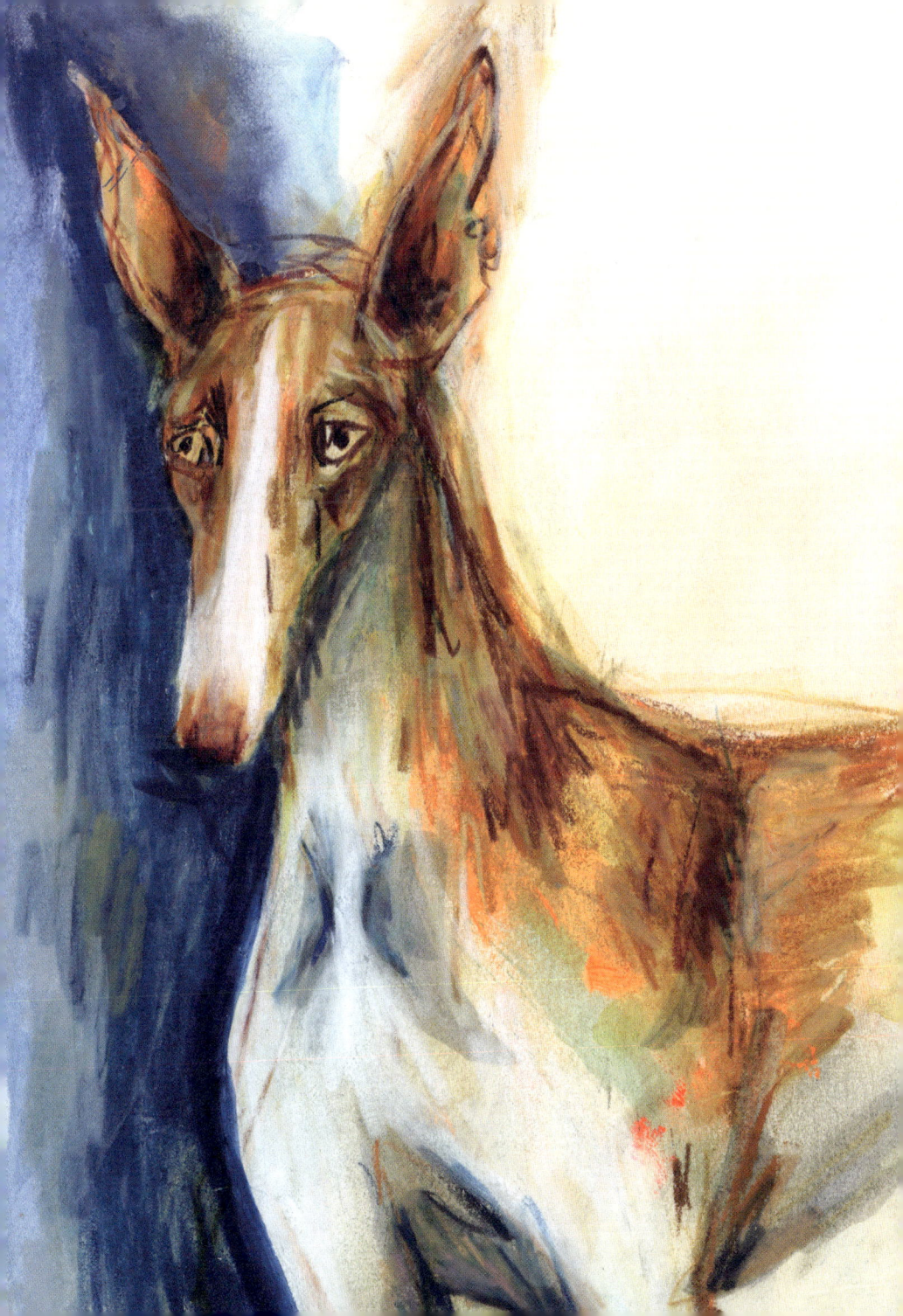

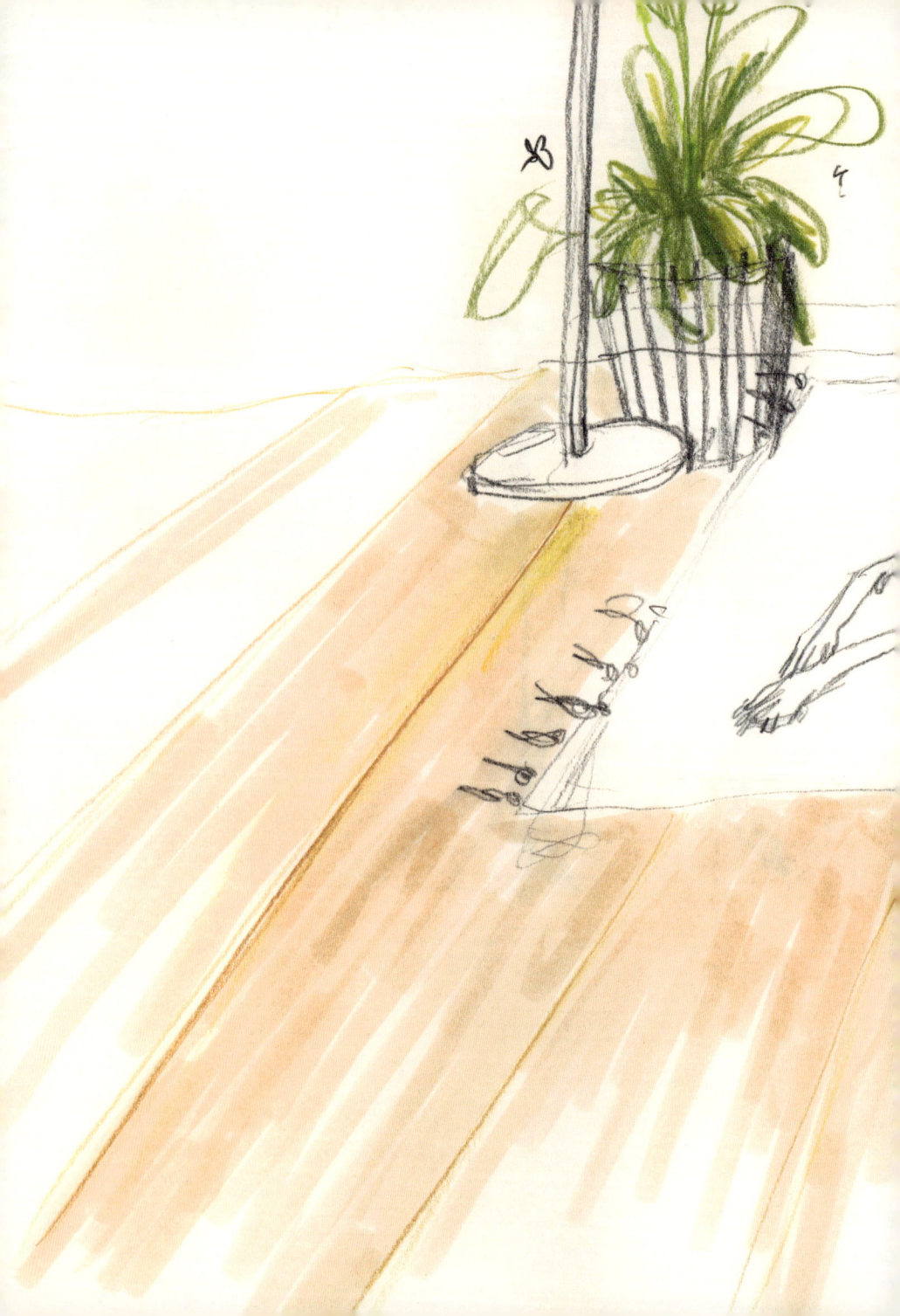

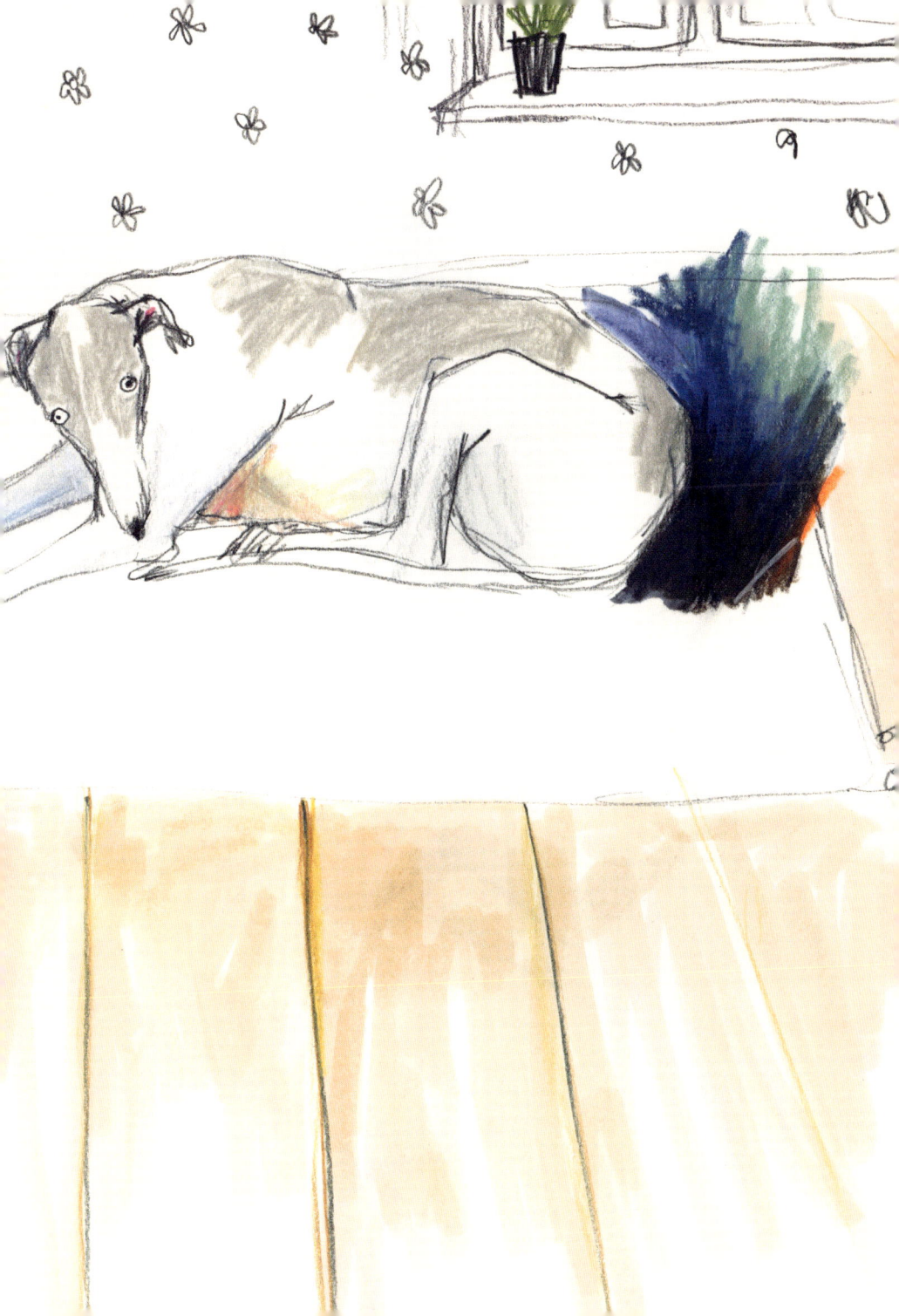

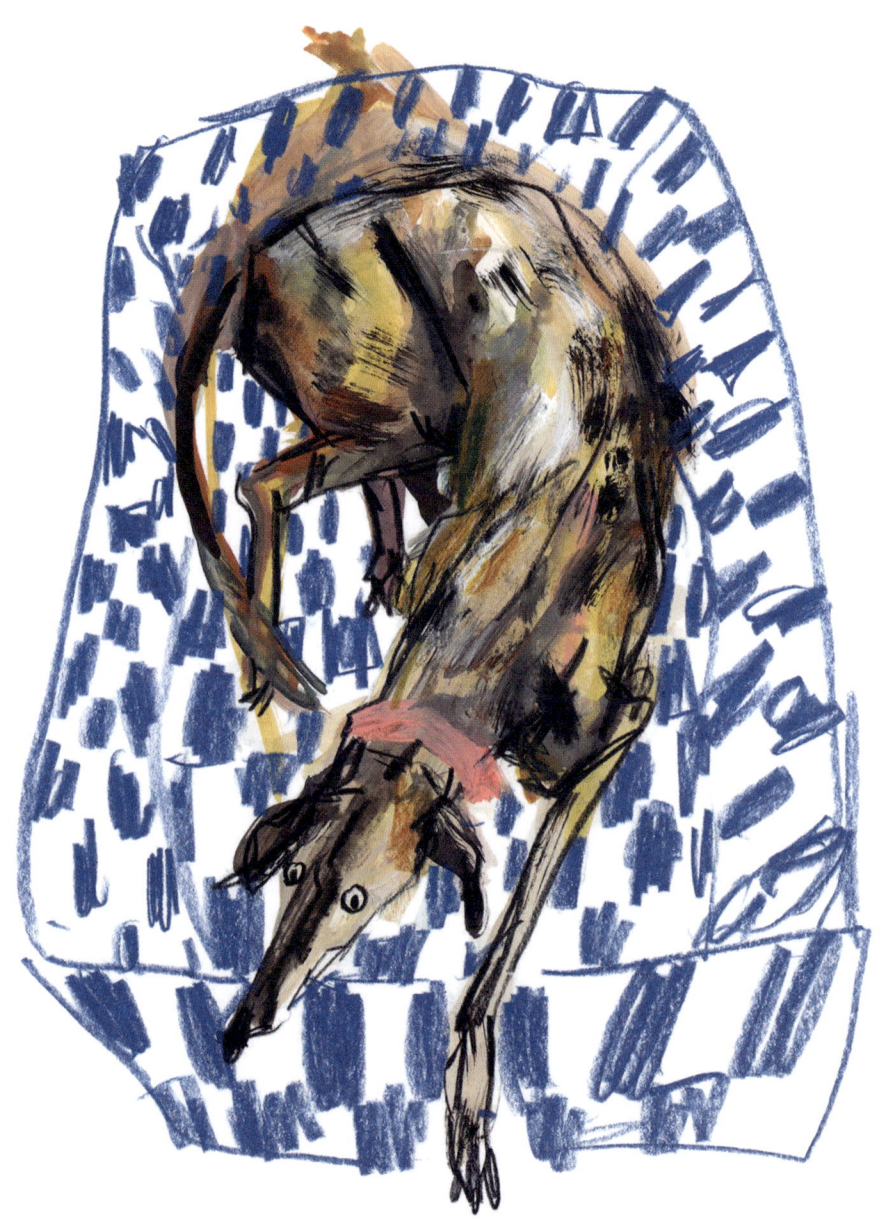

78

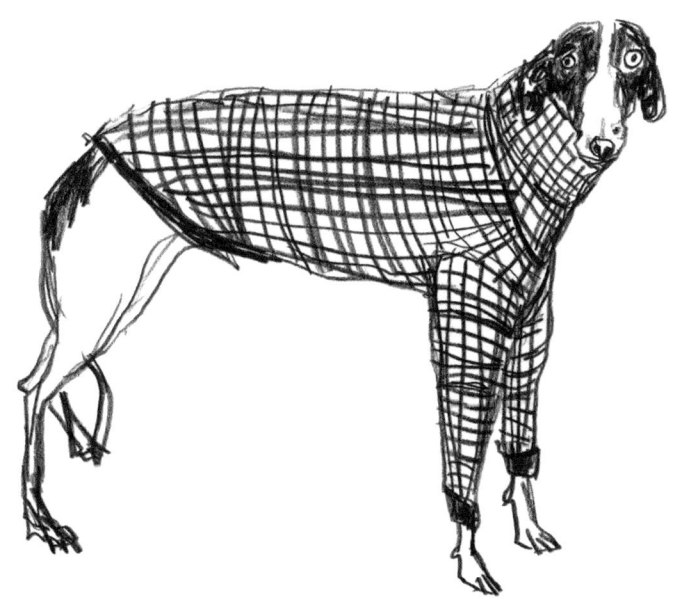

very cold

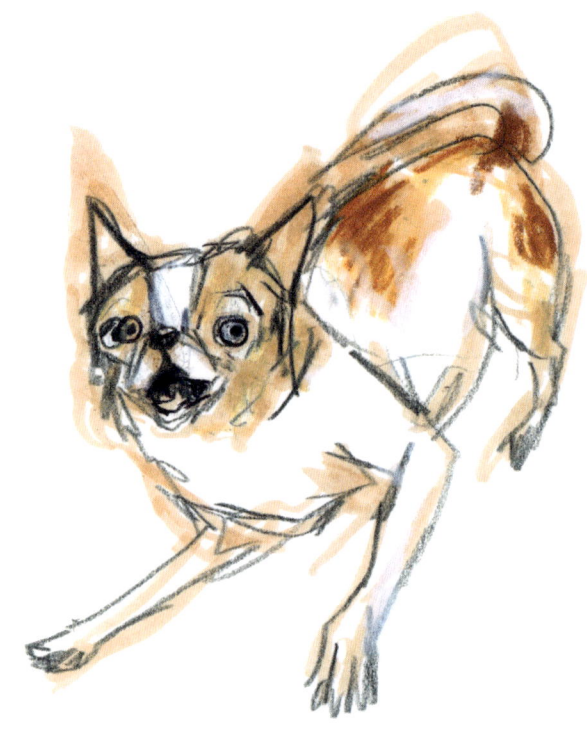

small bork

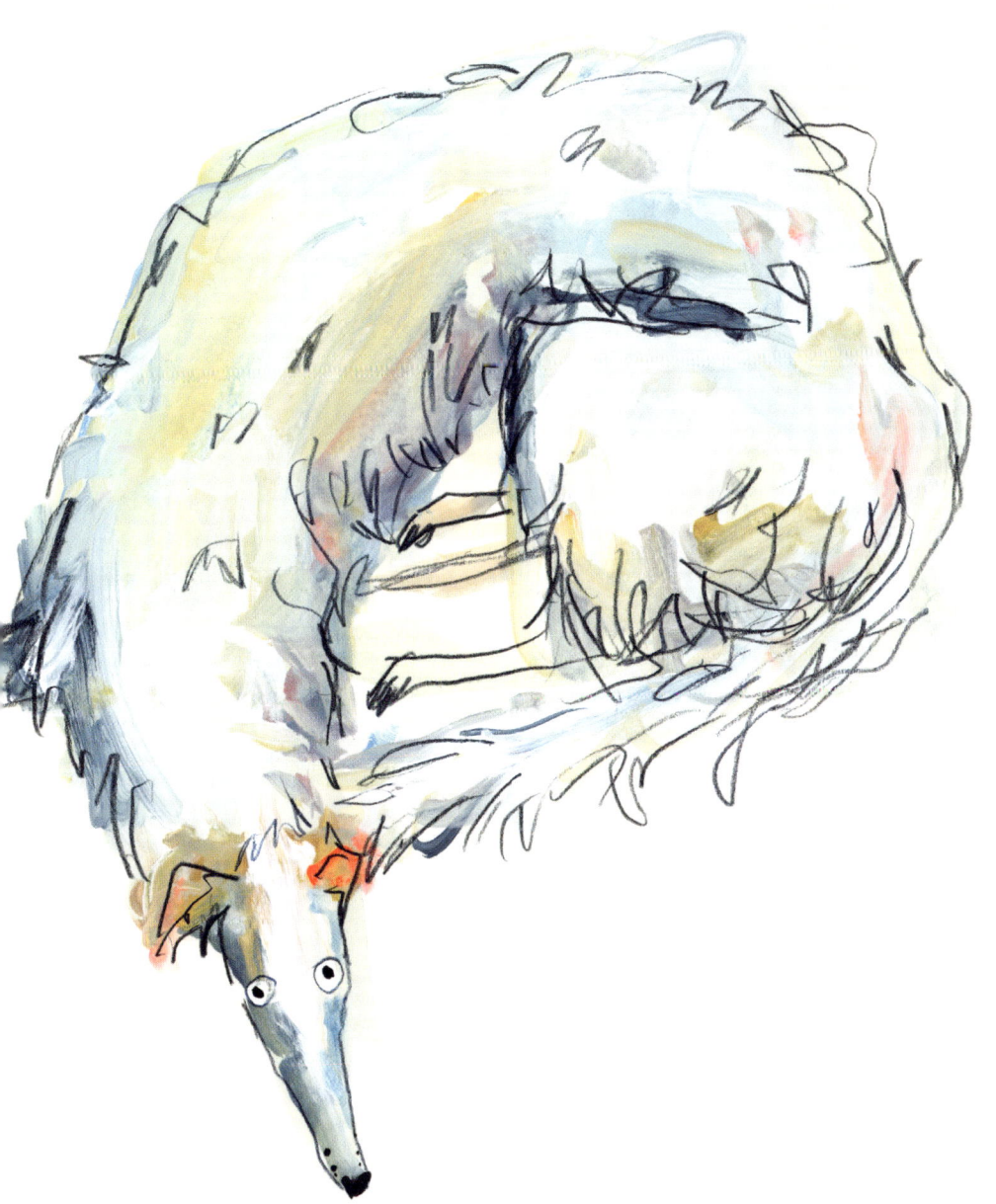

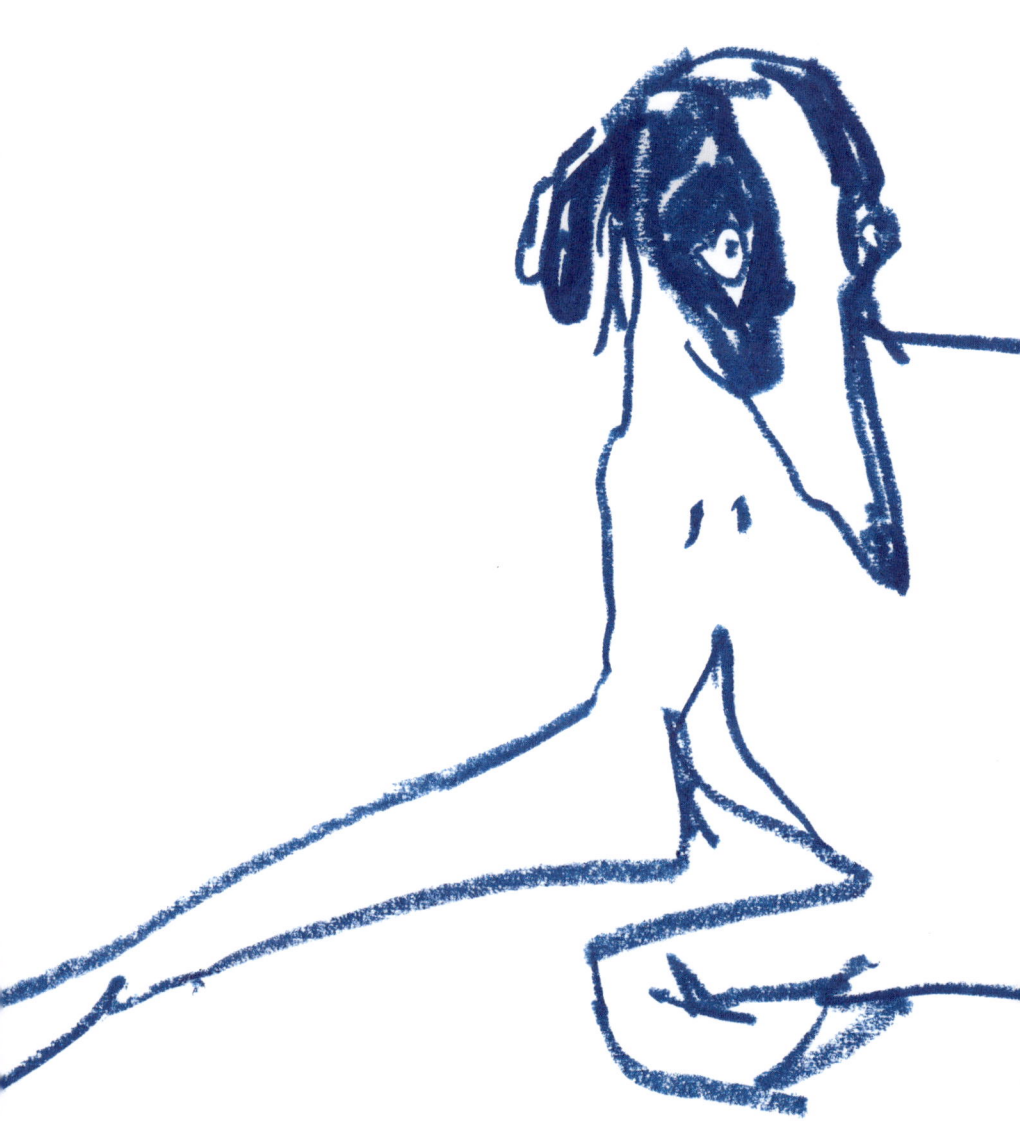

82

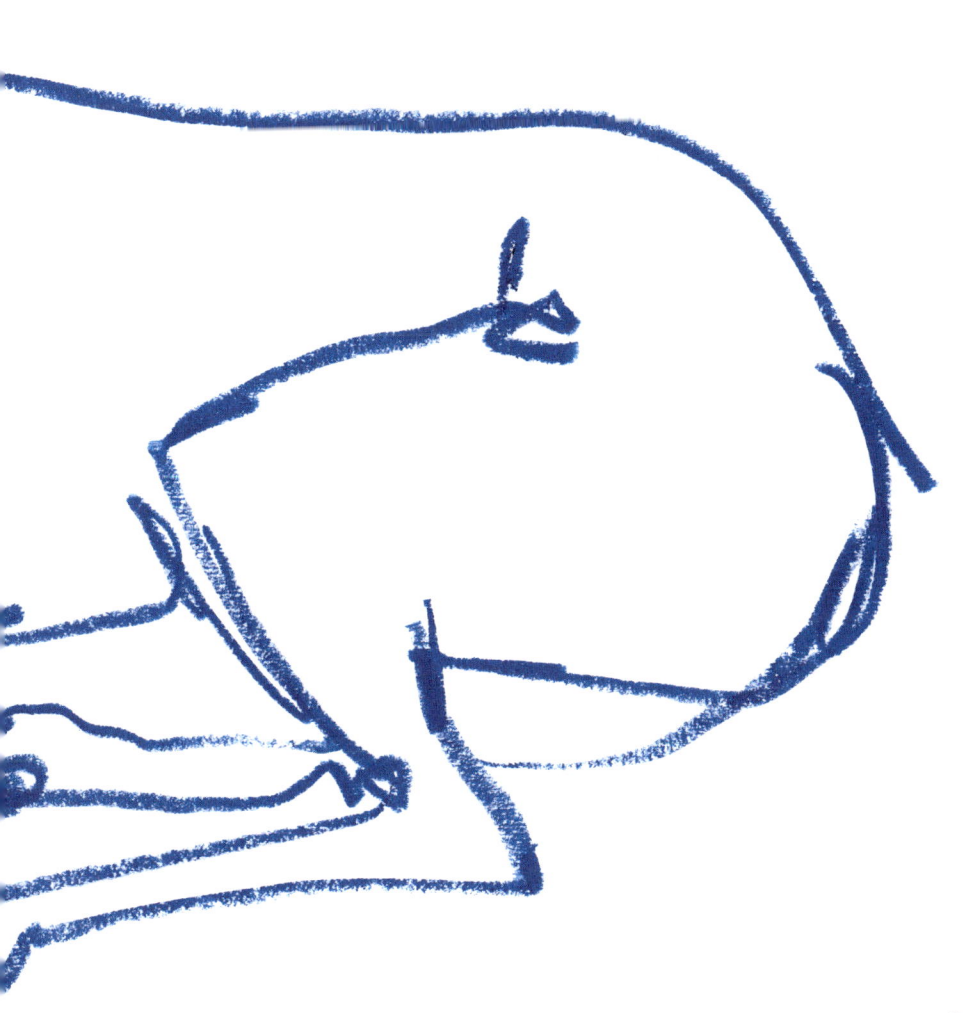

83

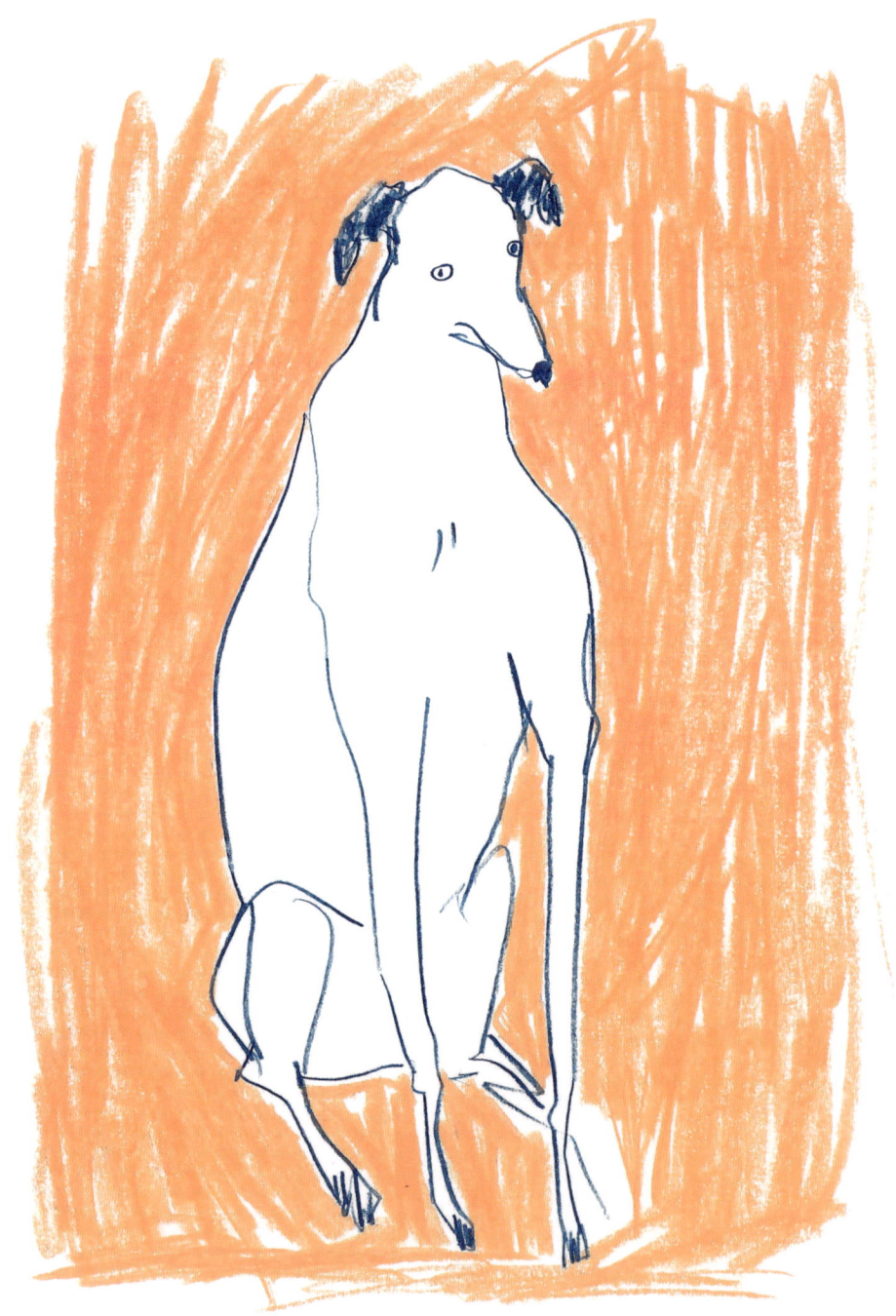

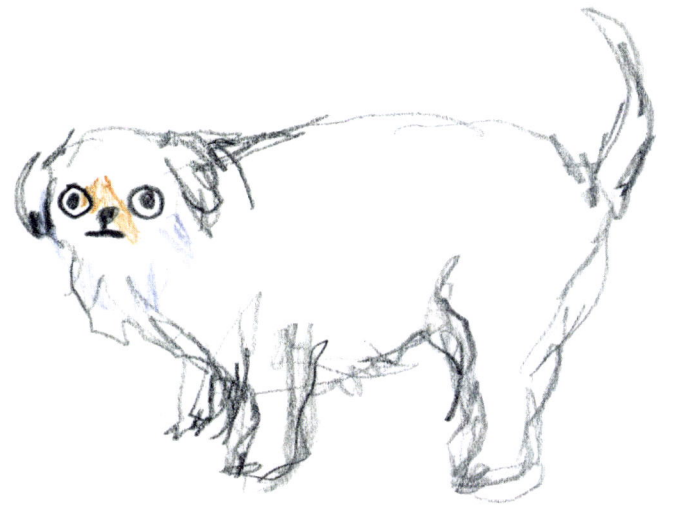

I was Told there would be cheese.

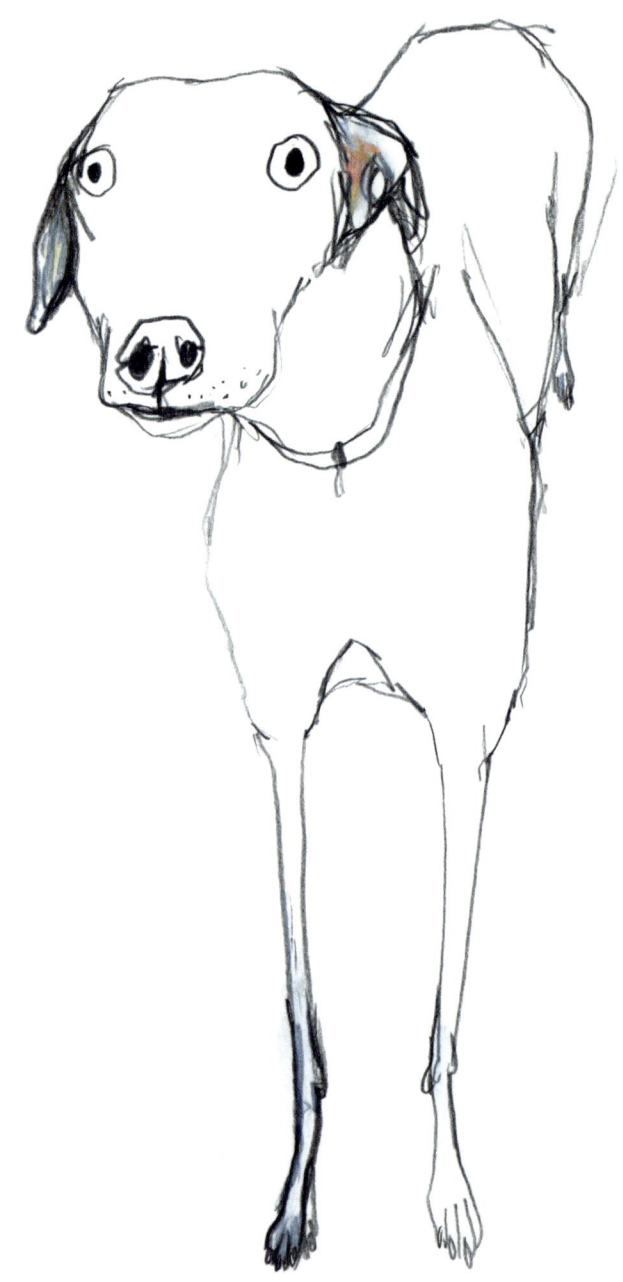

86

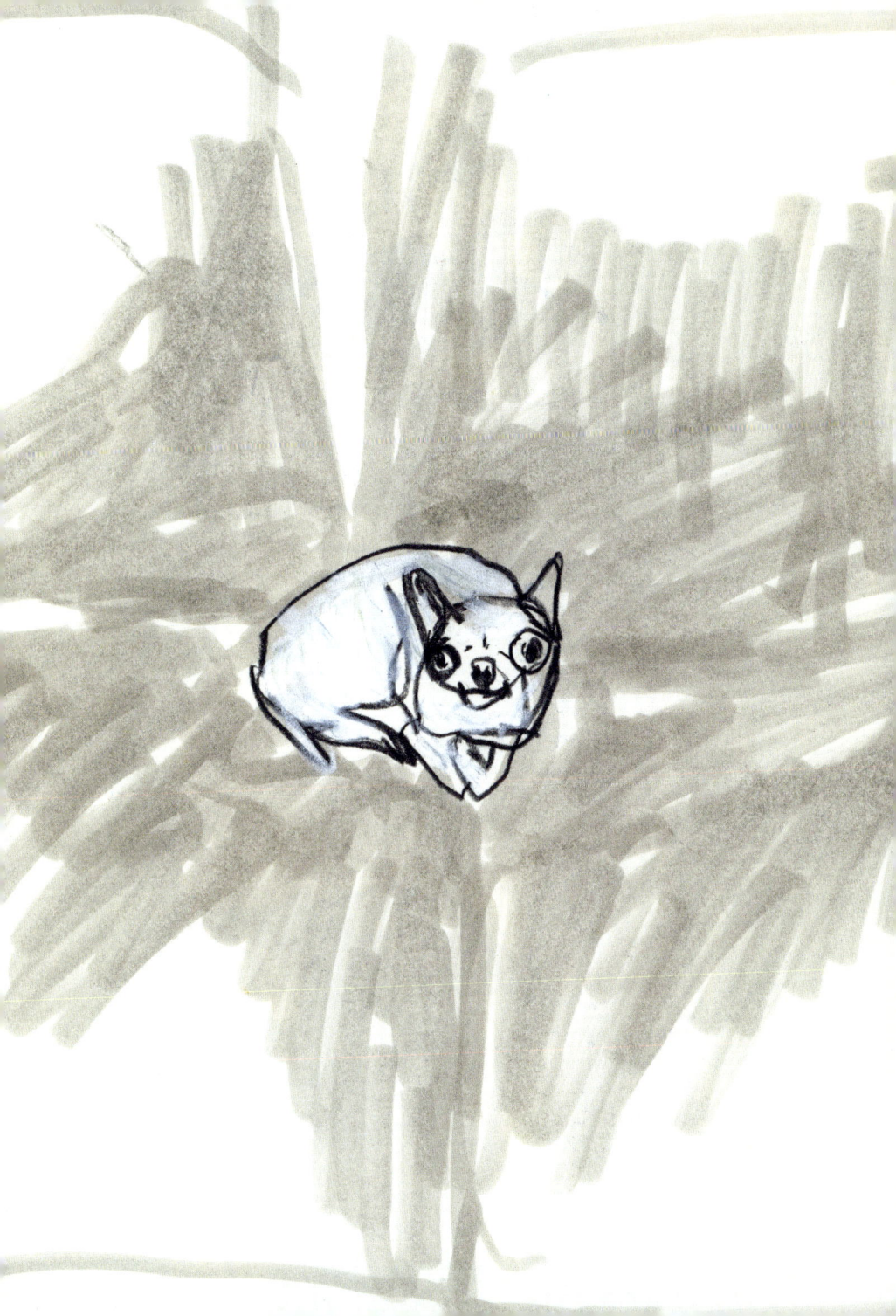

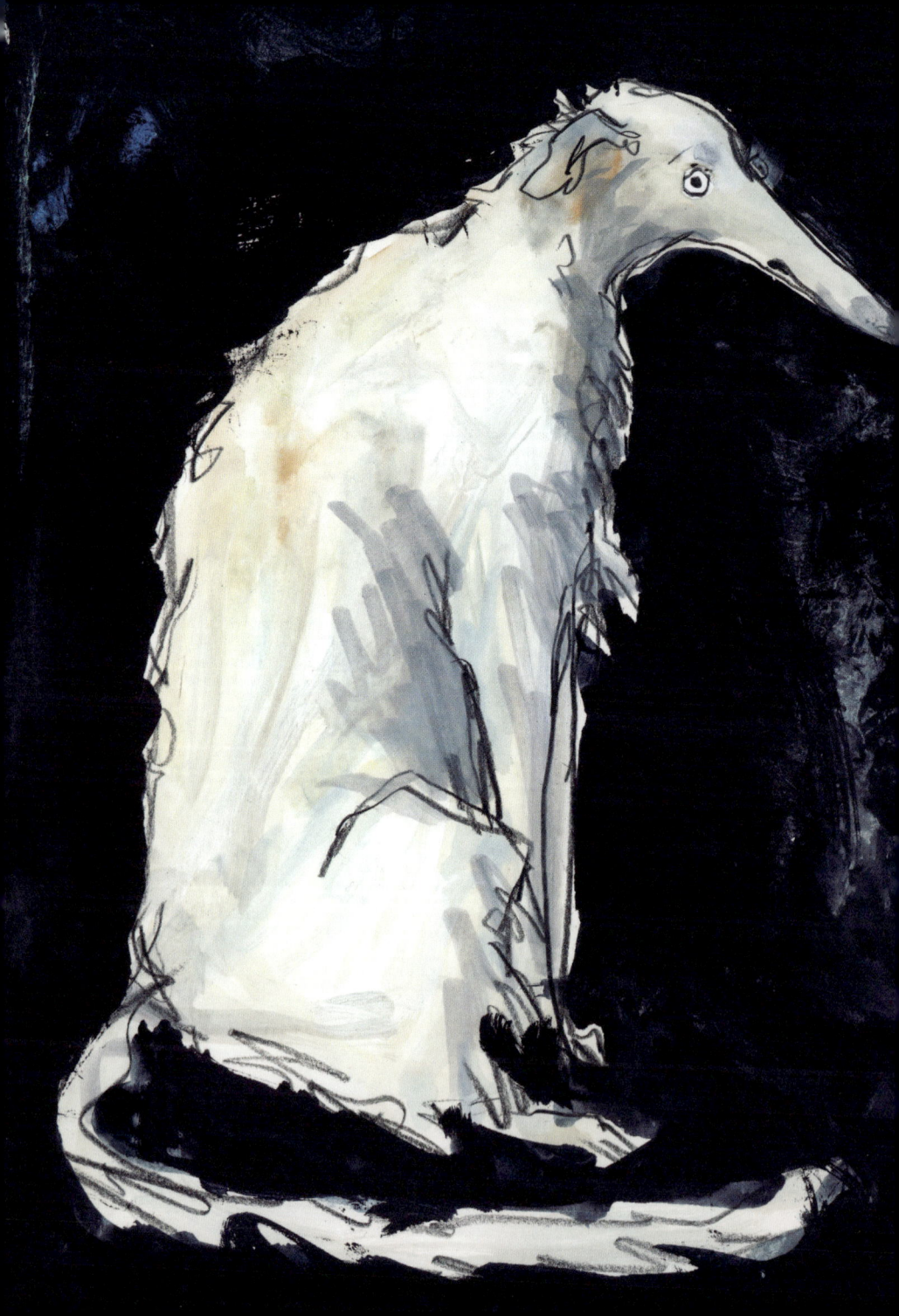

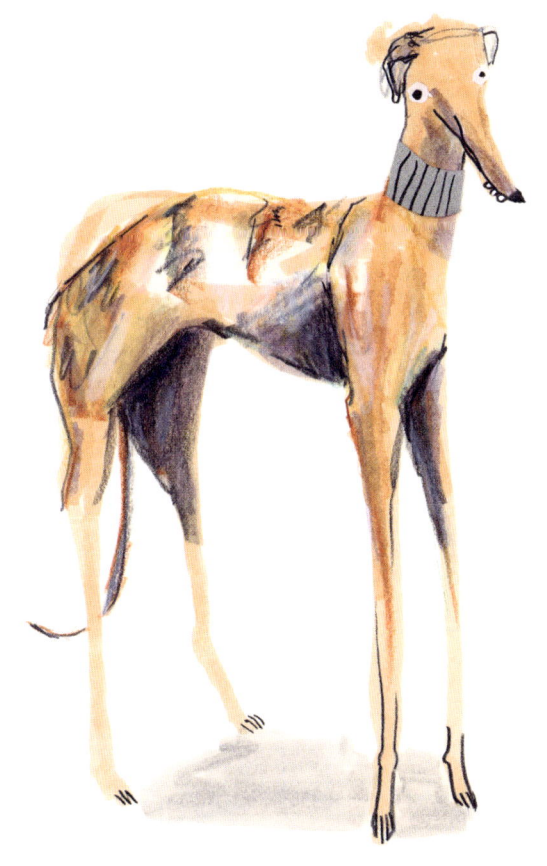

DOING GReat.

89

I LOVE IT WHEN YOU RUN

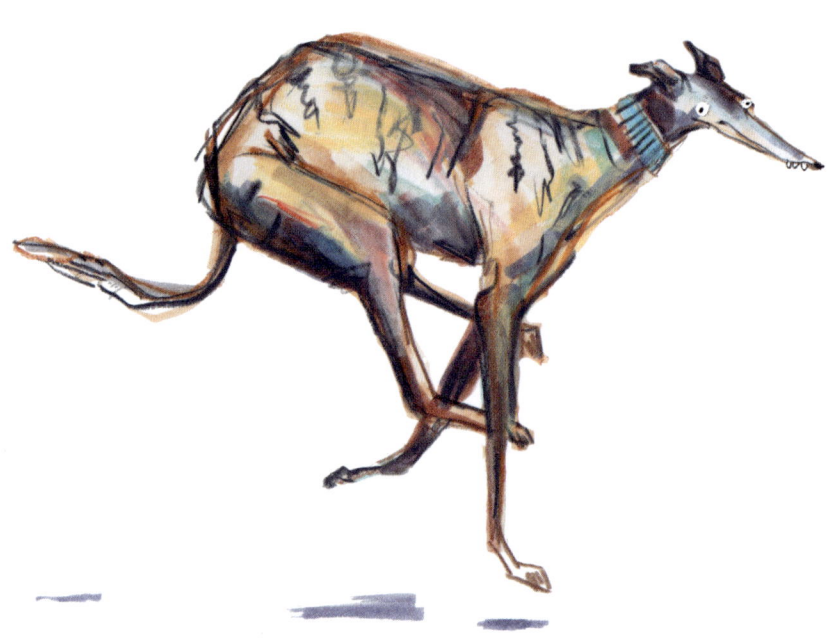

90

WITHOUT A CARE IN THE WORLD.

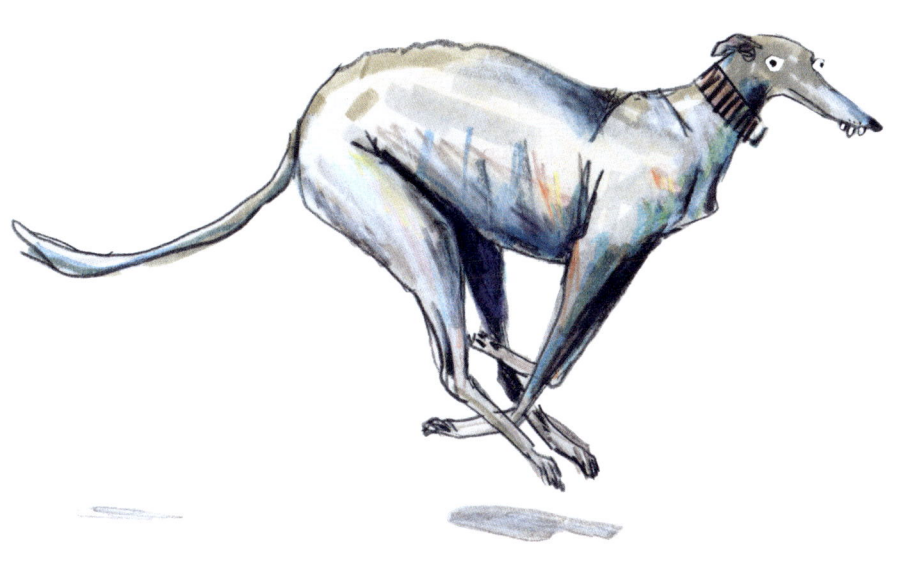

91

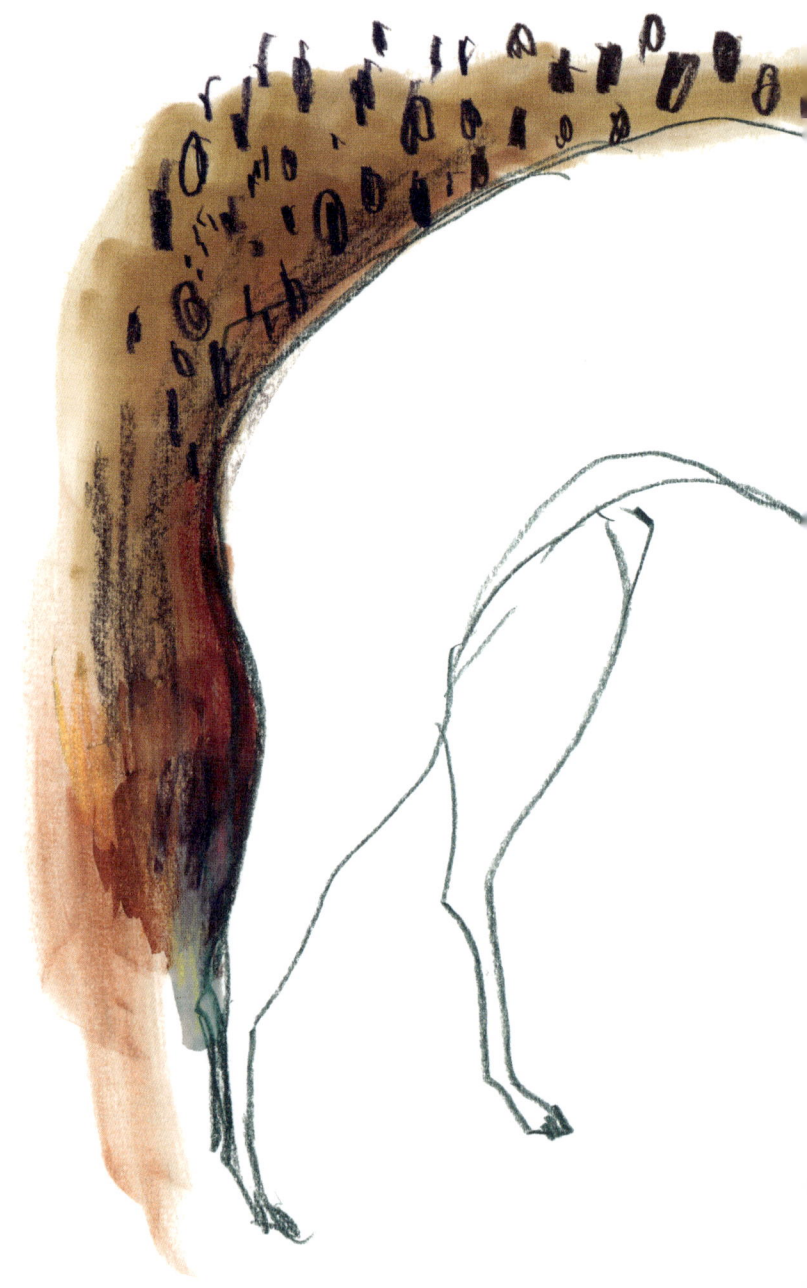

92

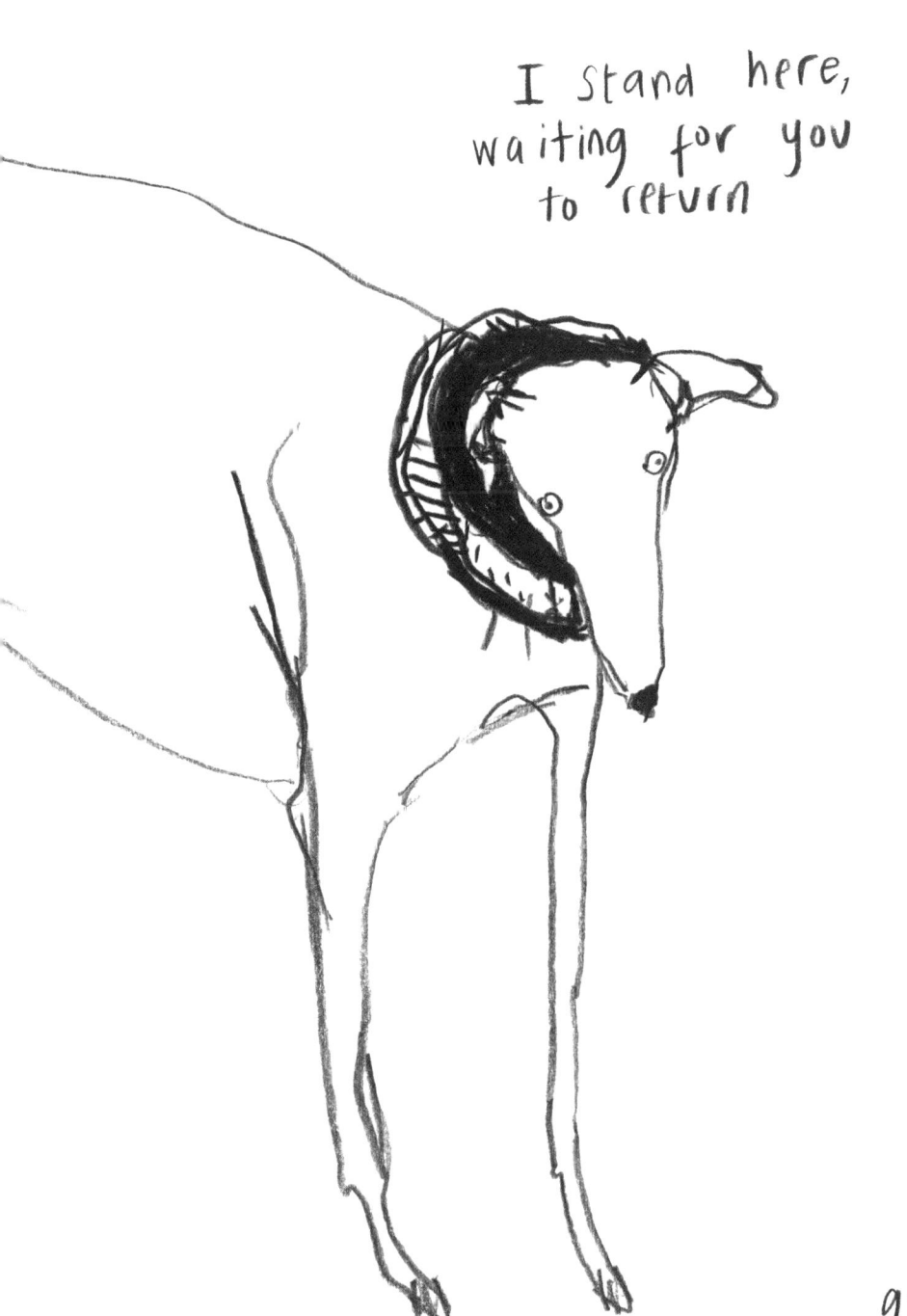

I stand here,
waiting for you
to return

93

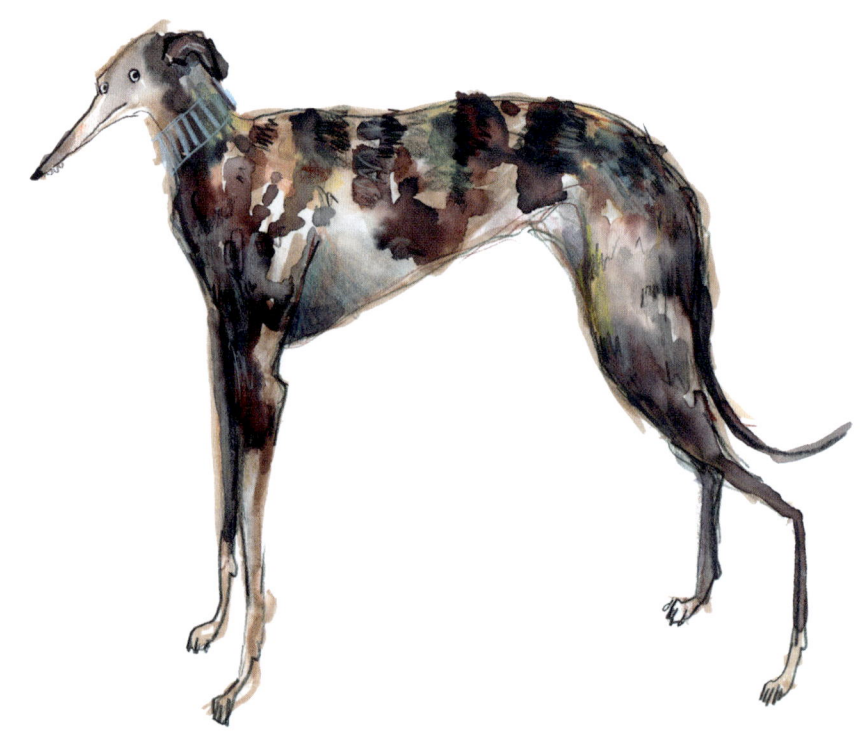

SUSPICION

94

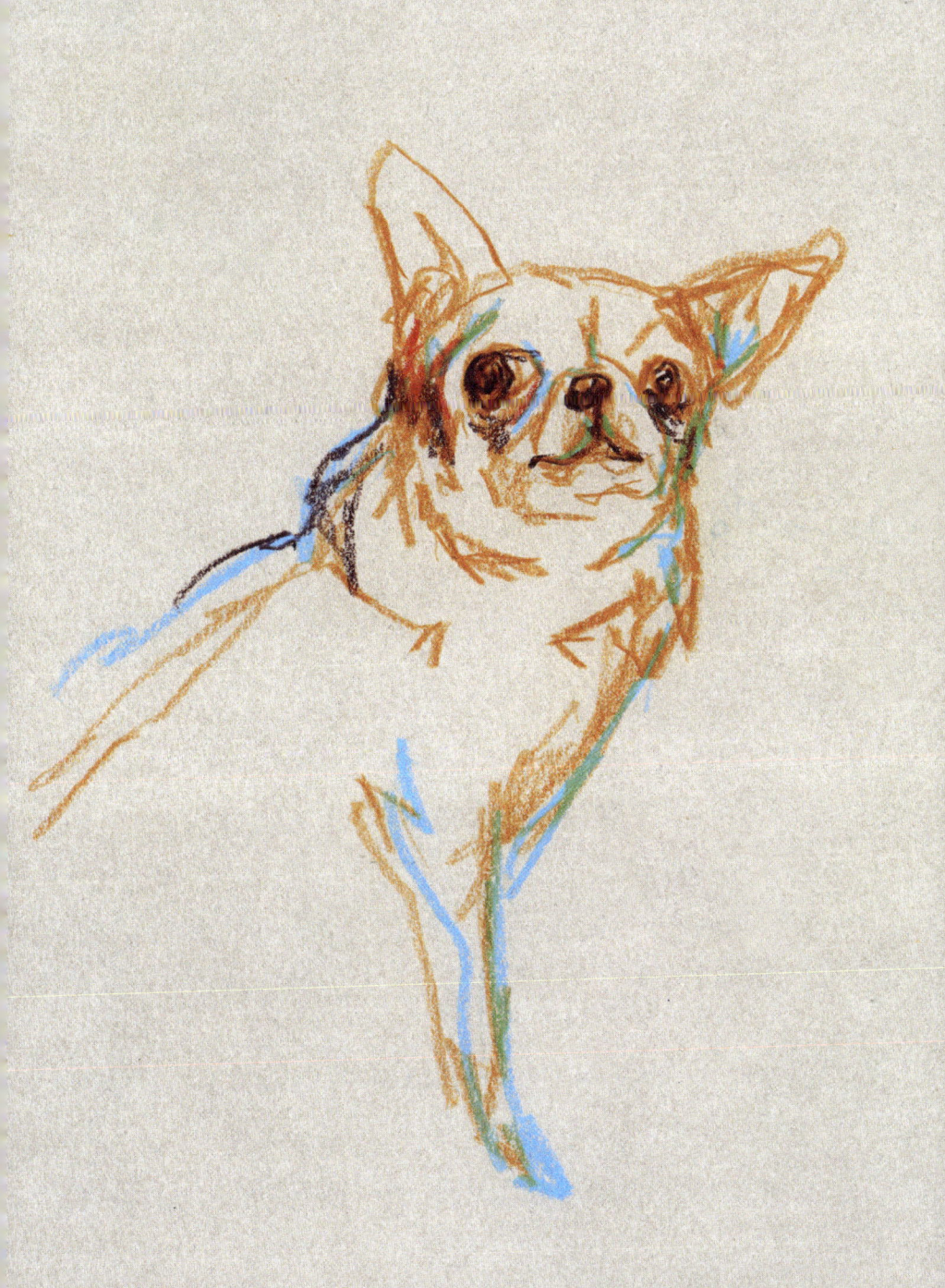

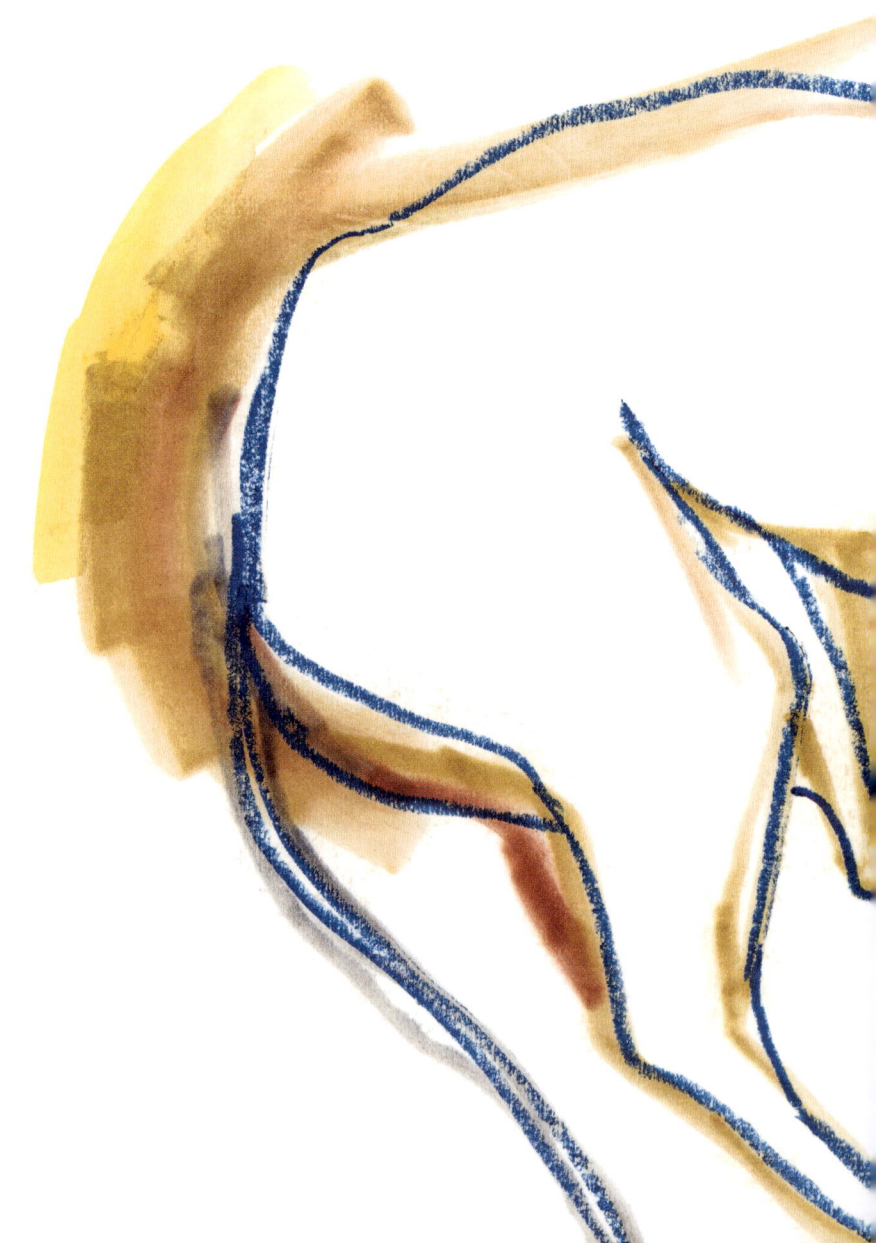

96

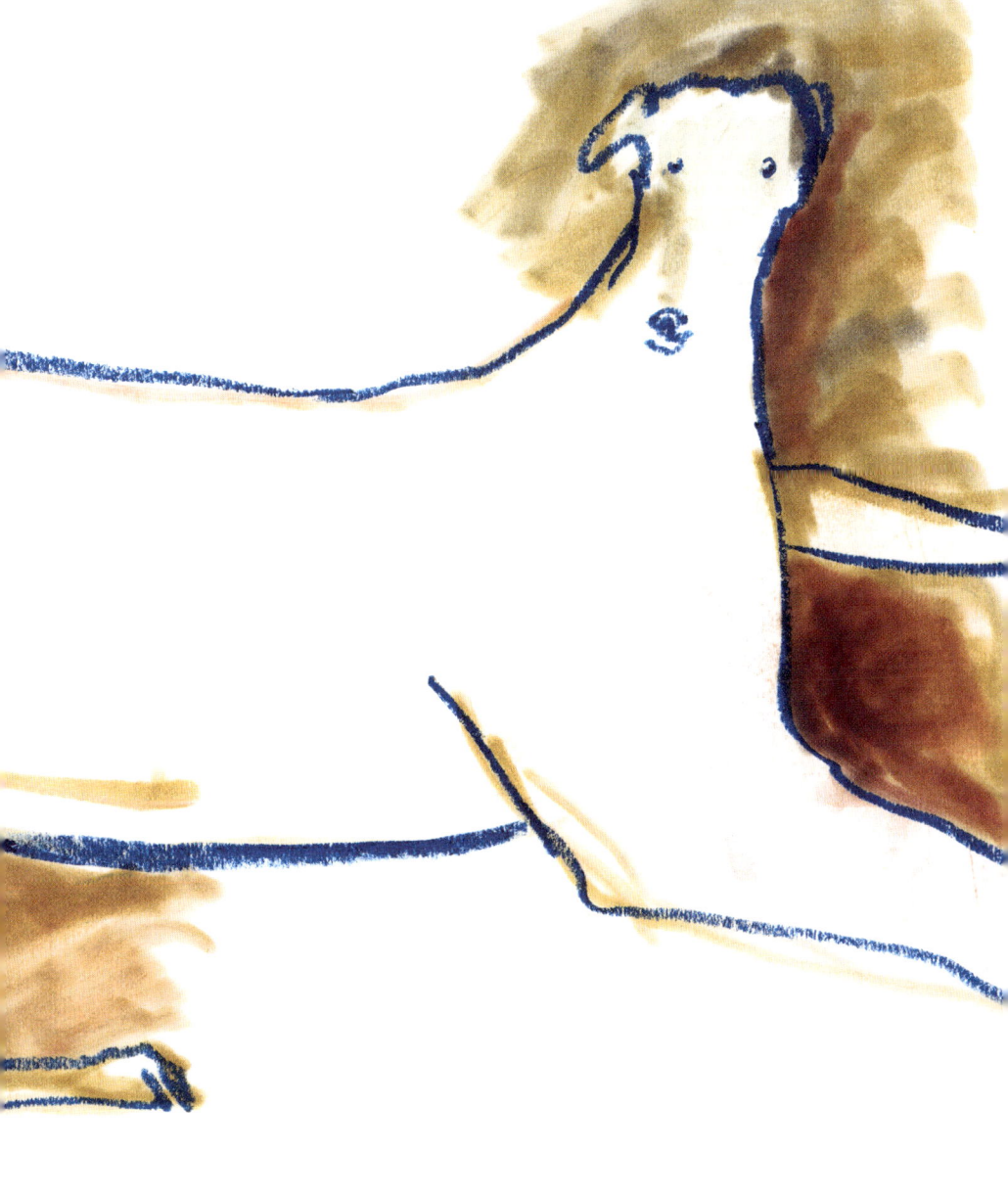

97

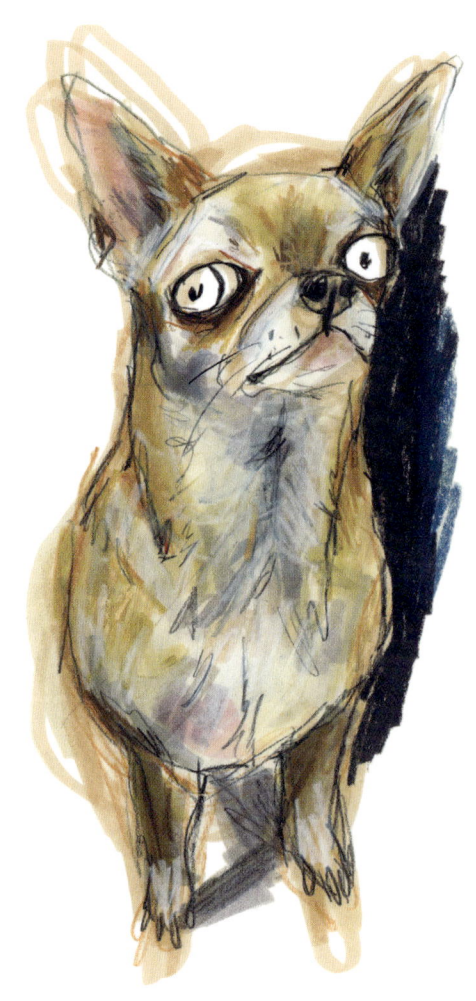

Nope

98

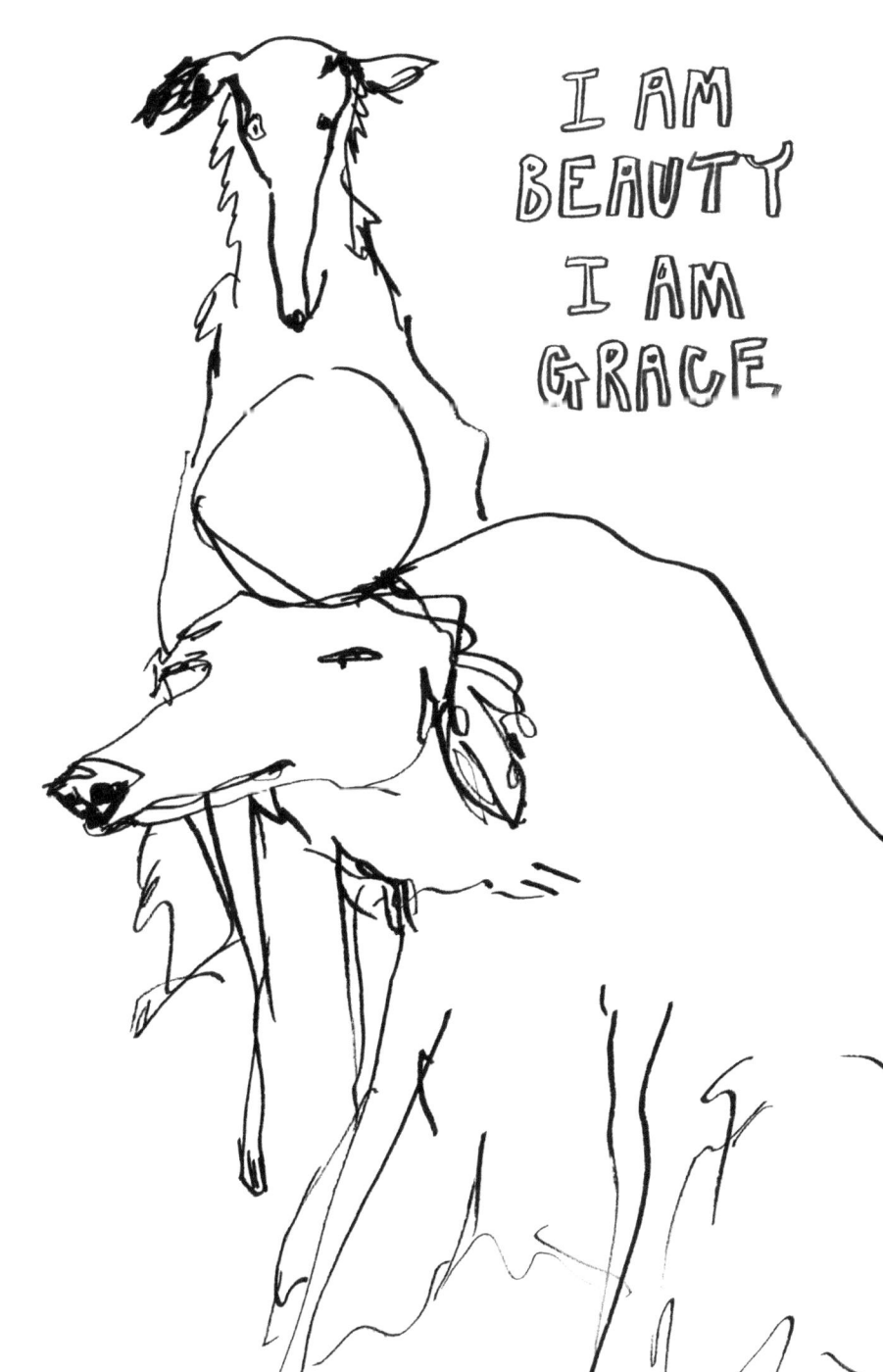

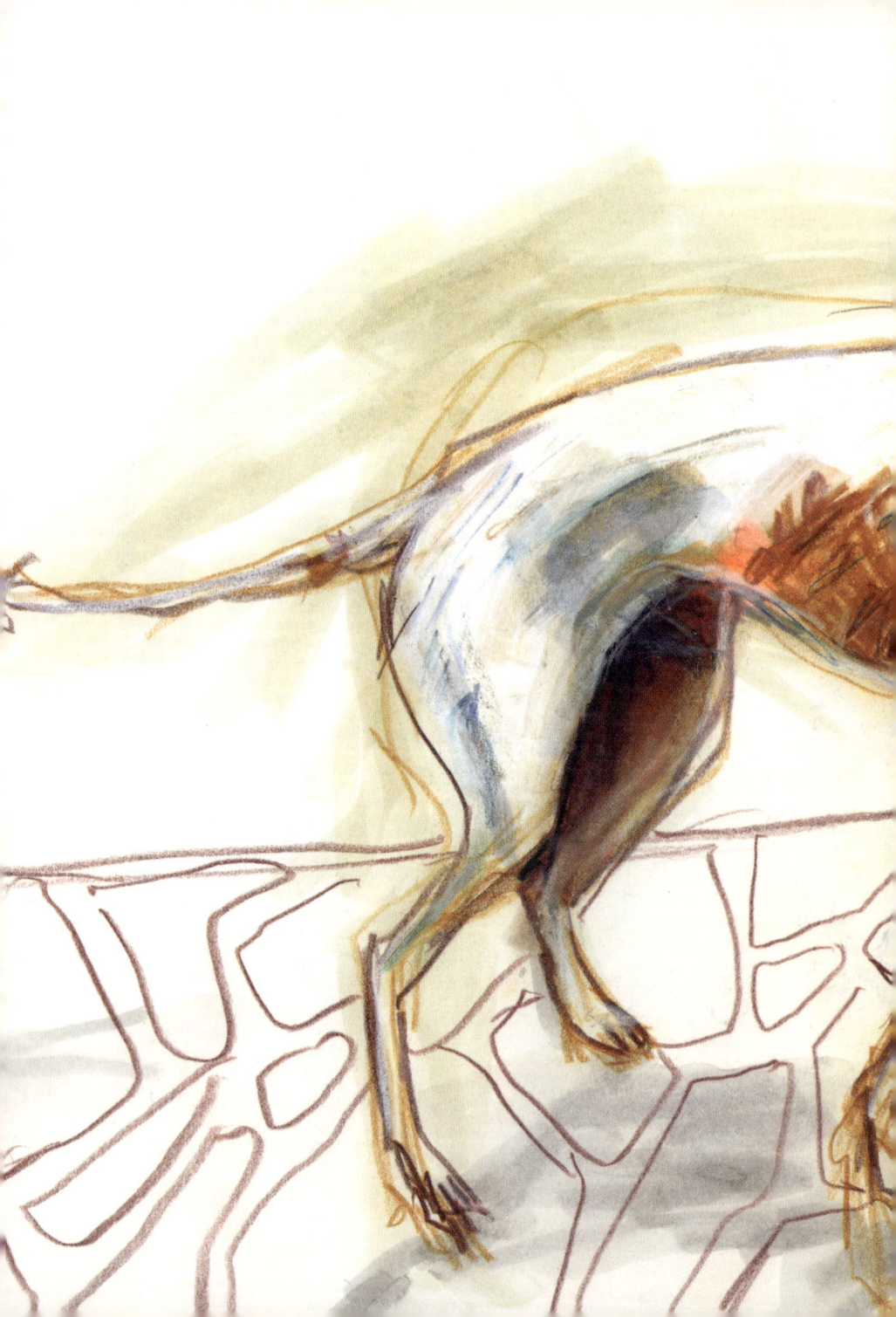

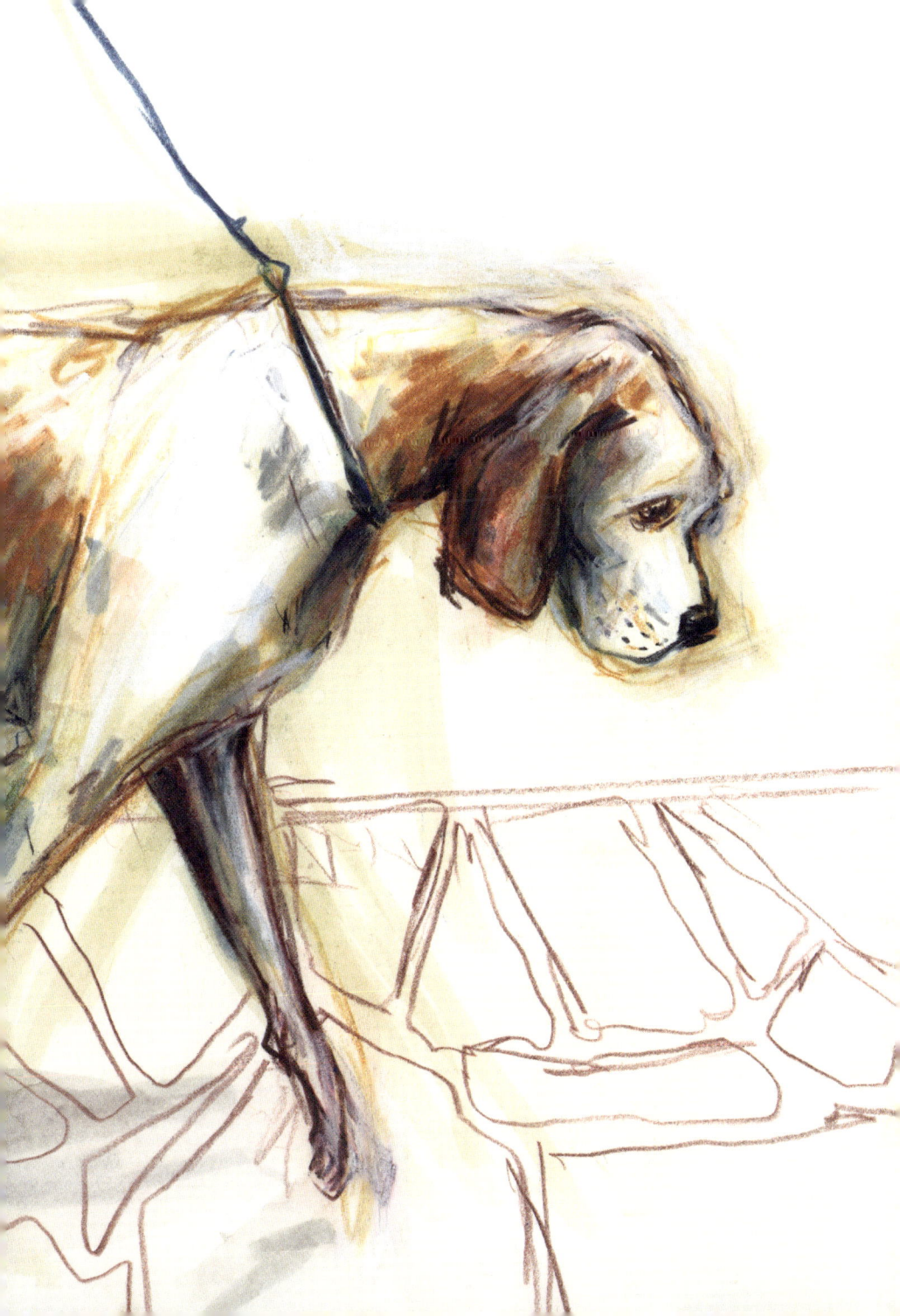

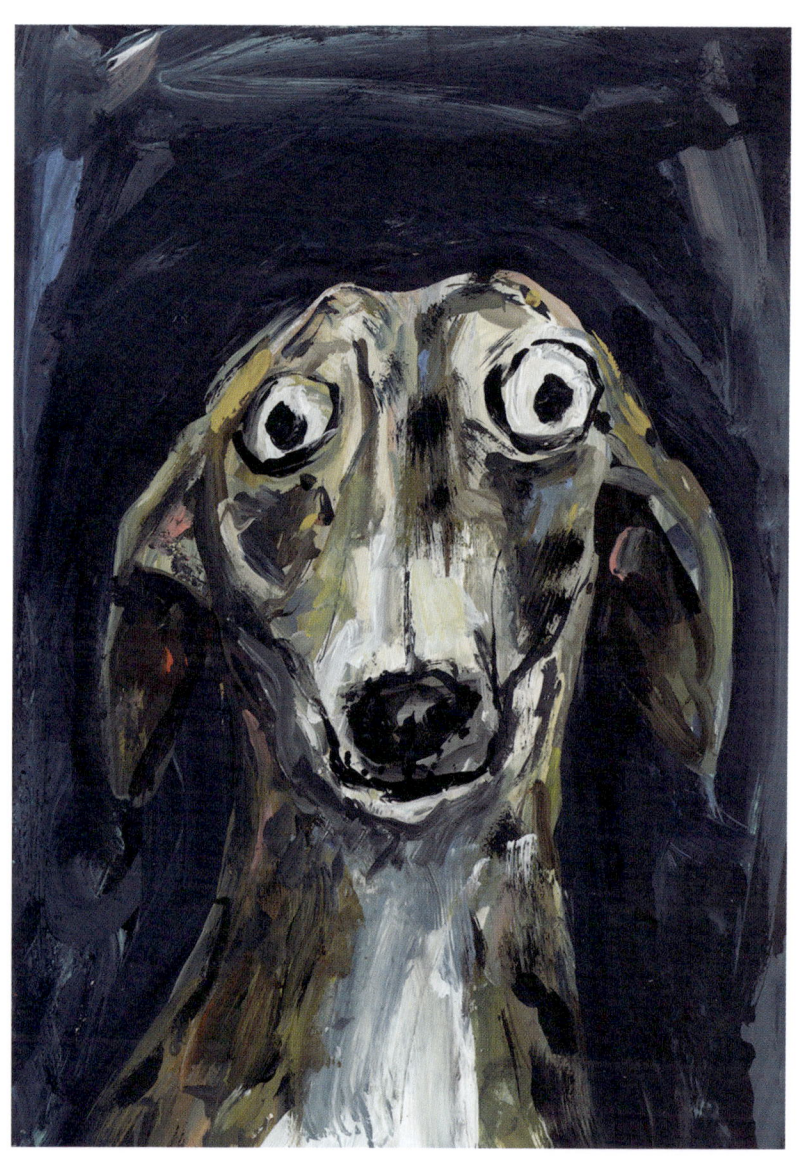

102

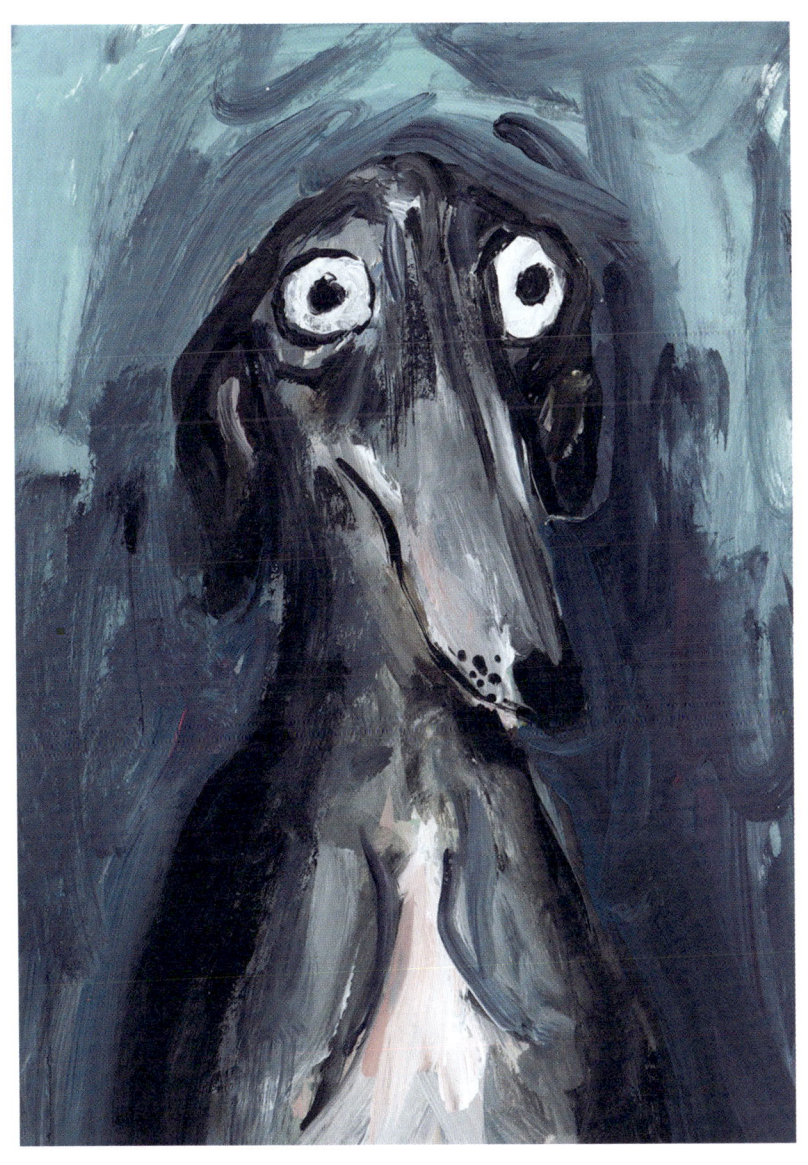

103

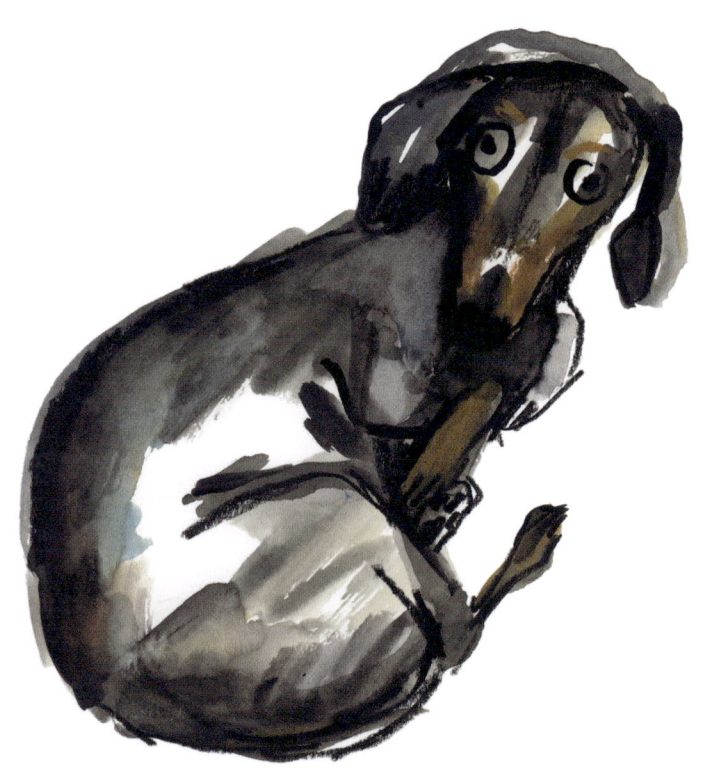

104

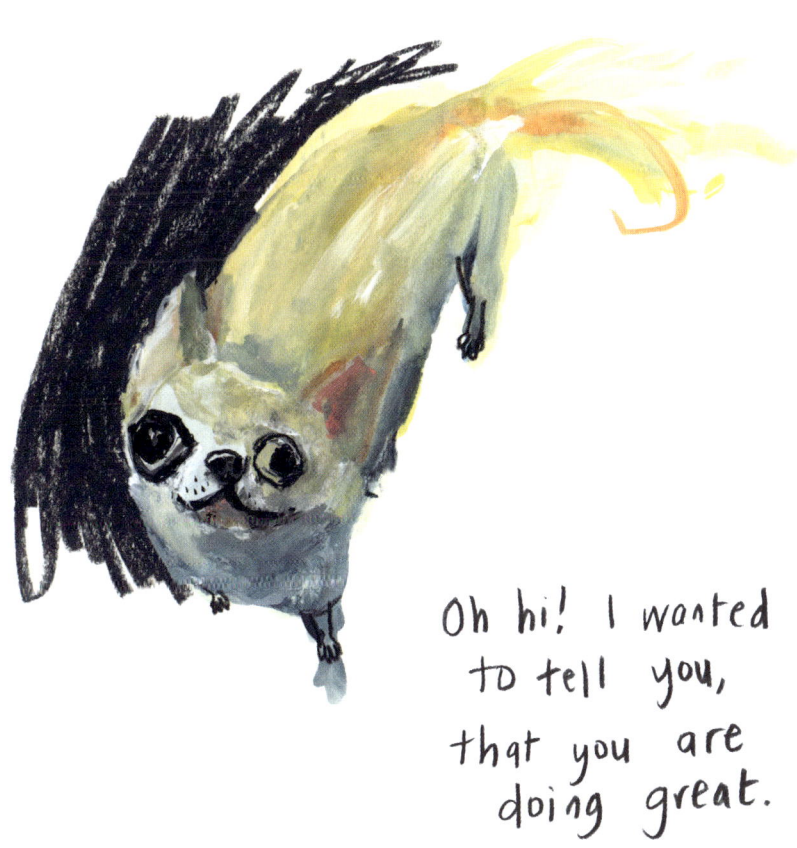

Oh hi! I wanted
to tell you,
that you are
doing great.

105

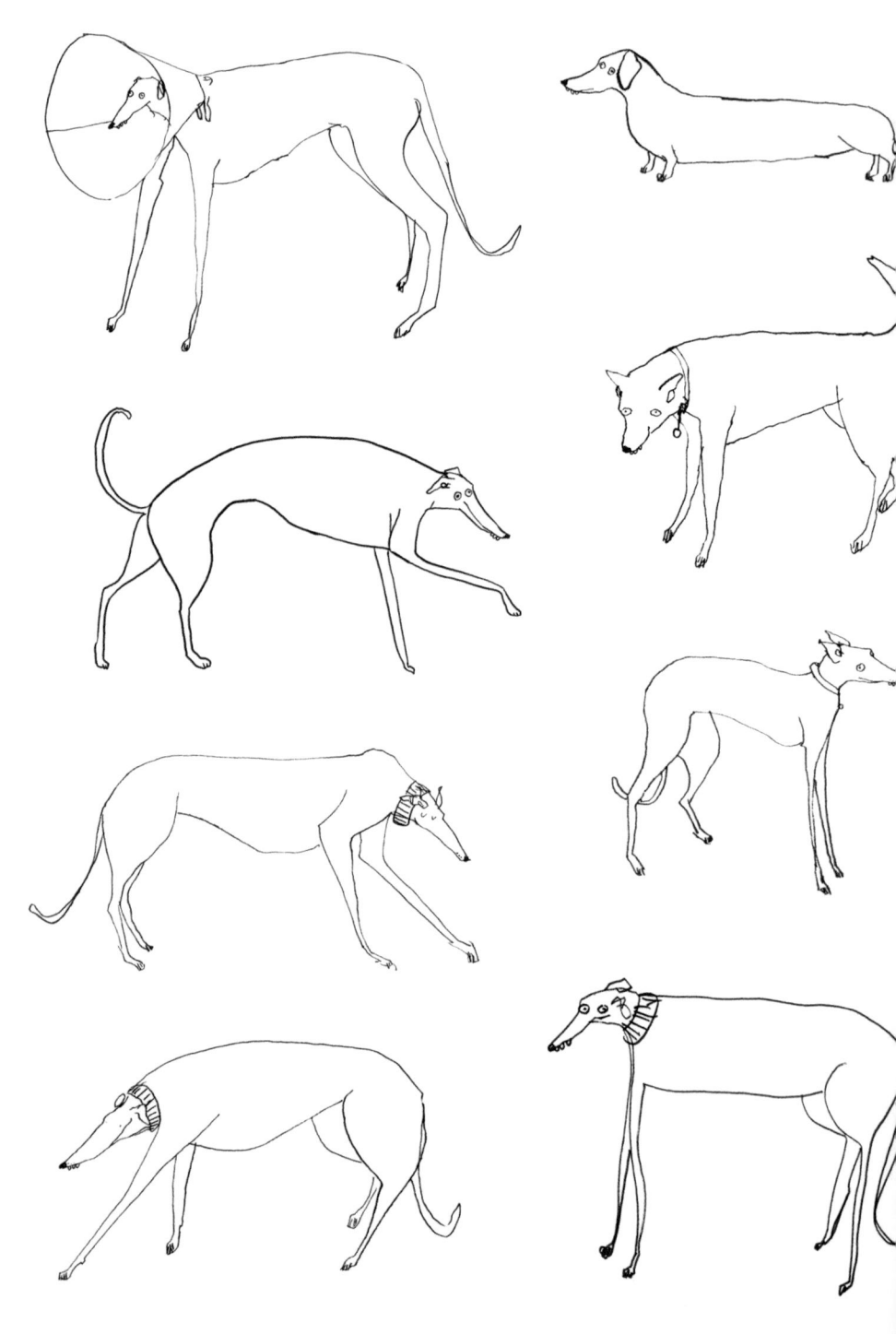

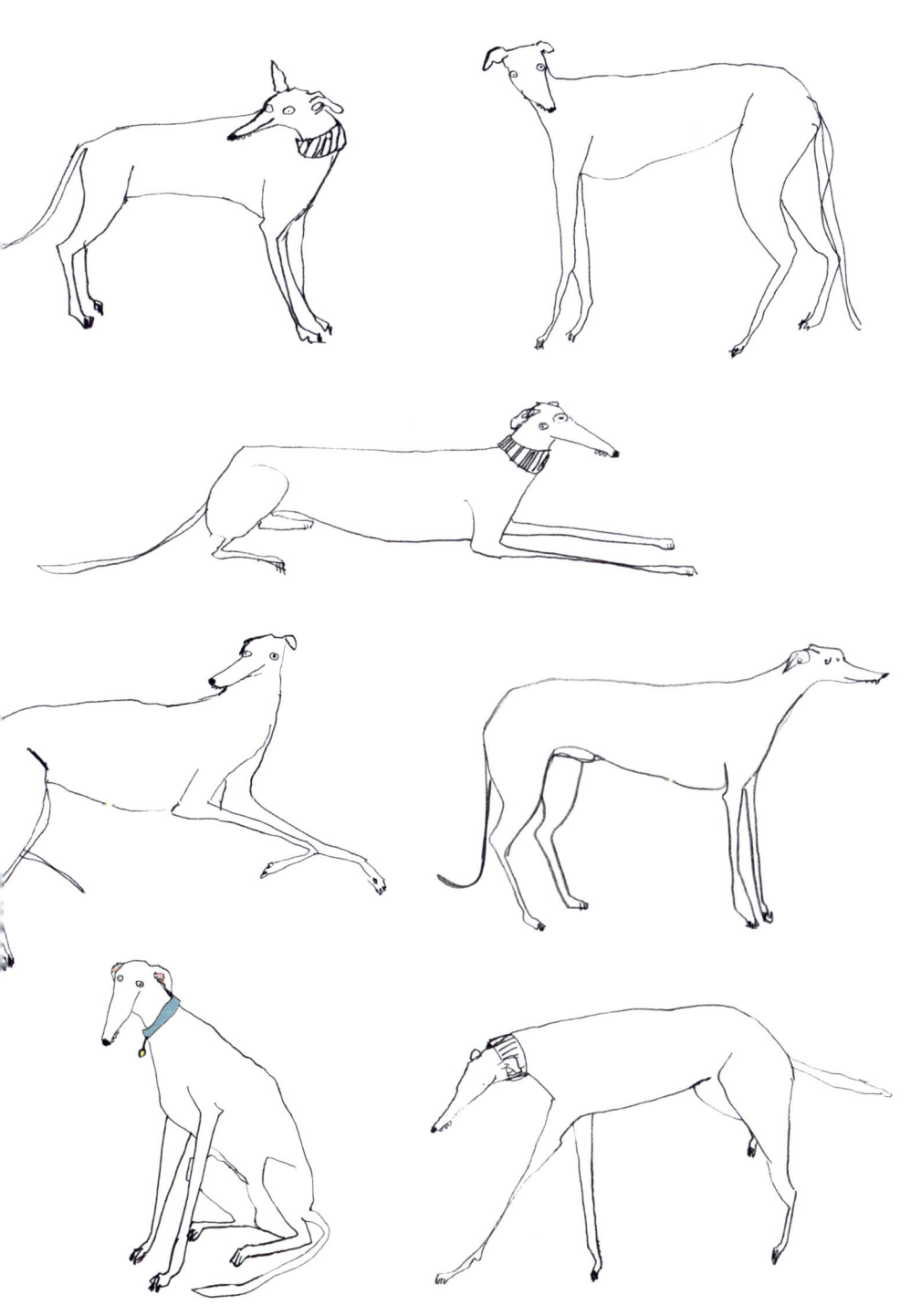

LOOk aT our Faces...

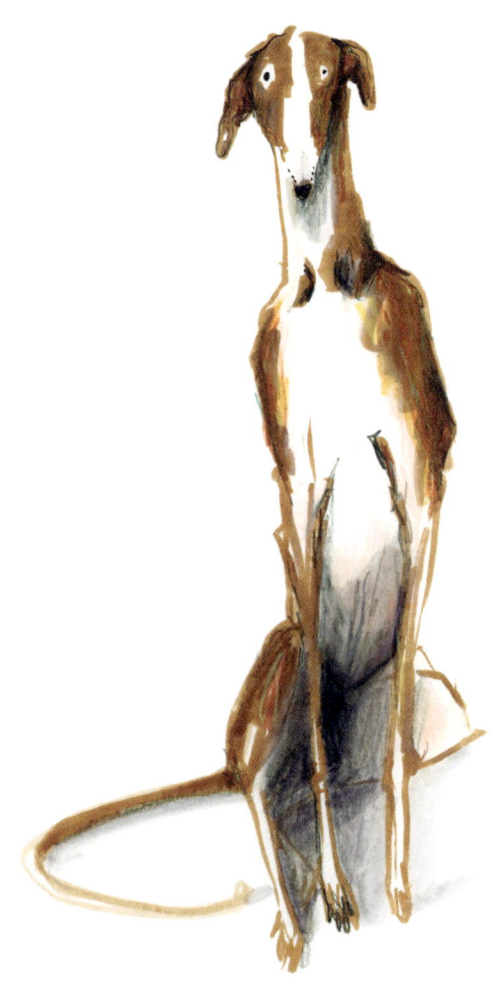

...and give us the food.

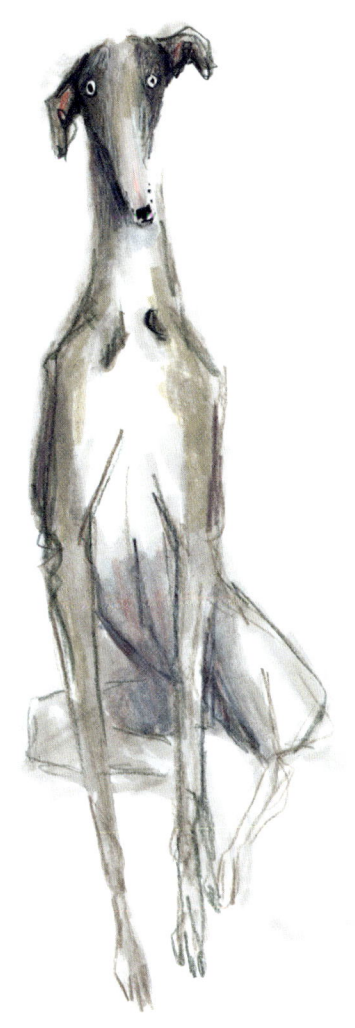

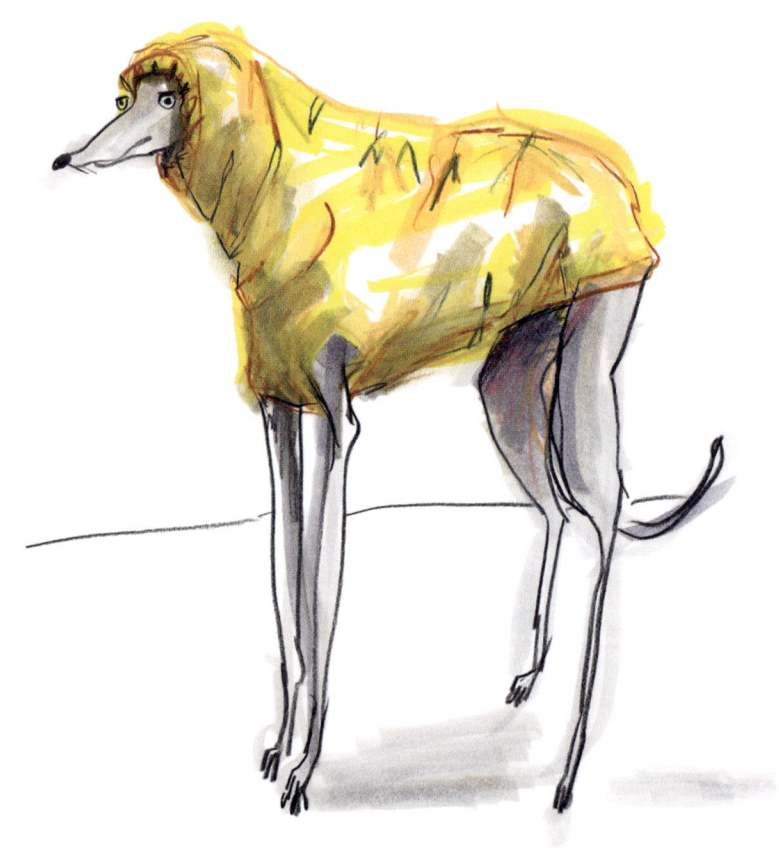

REGRET

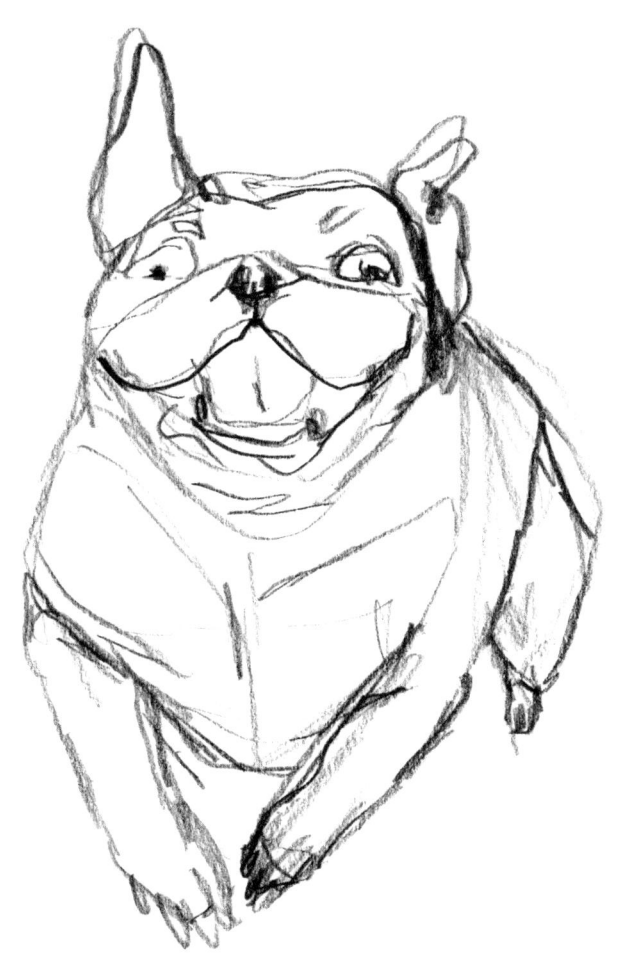

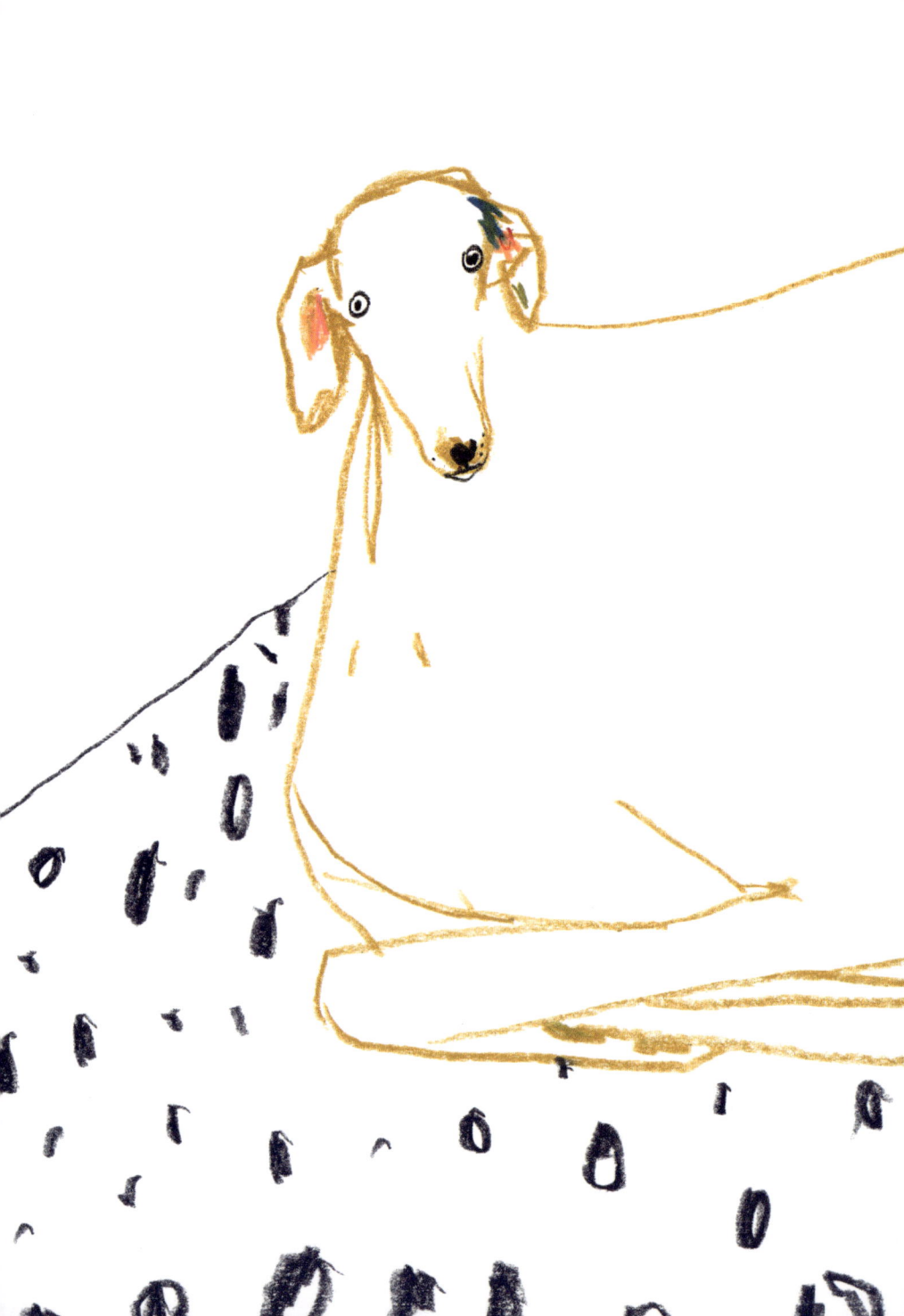

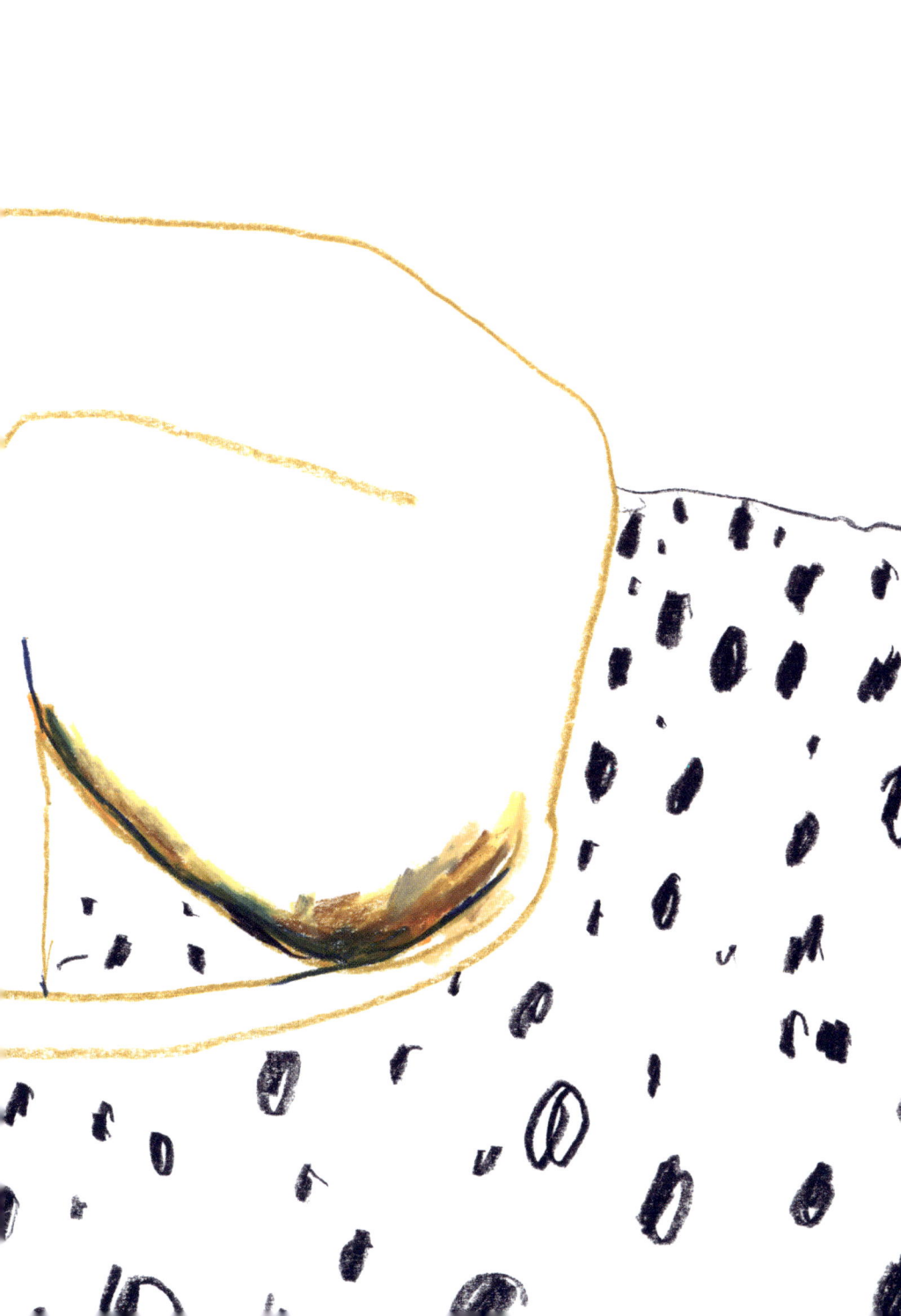

I am ready to
participate in life

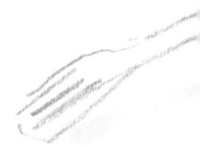

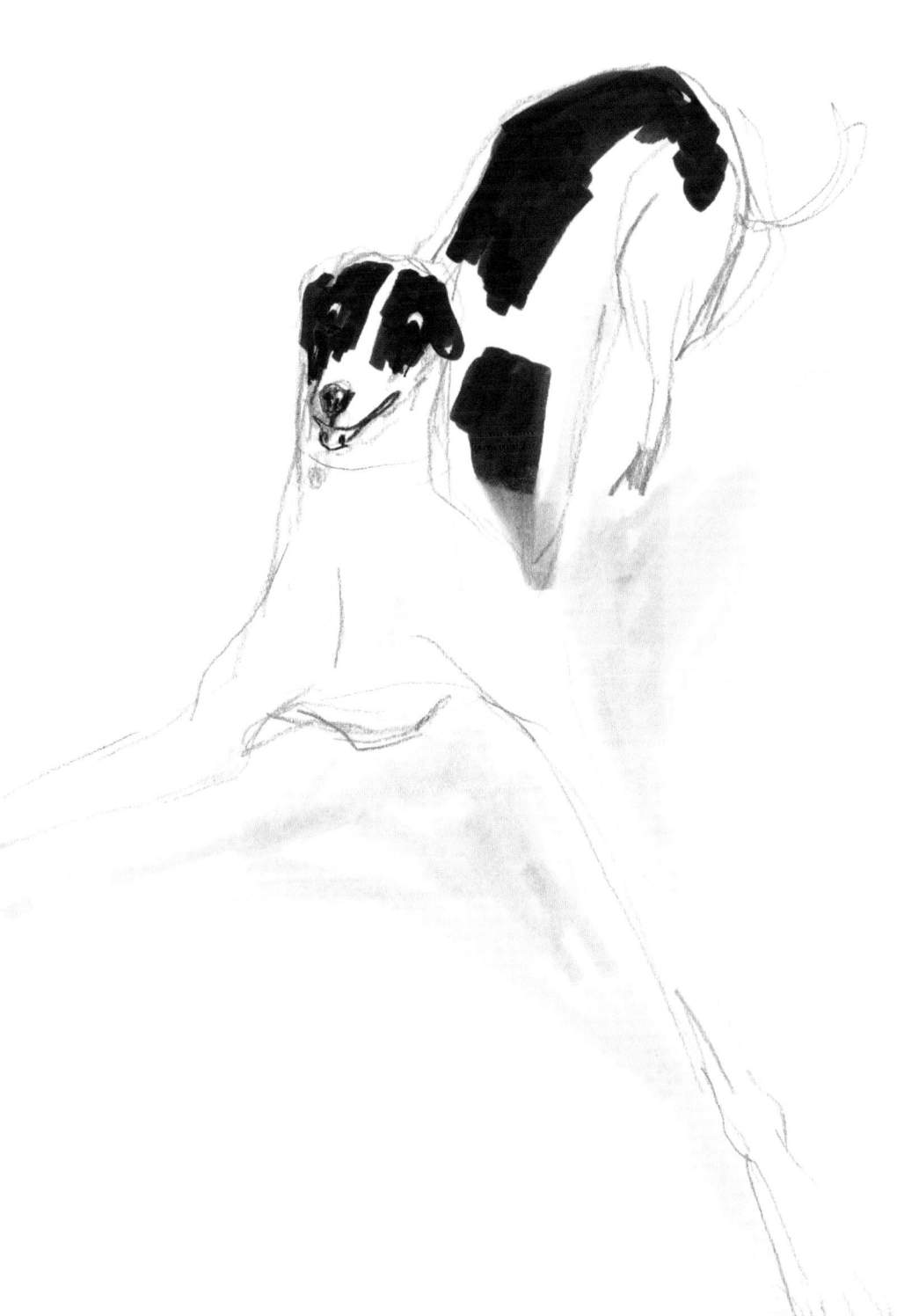

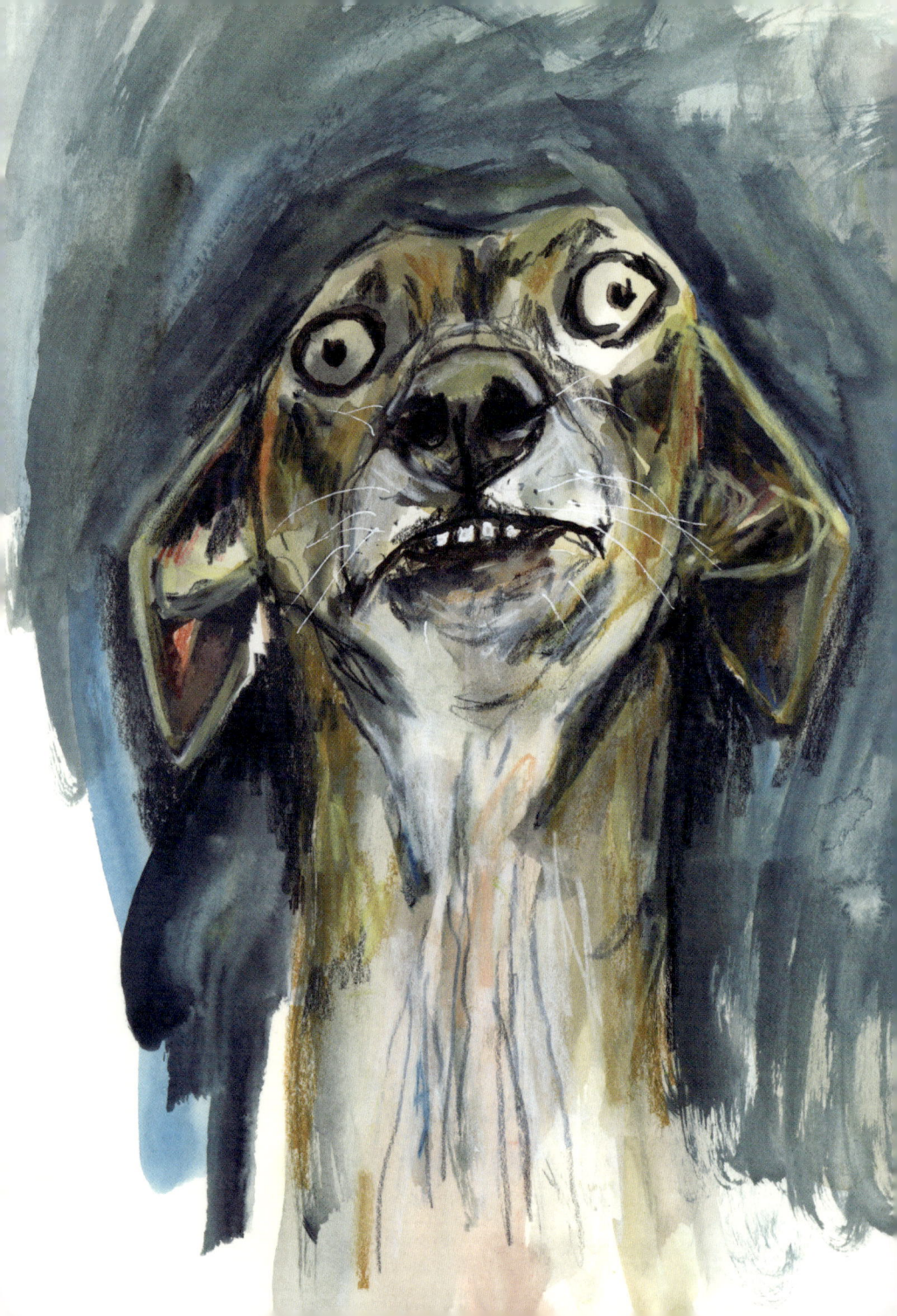

I wait

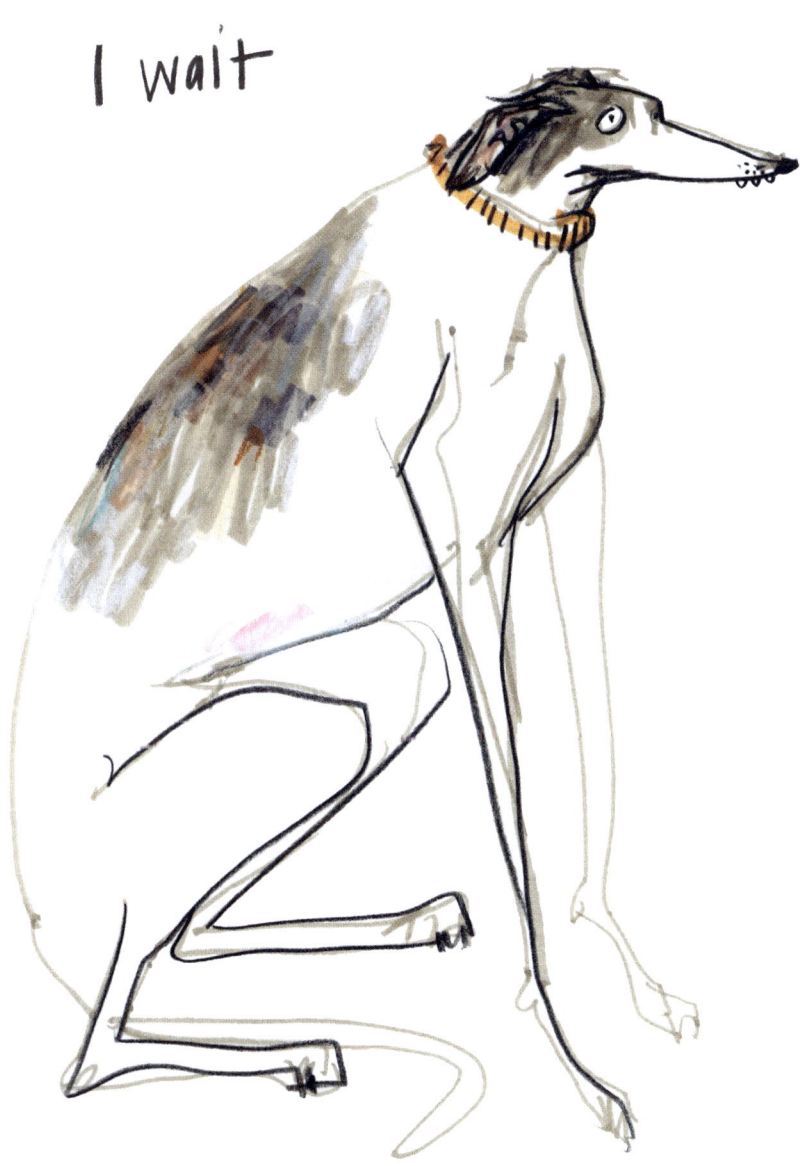

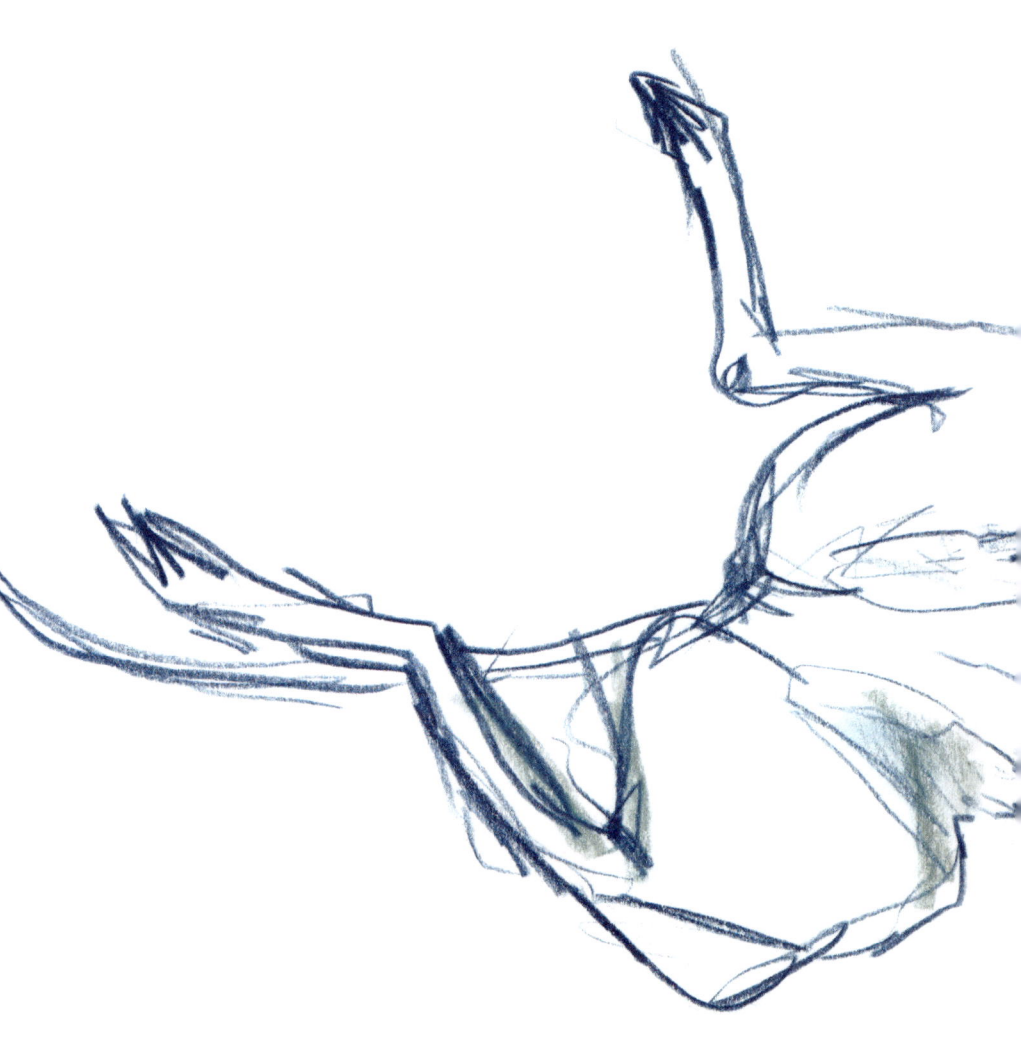

118

MODESTY.

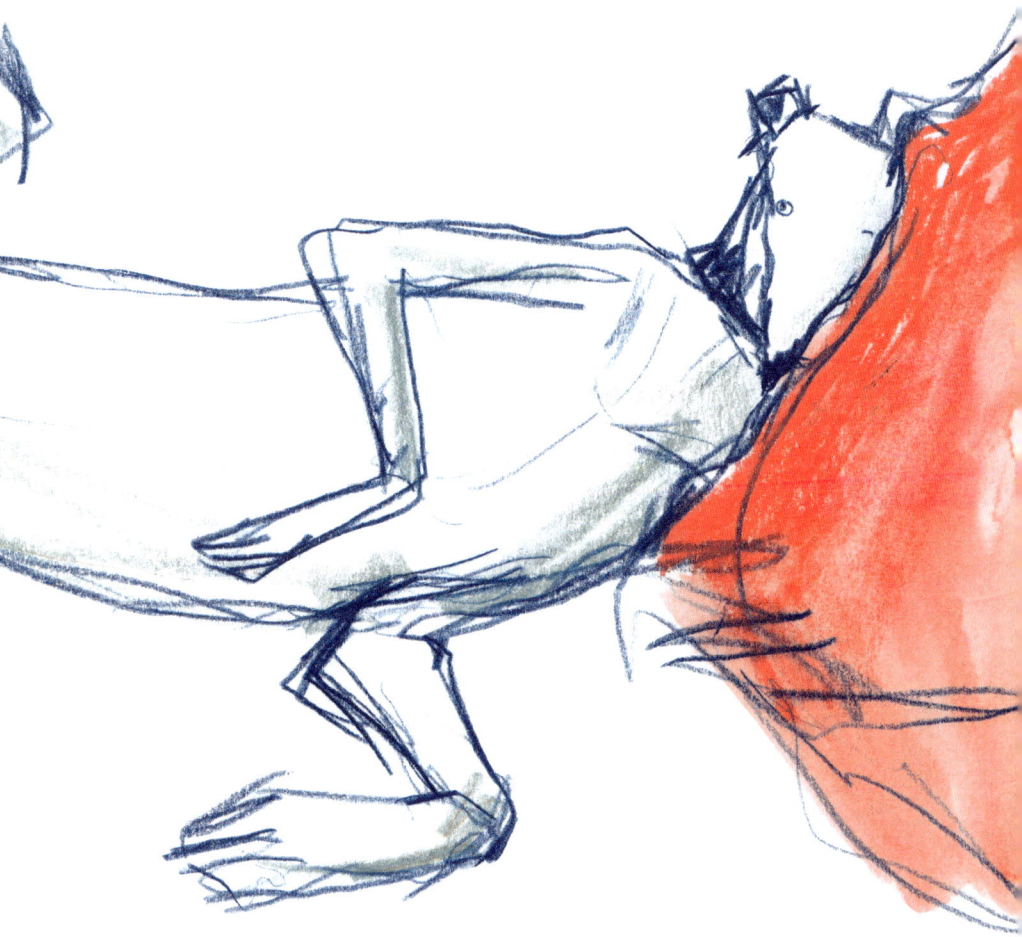

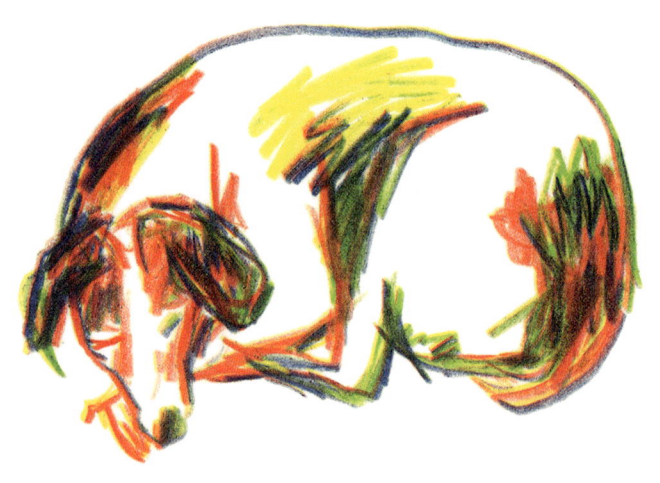

He sleeps

120

CARRY me,

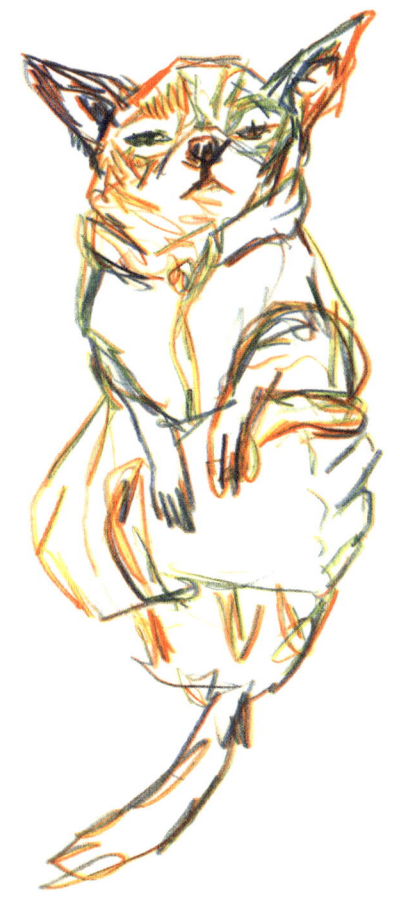

like the princess I am

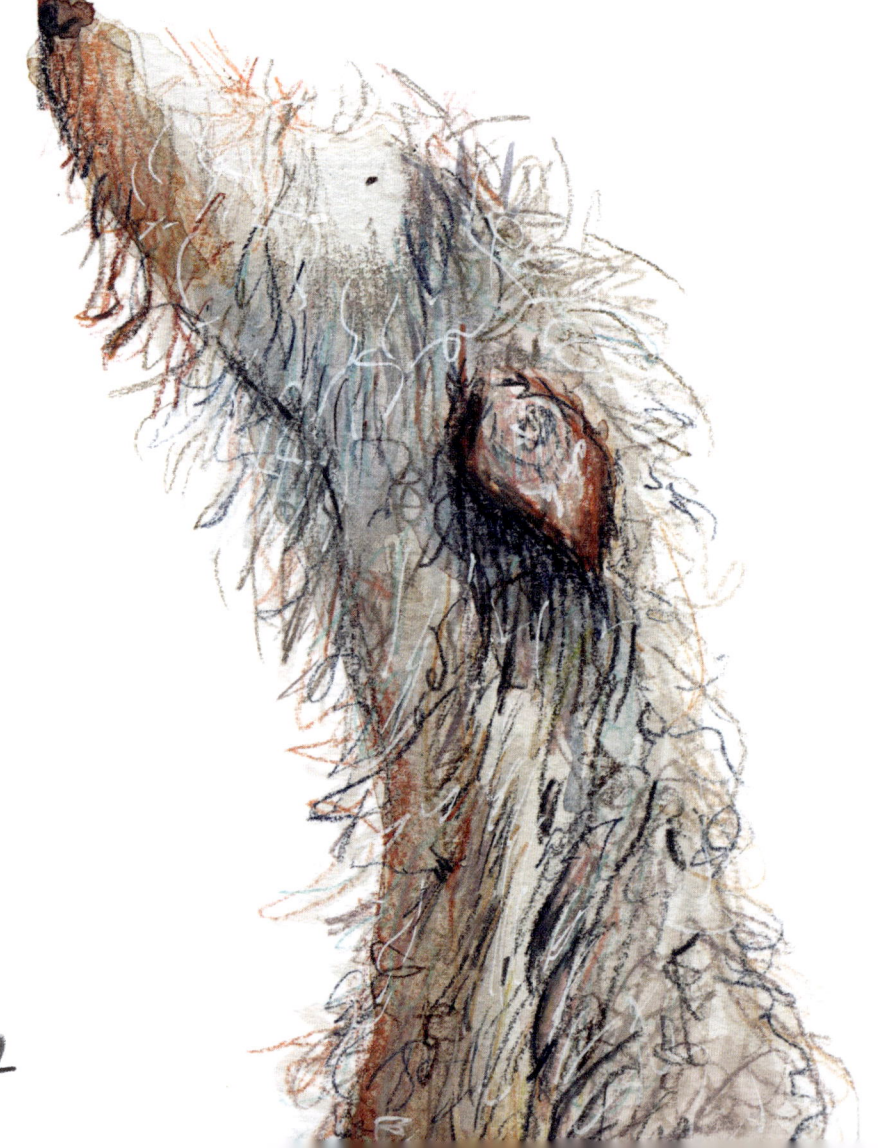

122

DO NOT Question
the **small,**

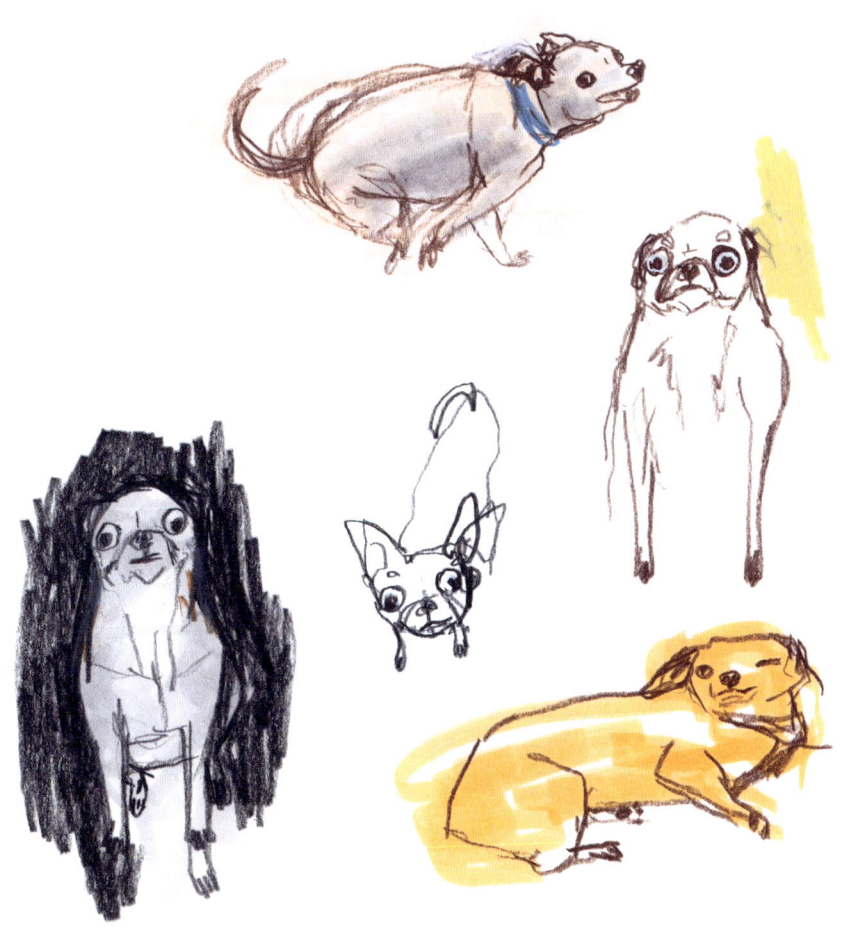

for they are very mighty

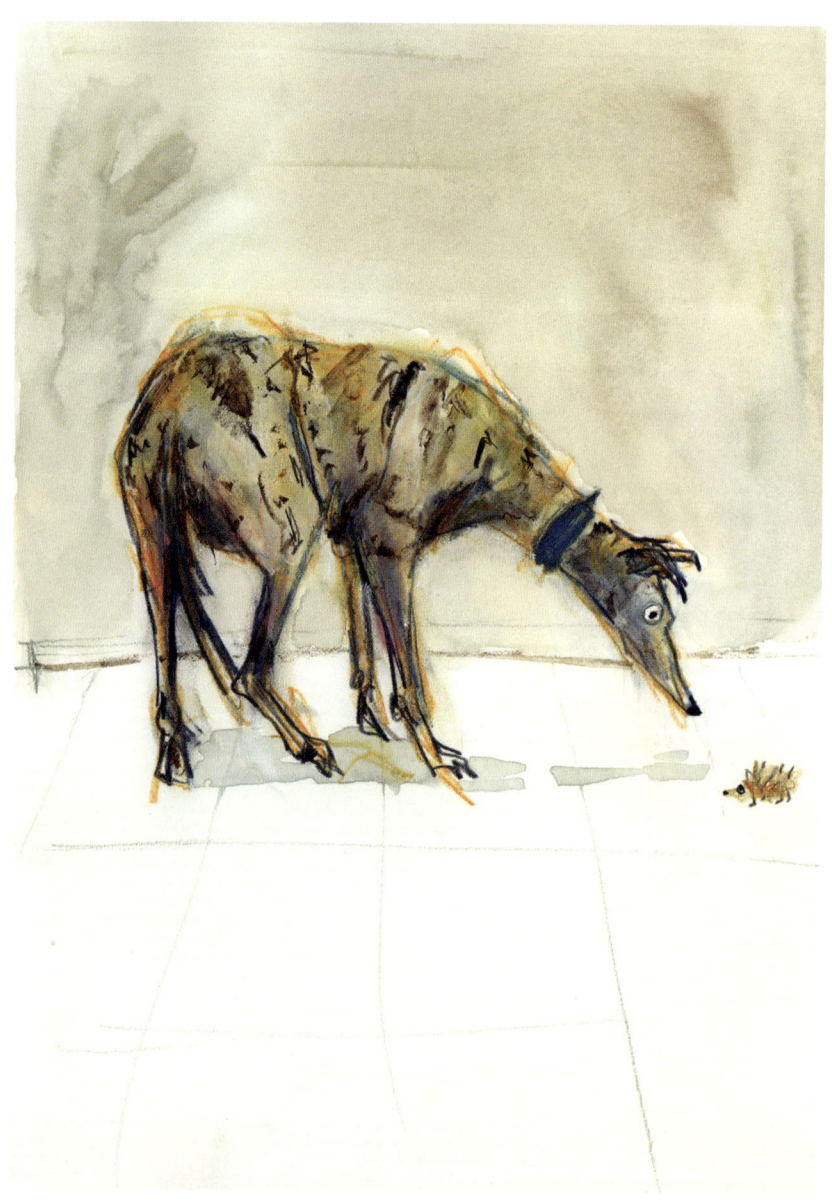

124

LittIe

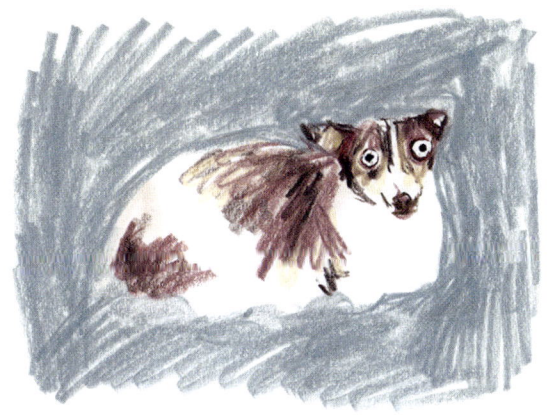

FIoofy

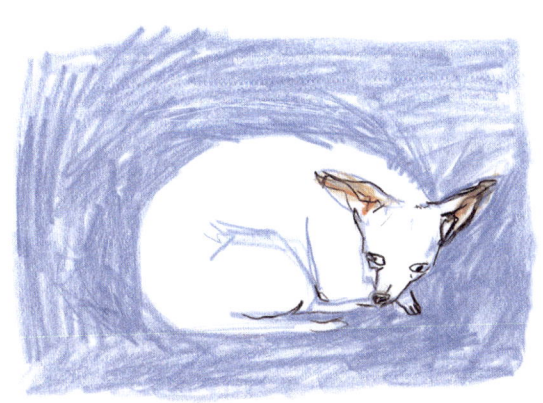

cRoissants

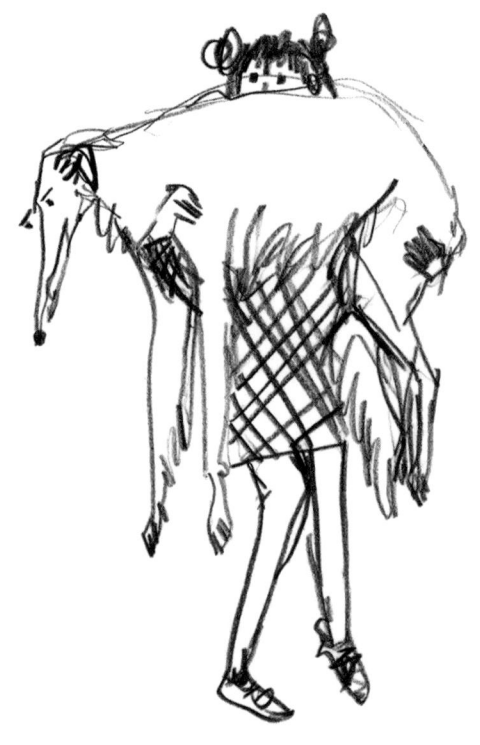

PLEASE DON'T MAKE ME DO STUFF

126

I SIT.
For you.

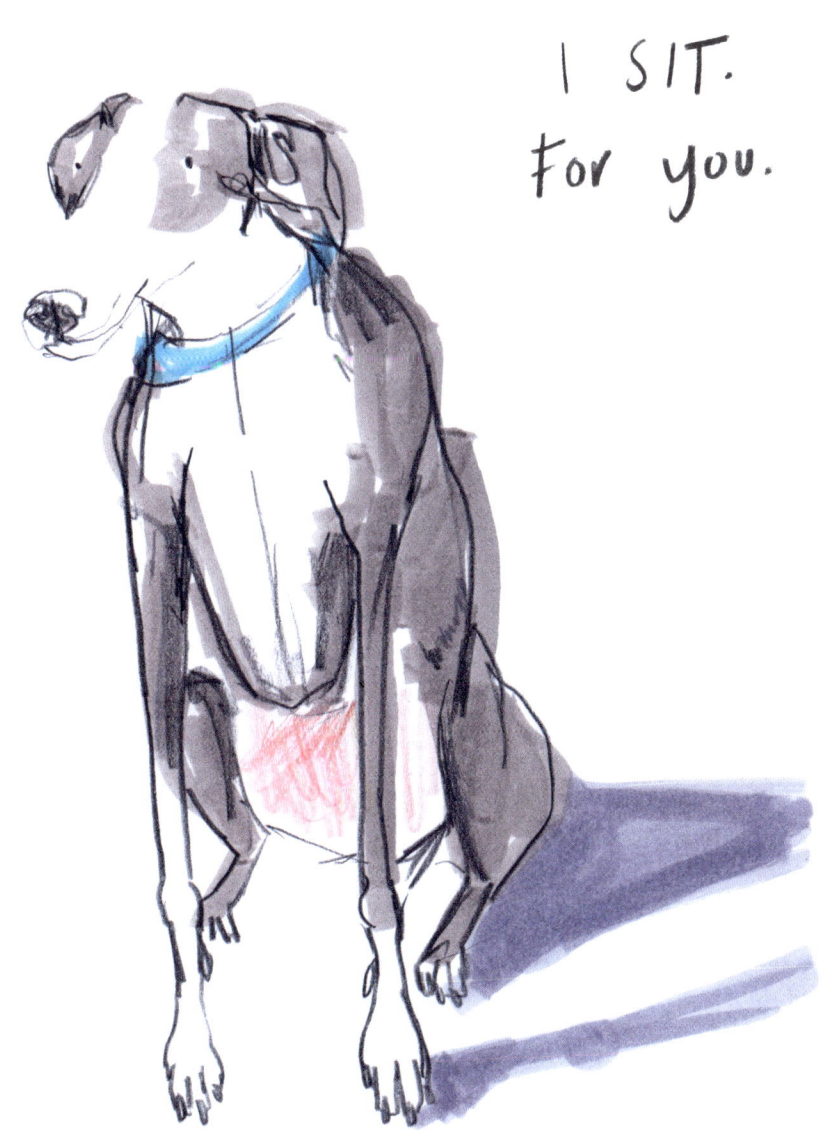

127

A peeping eye

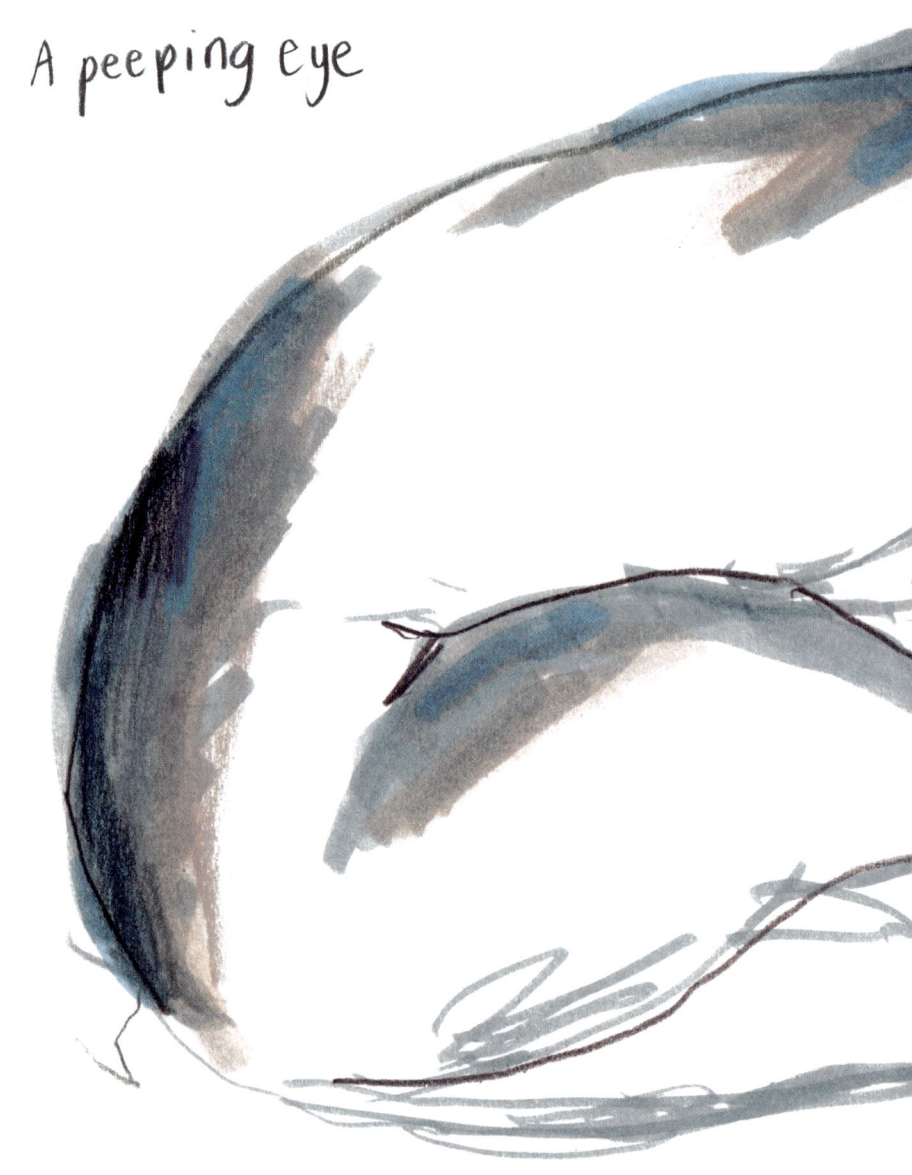

and a snaggly tooth.

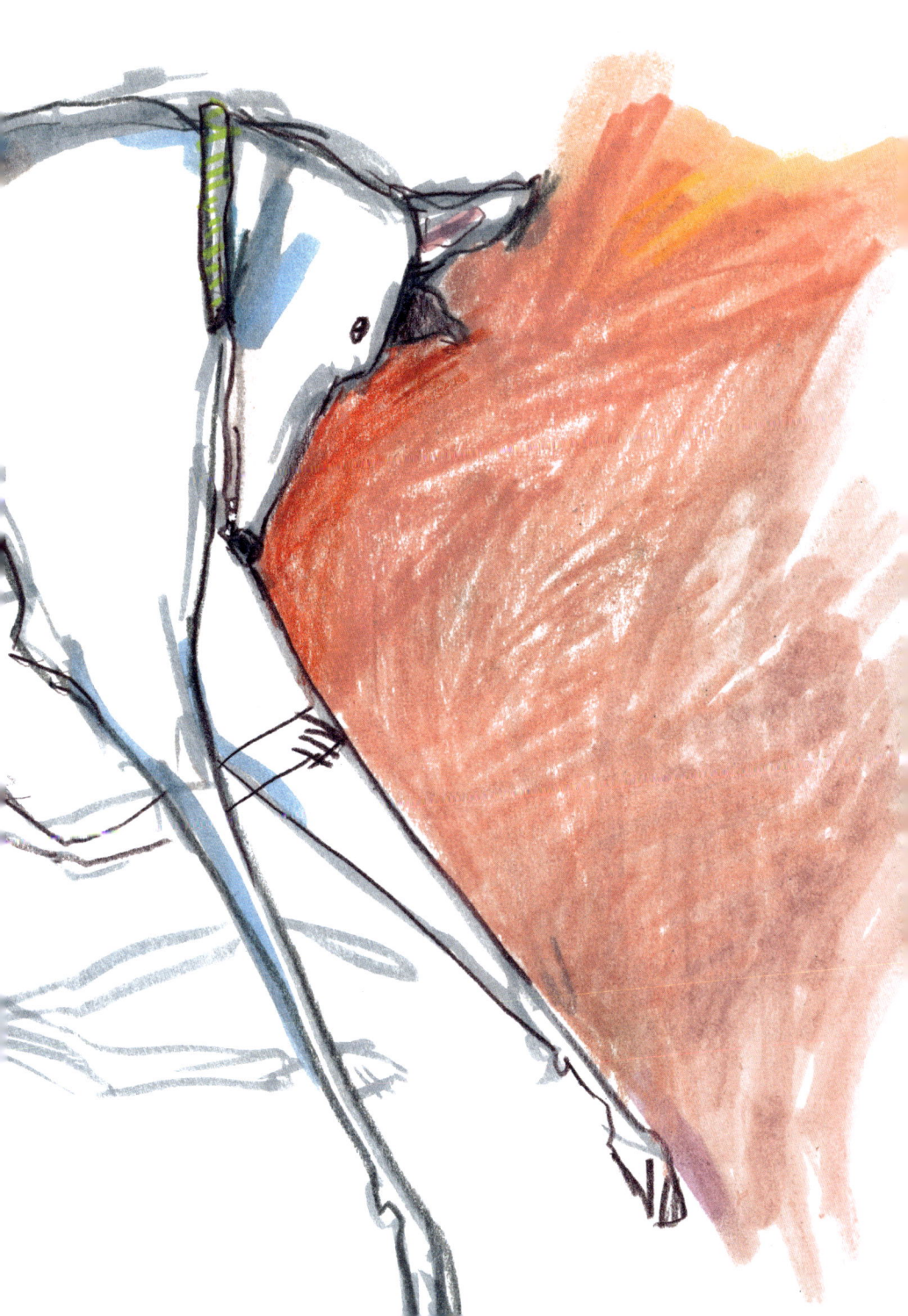

WAITING FOR MY

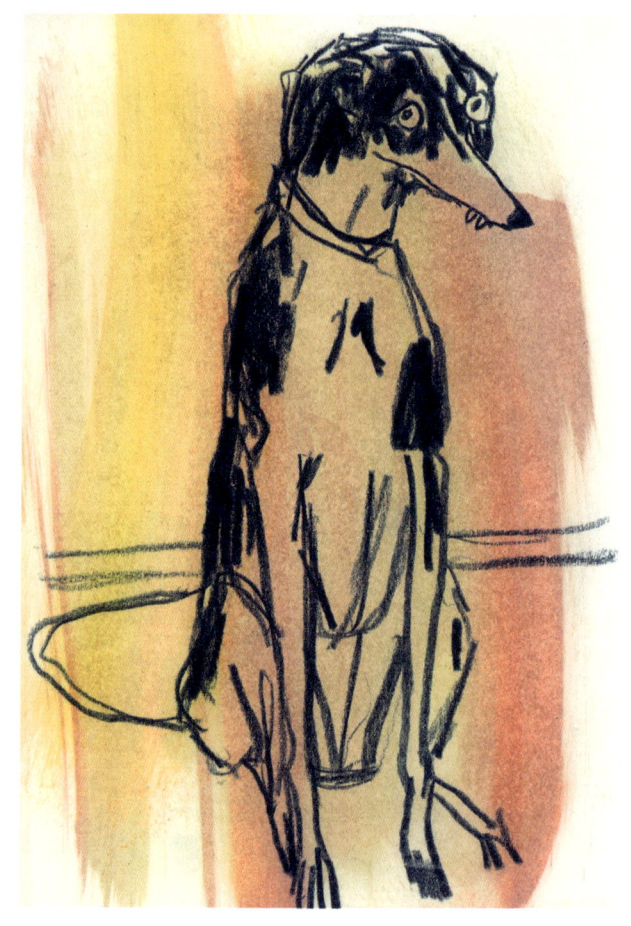

GOODBOI TREAT.

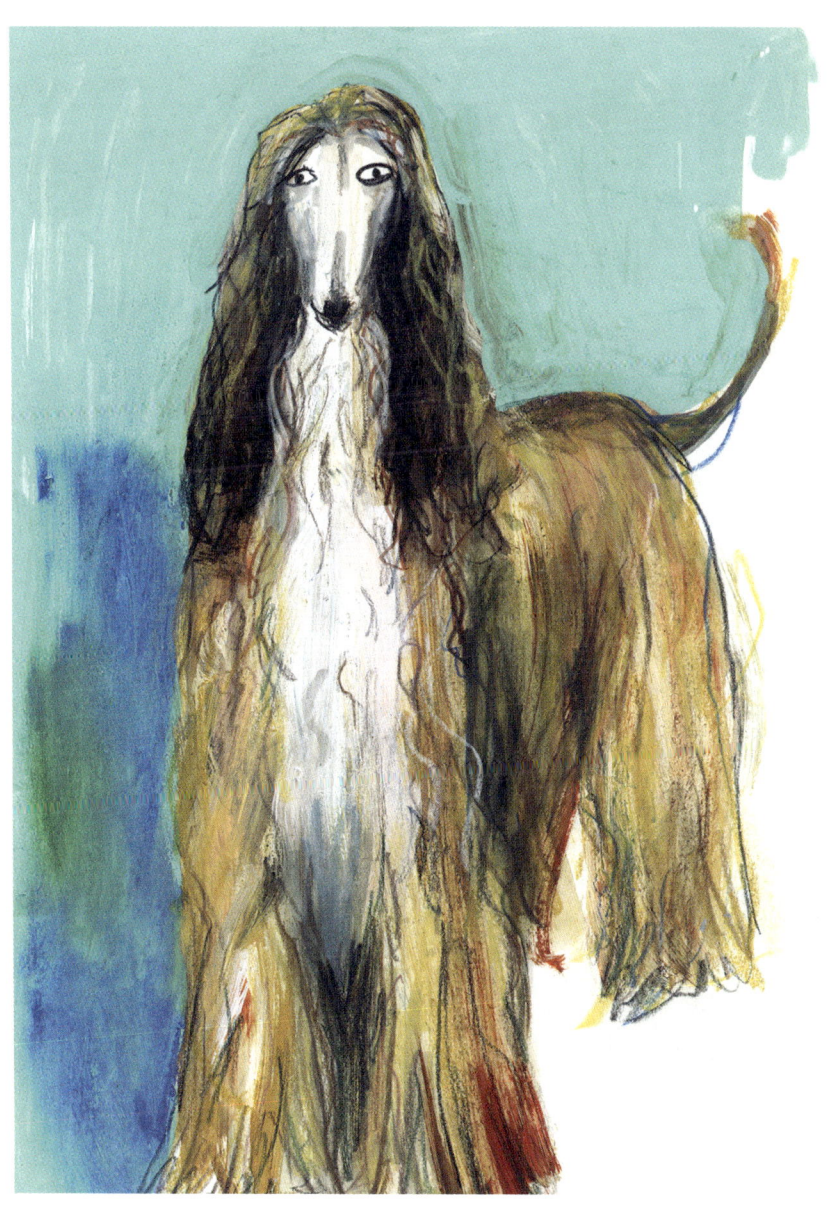

131

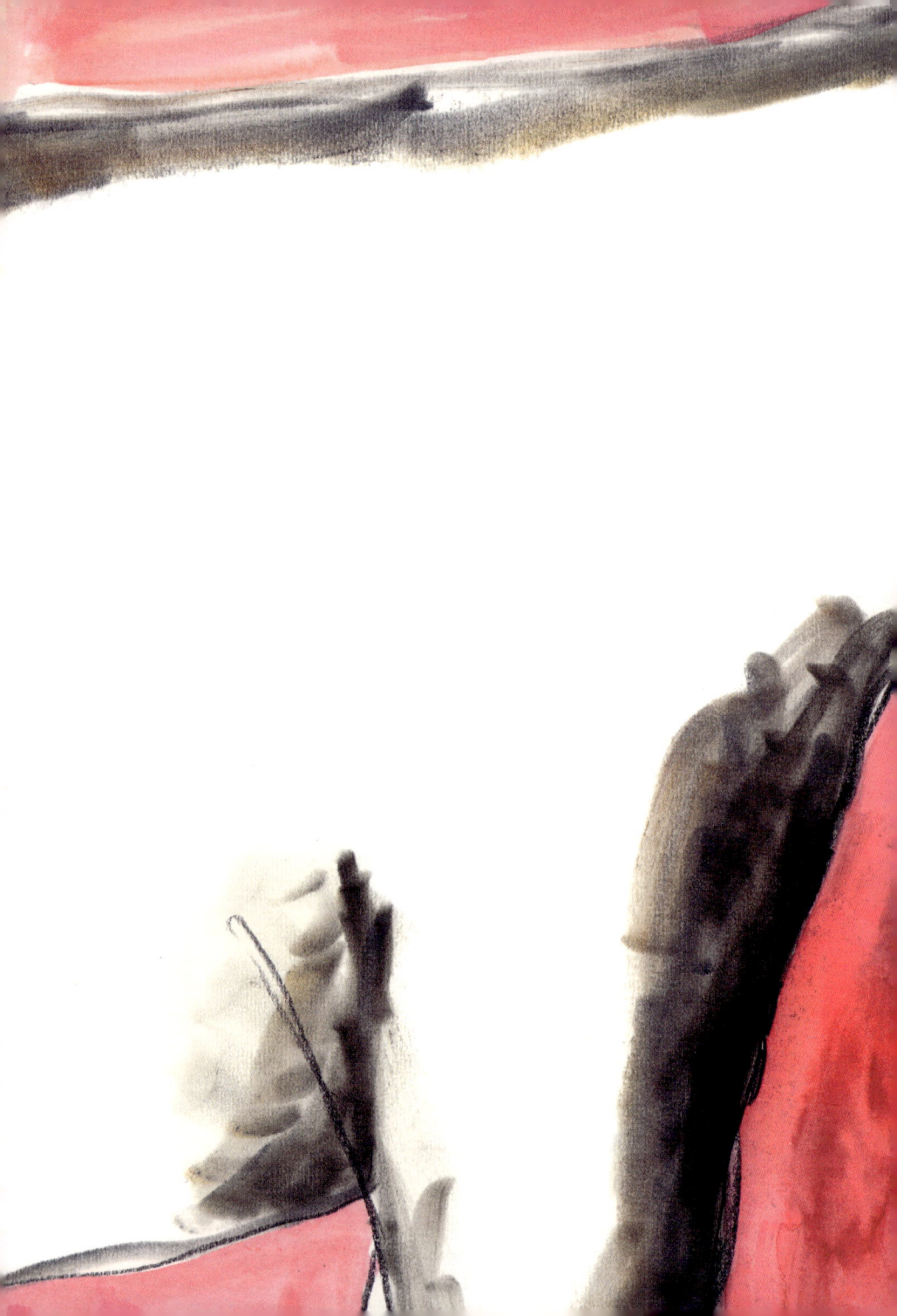

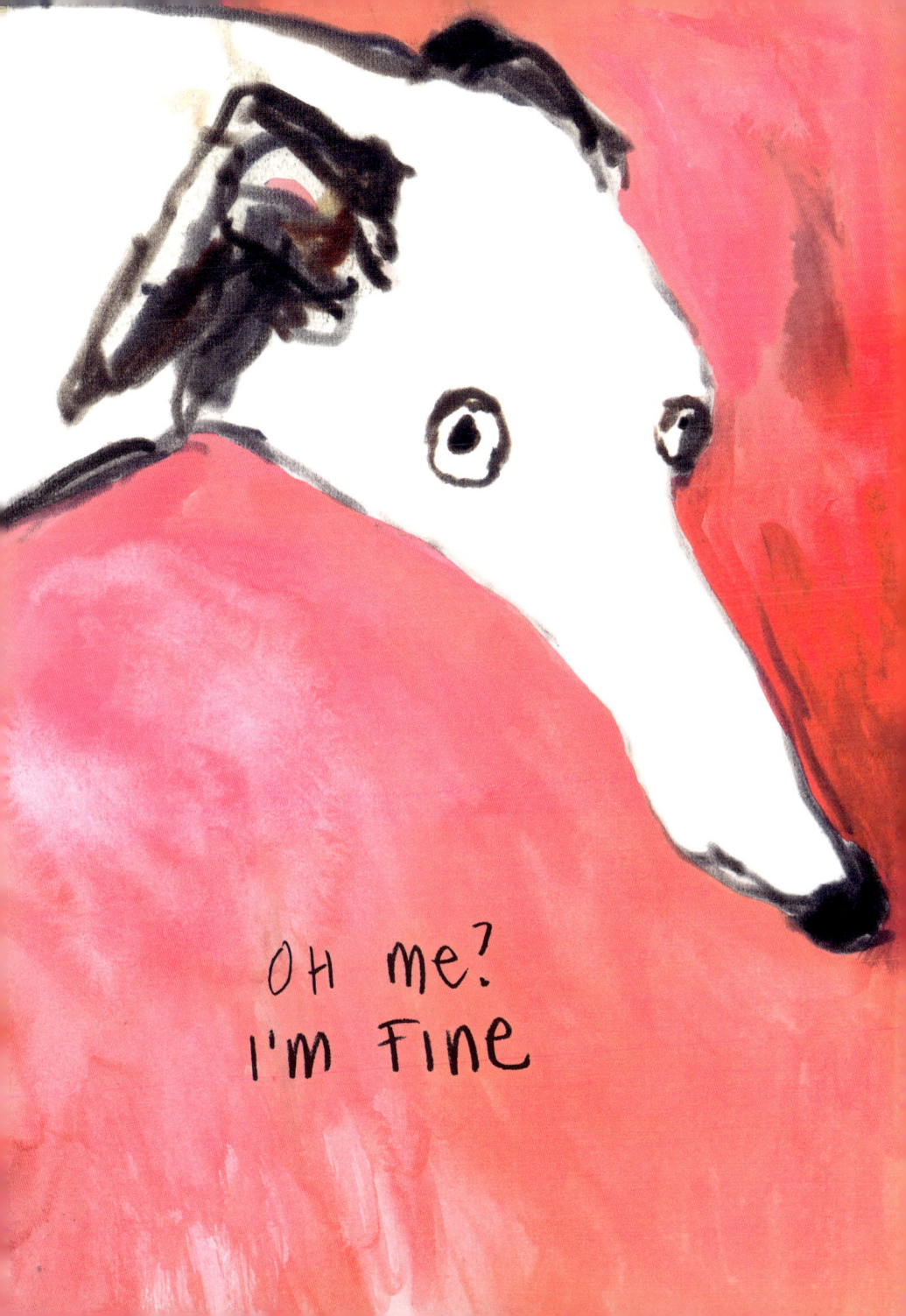

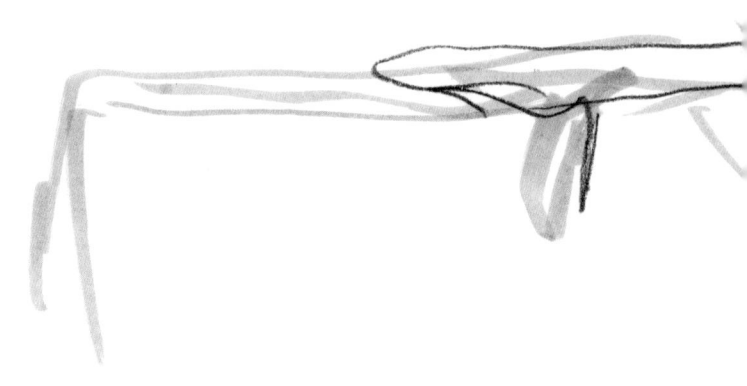

I see you have a tasty snack,
and I have no such tasty snack.

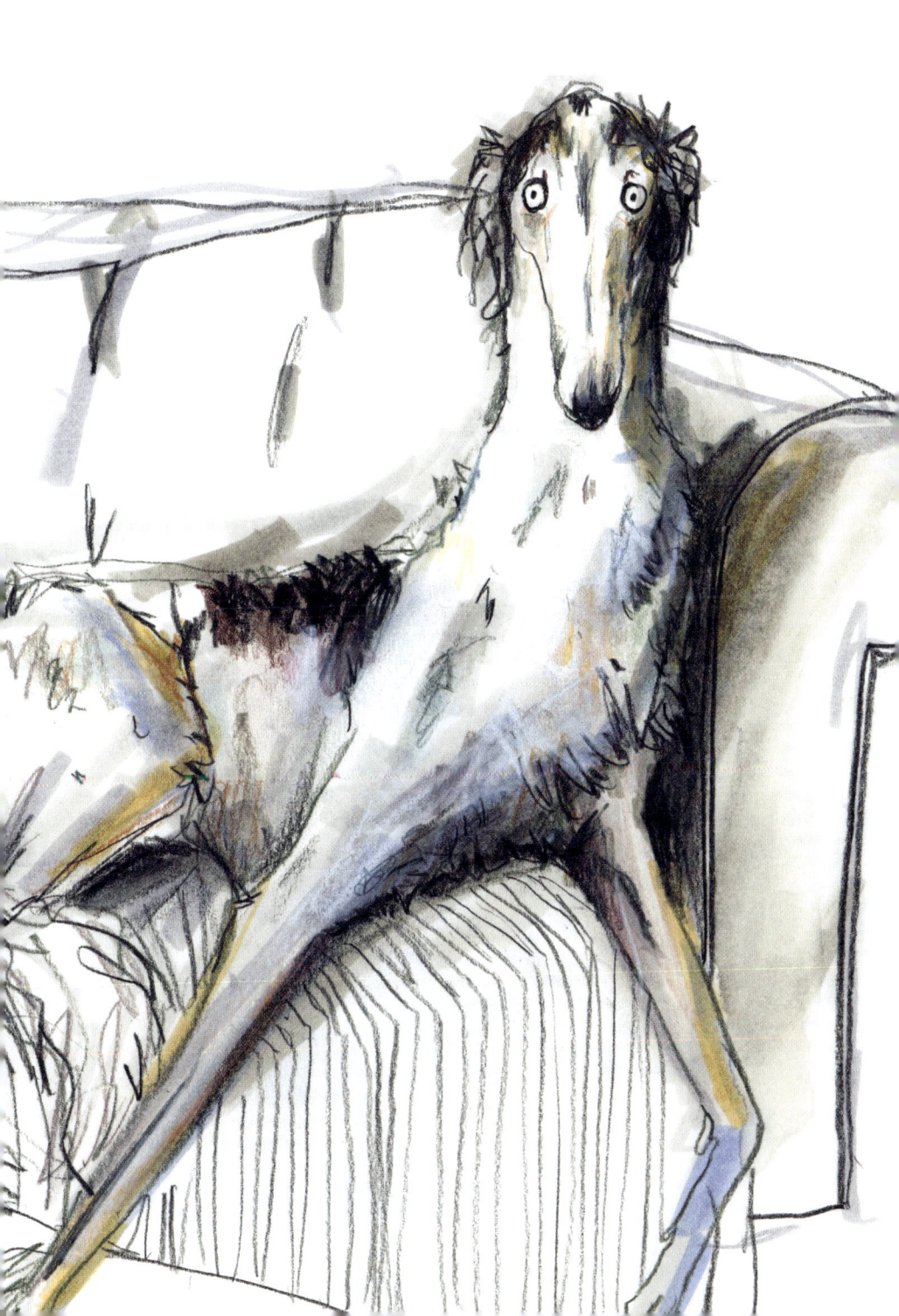

THIS IS MY TUMMY.
I AM VERY PROUD
OF IT.

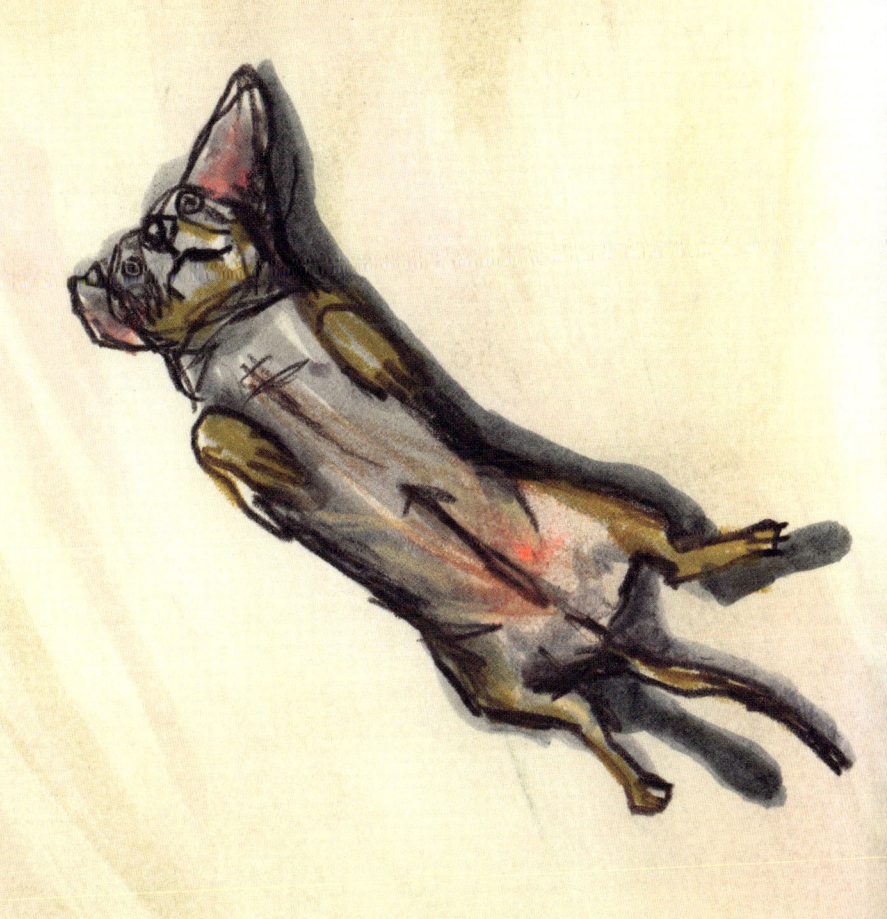

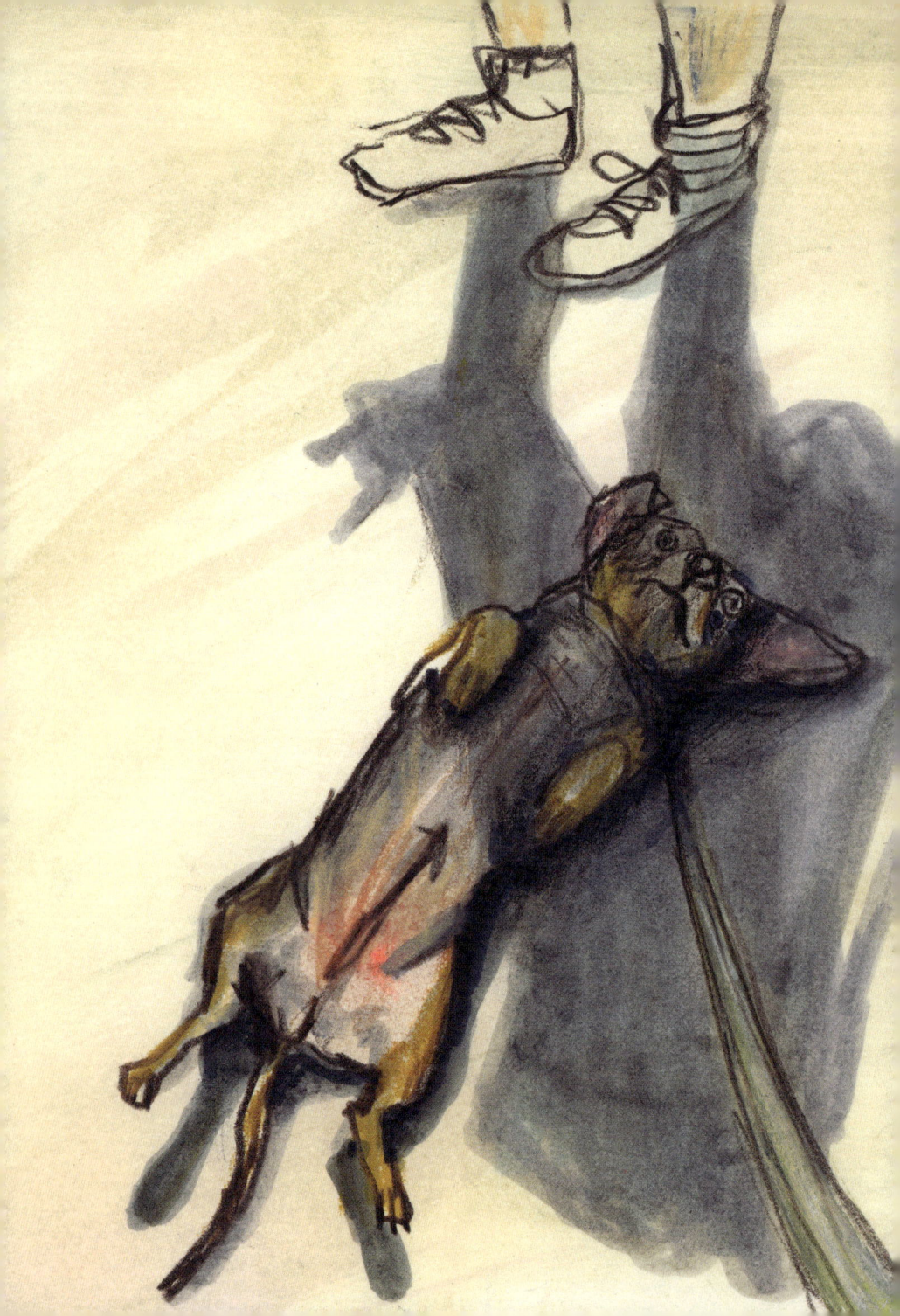

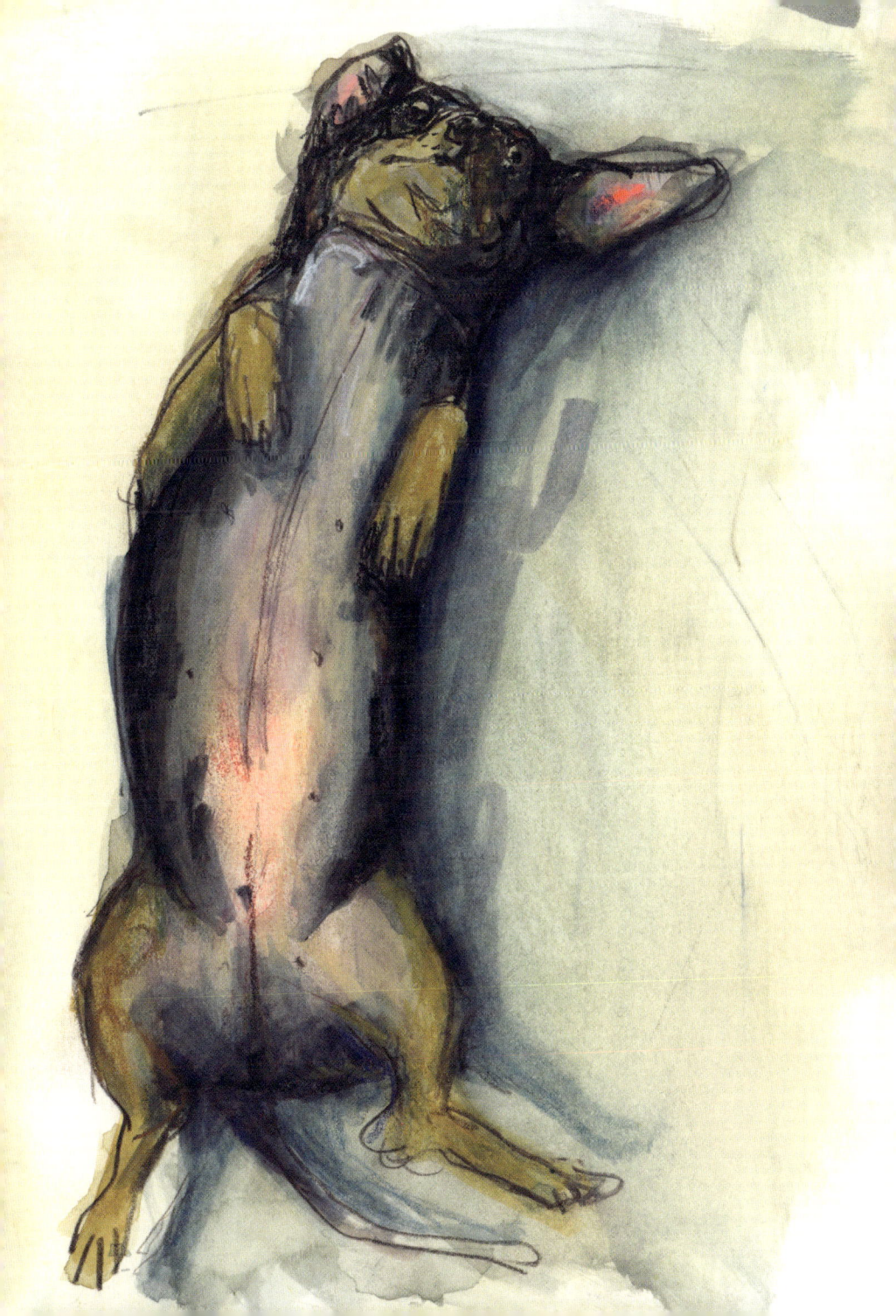

I see you.

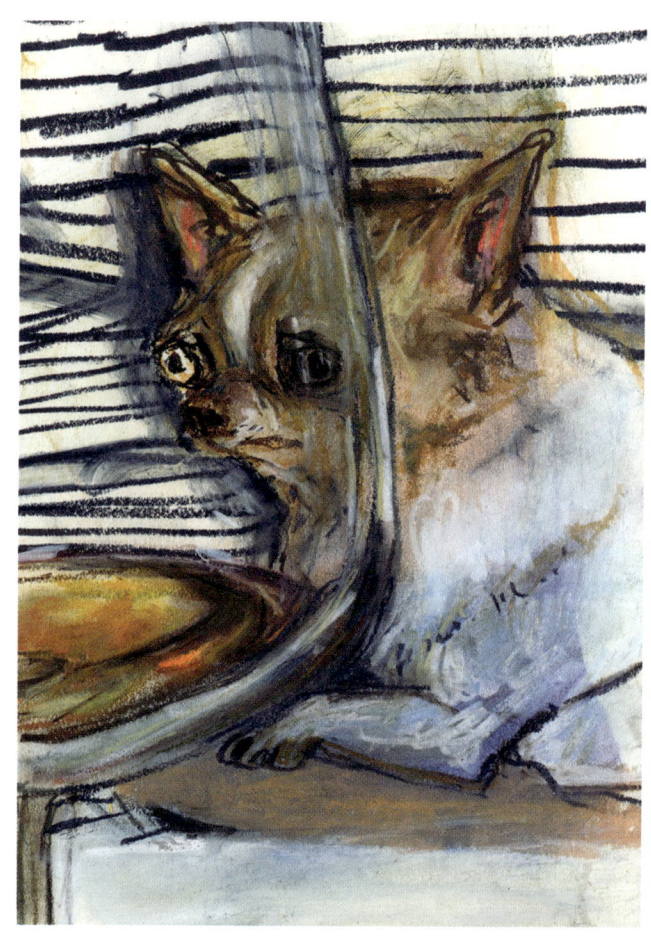

watching me.

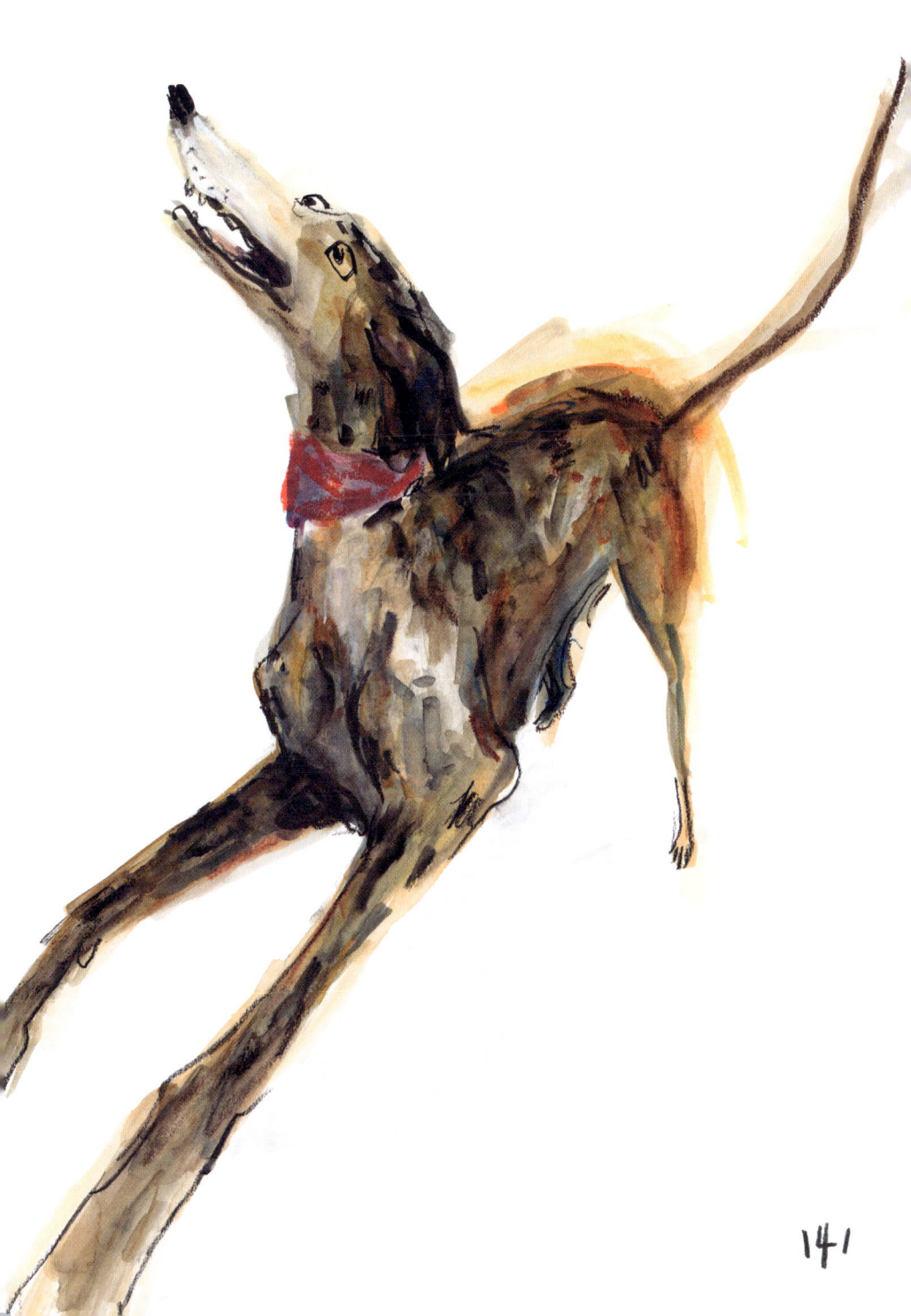

141

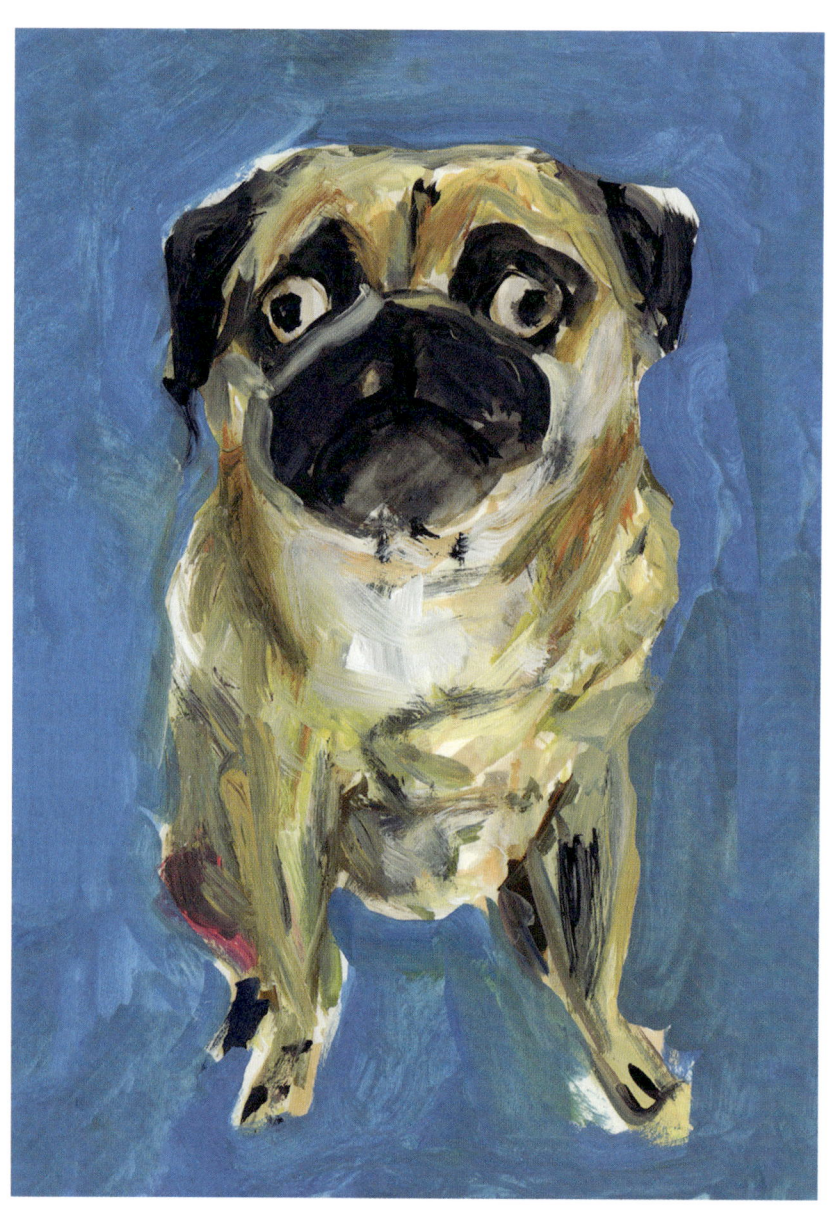

142

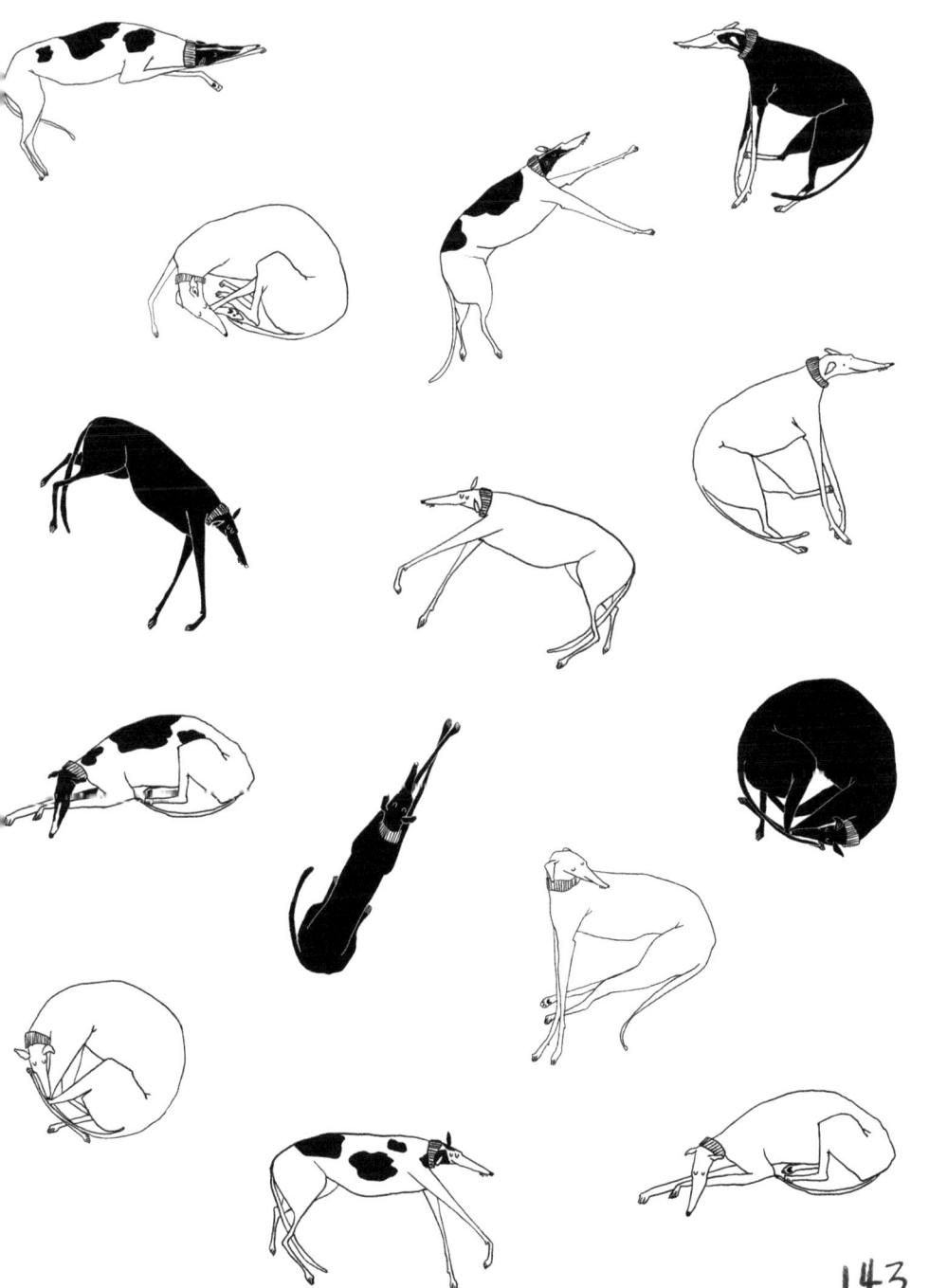

143

Tippy
tappy
tiny
feet

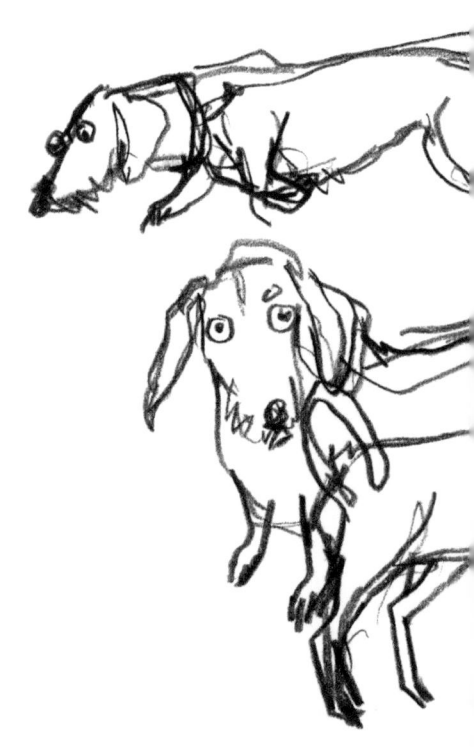

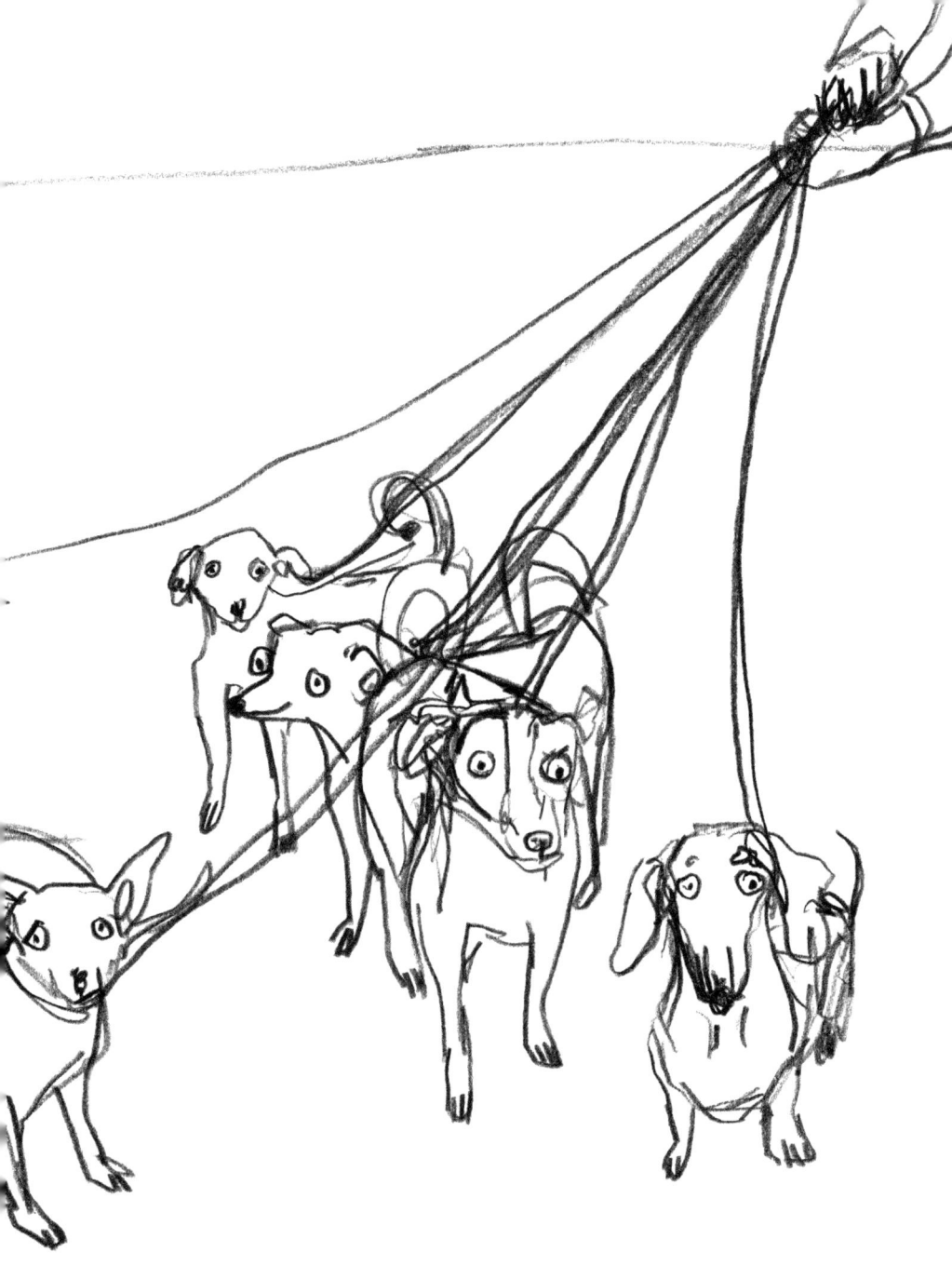

145

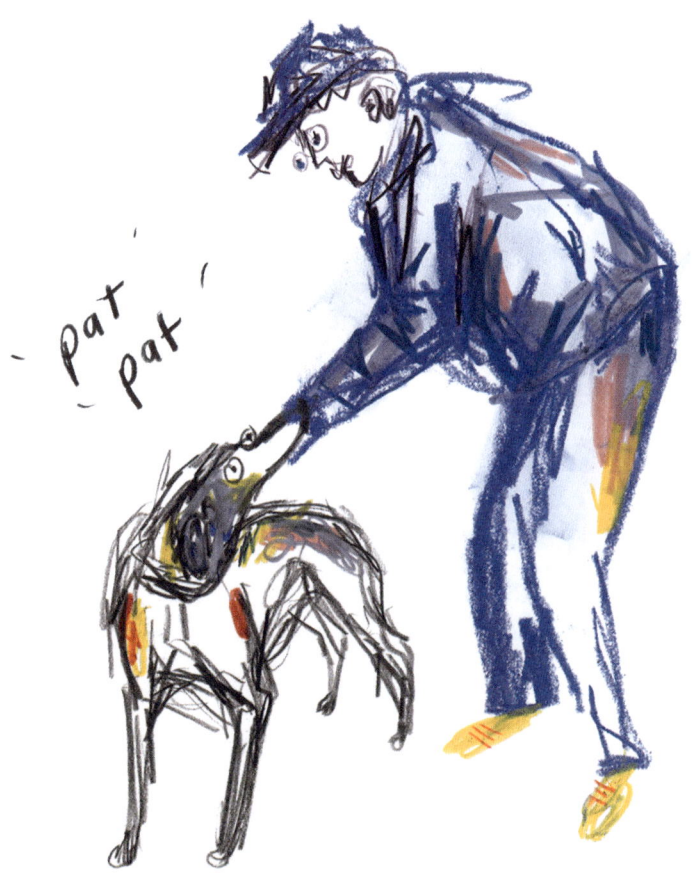

`pat`
`pat`

146

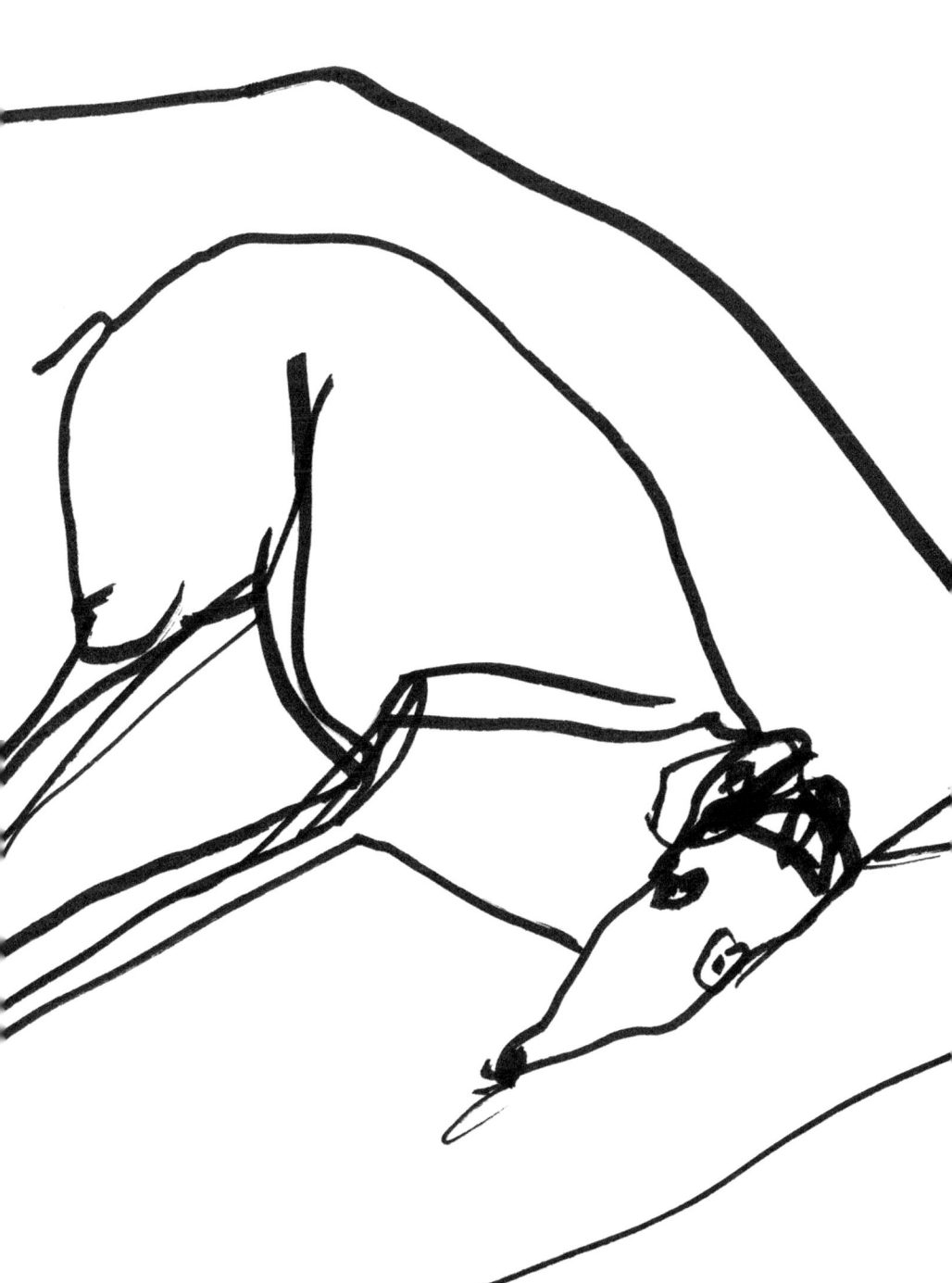

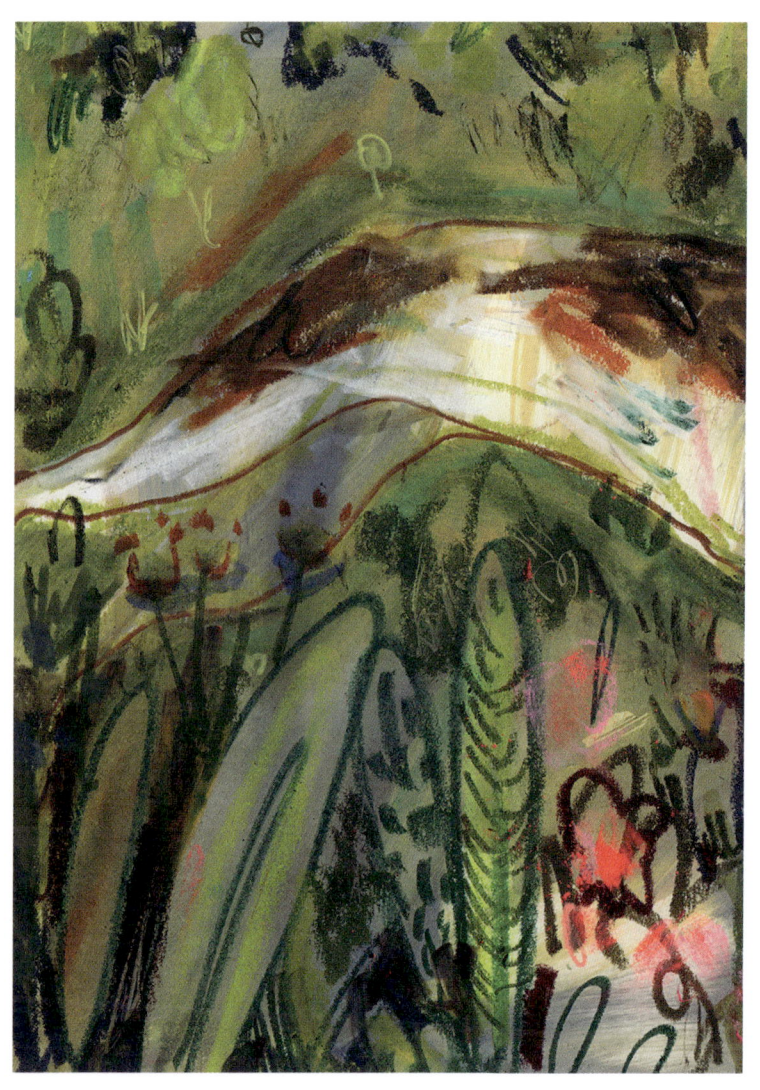

148

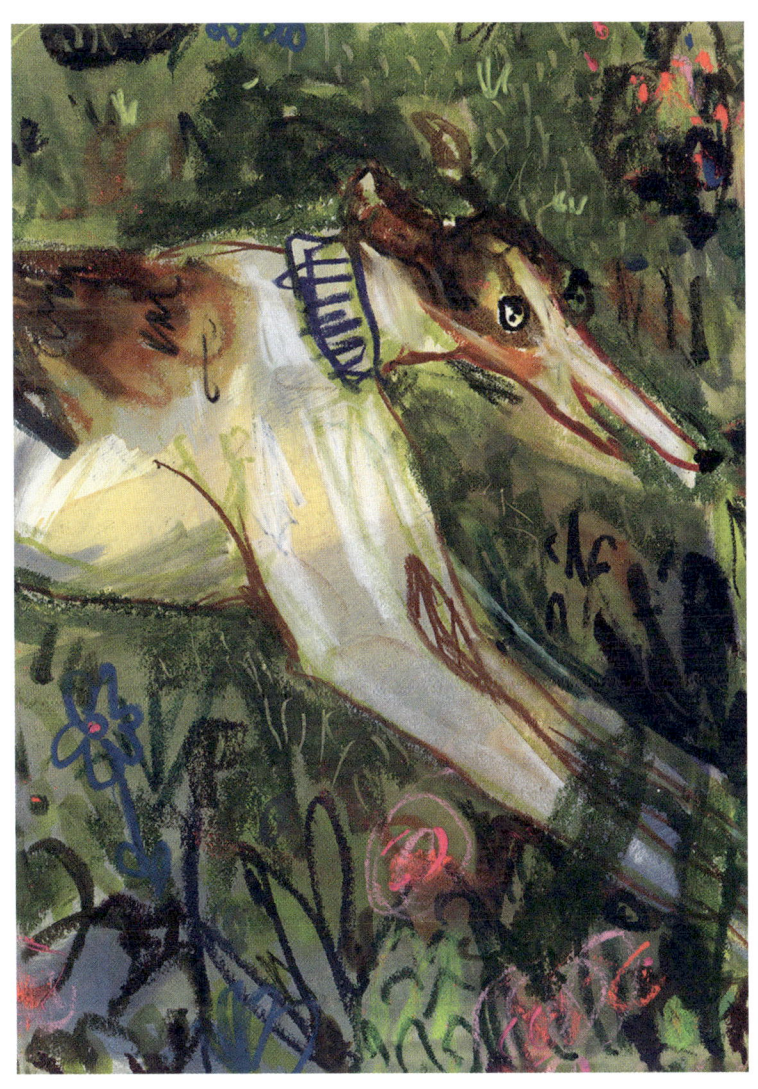

149

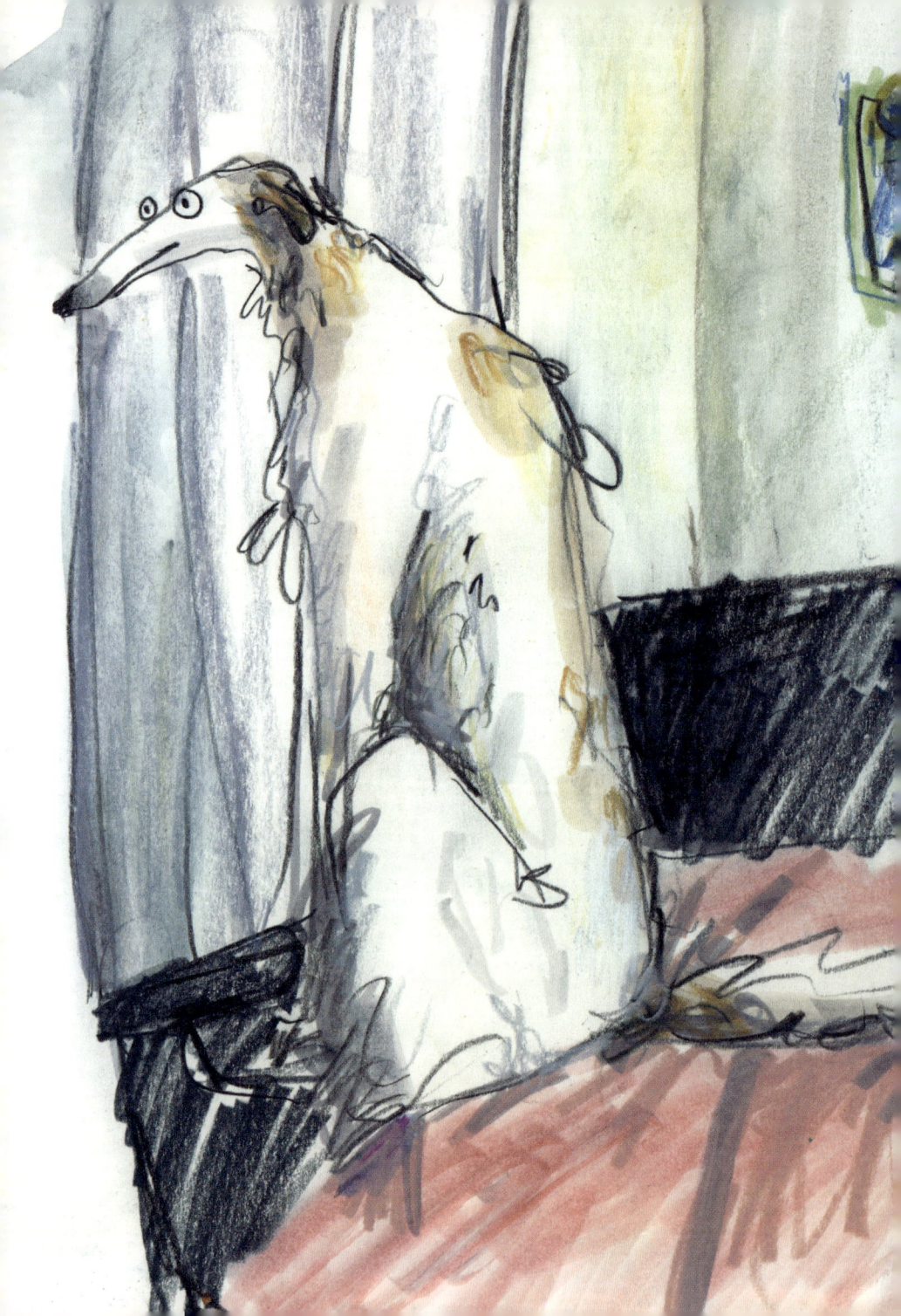

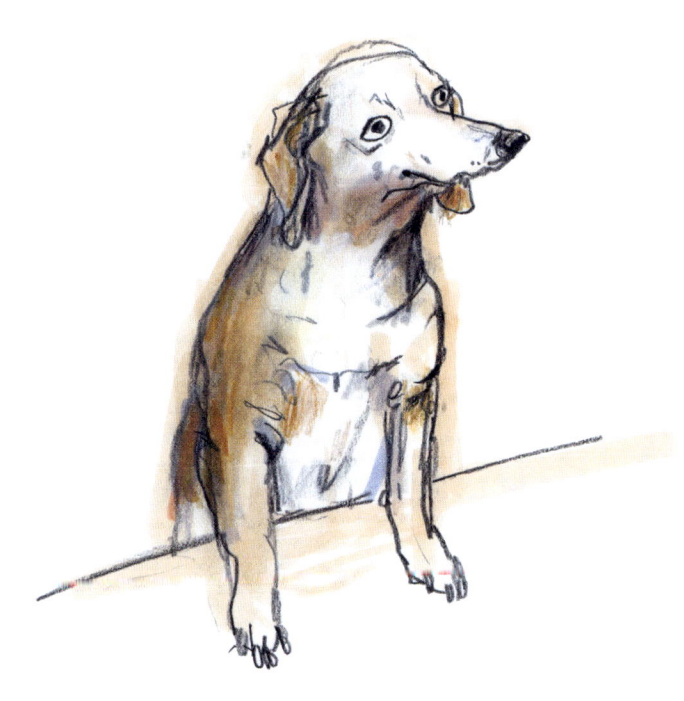

Do you have treats?

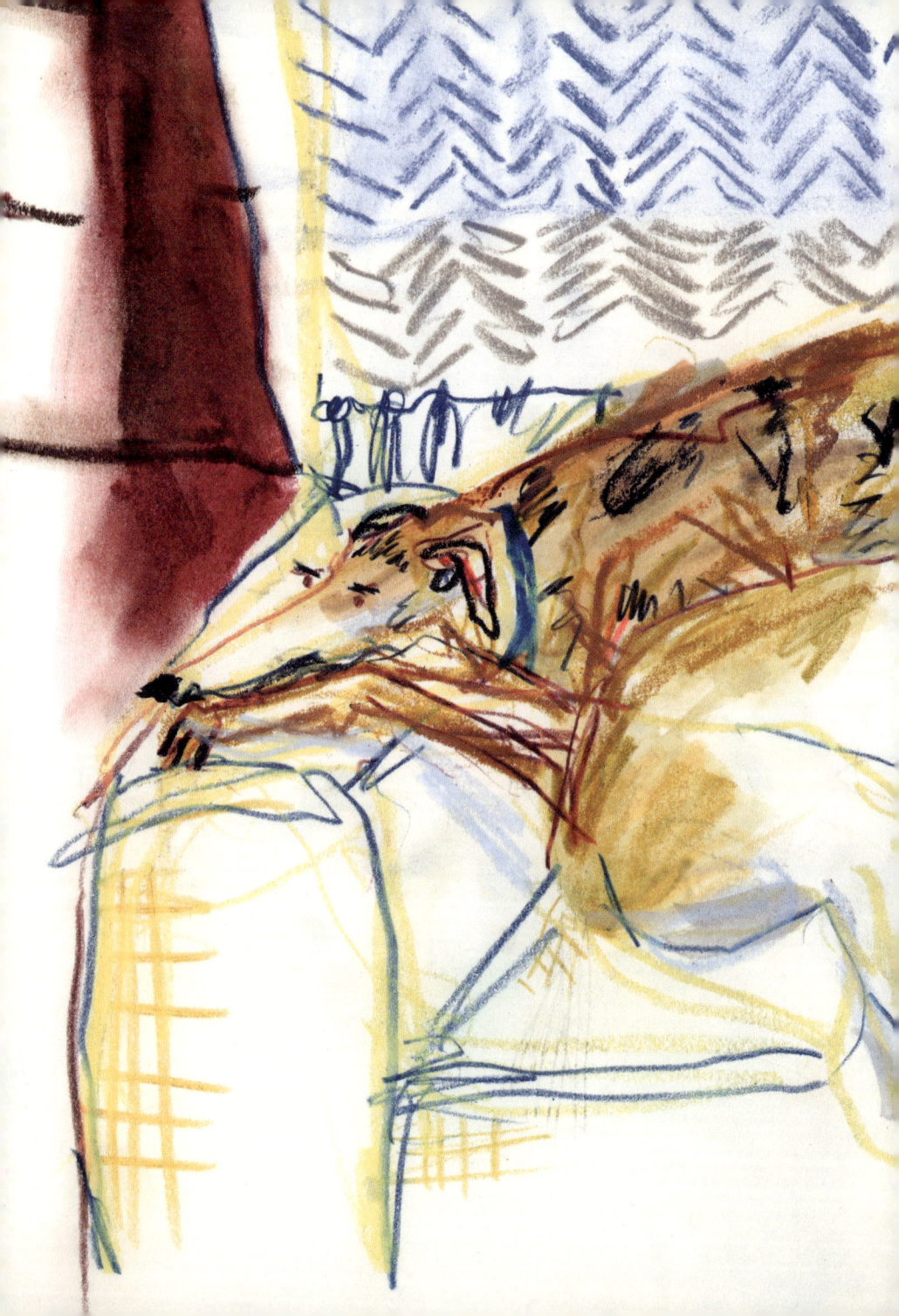

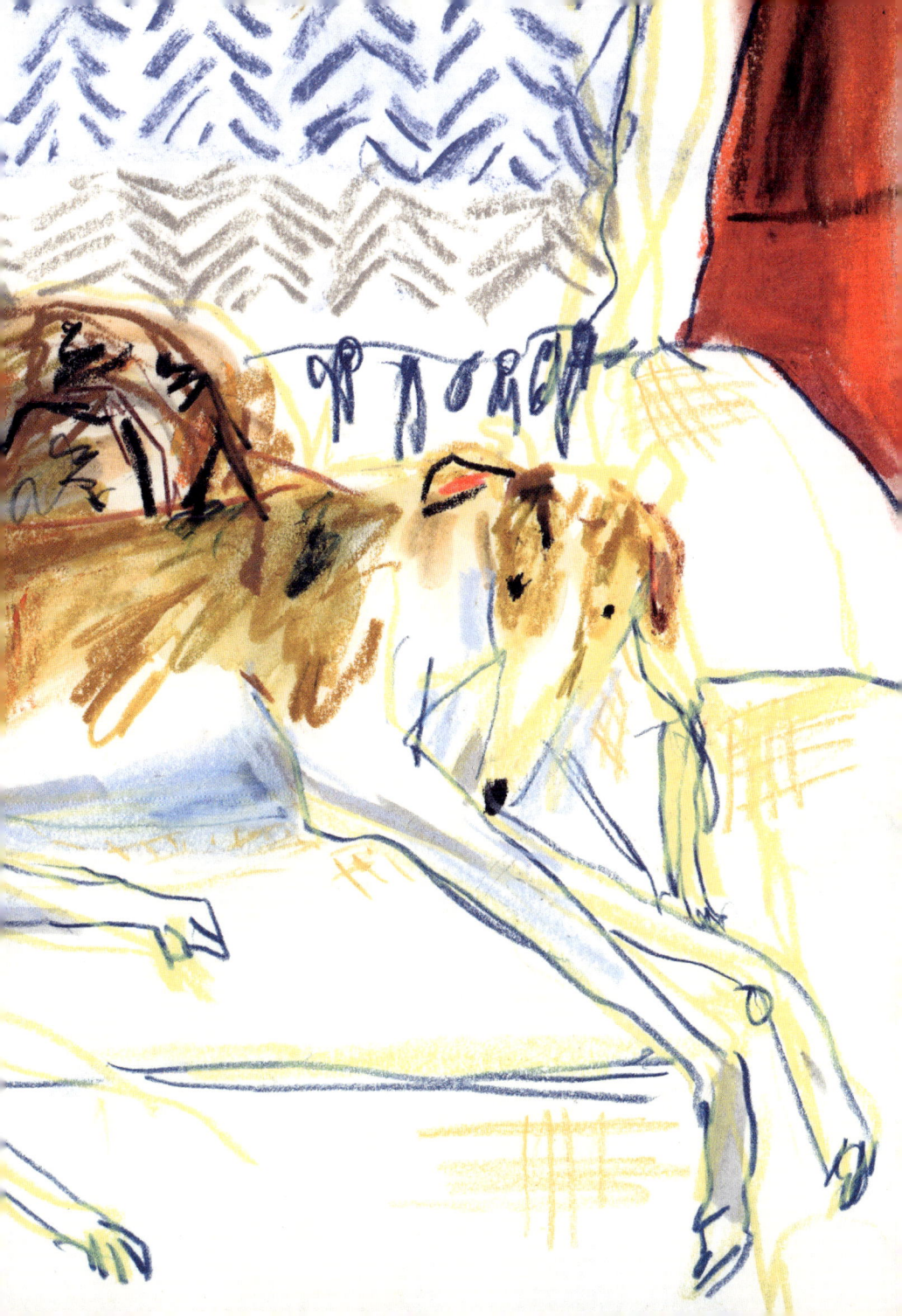

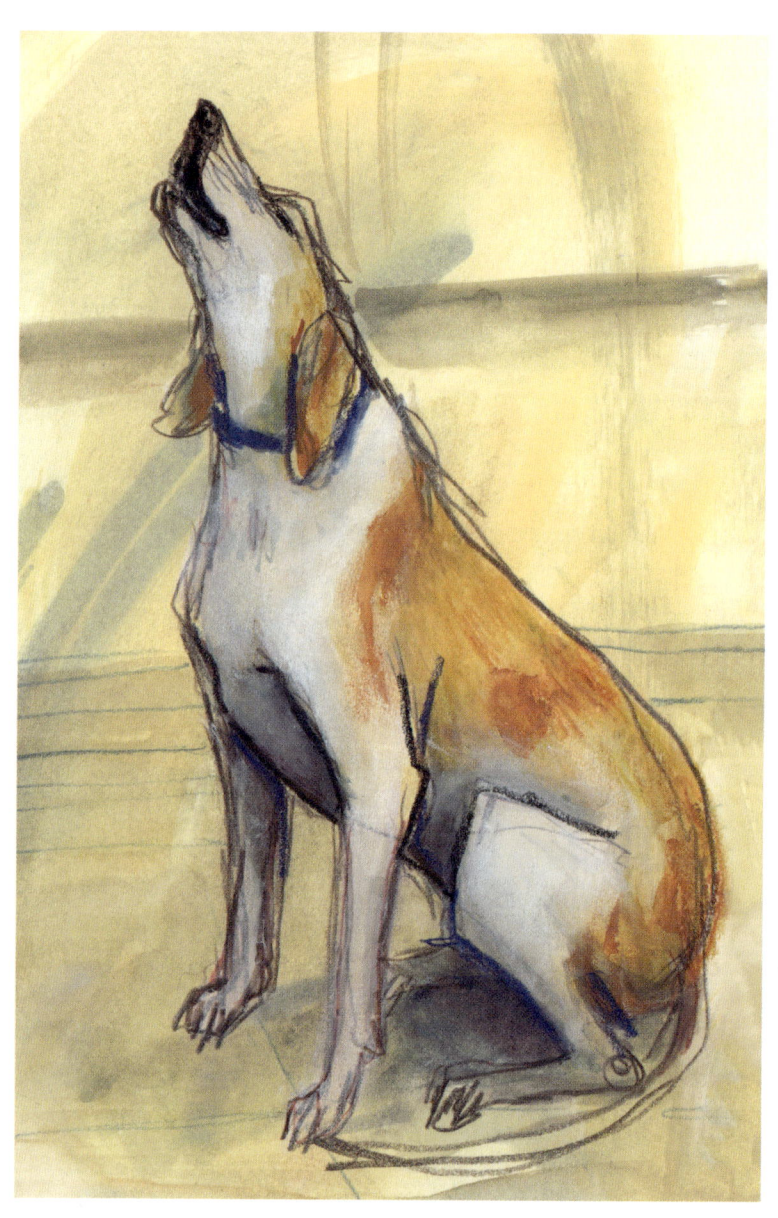

154

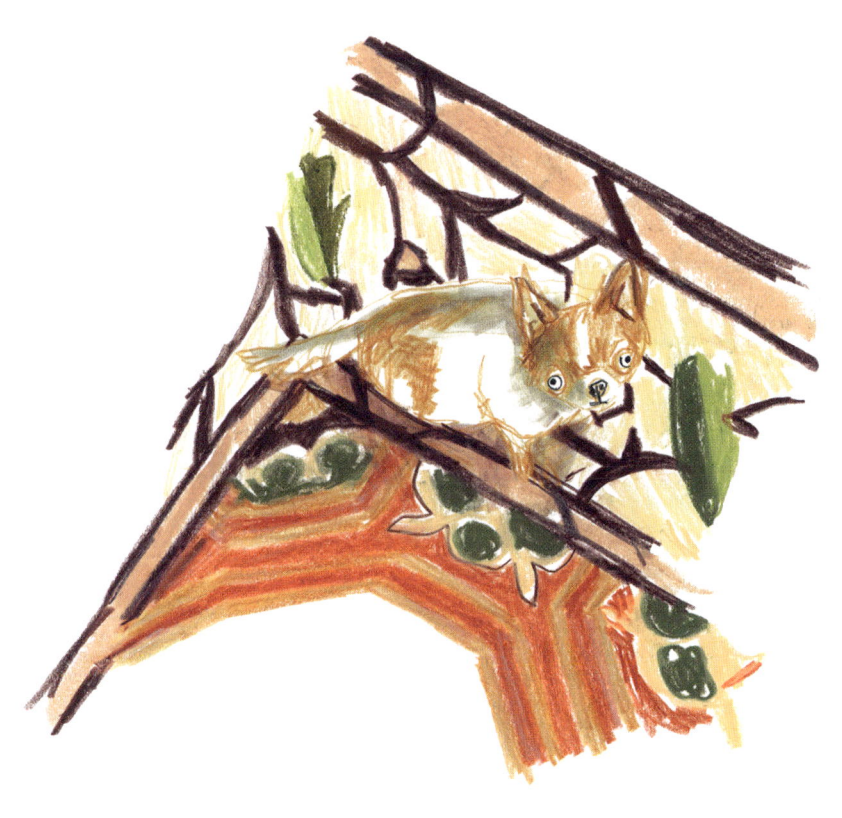

You are very big

155

speed demon

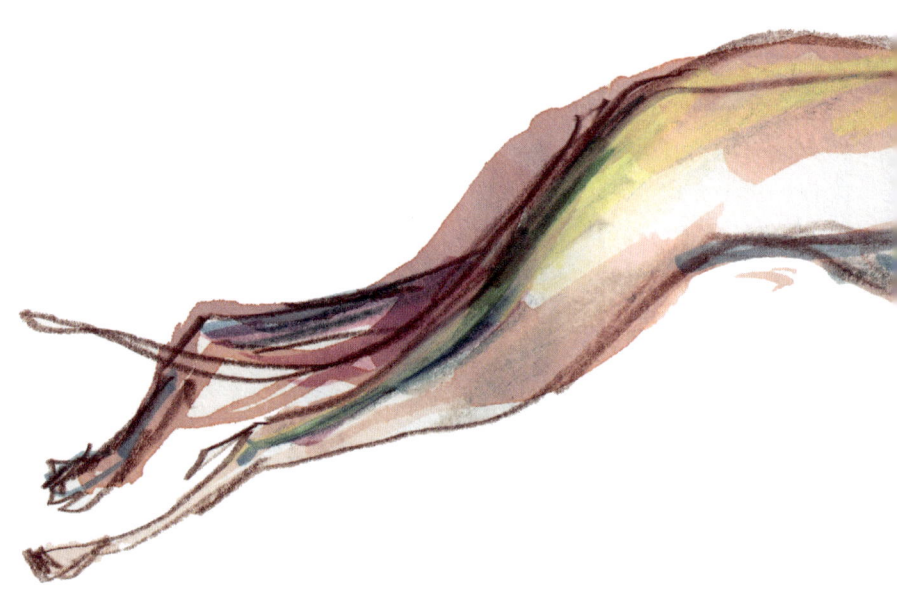

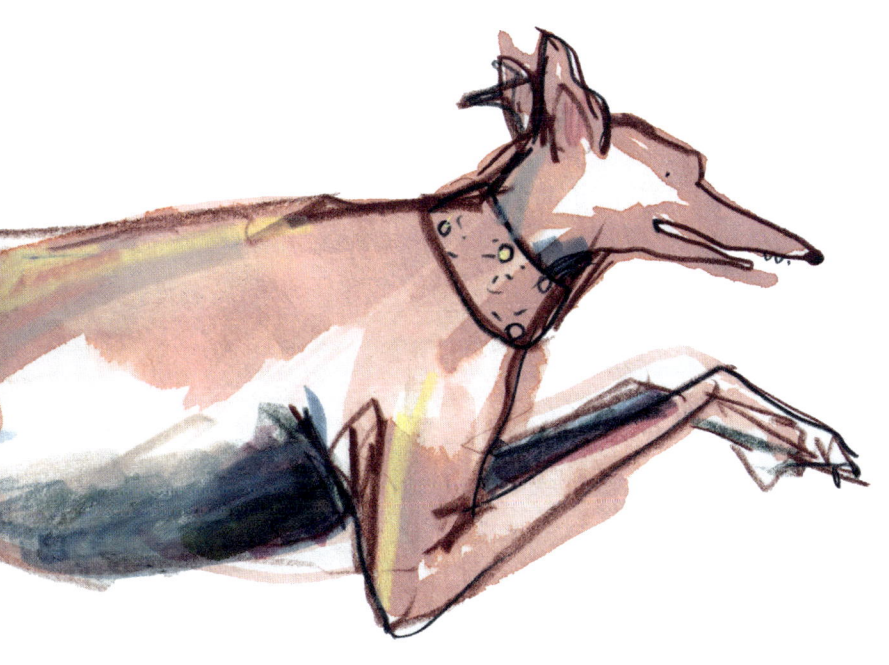

157

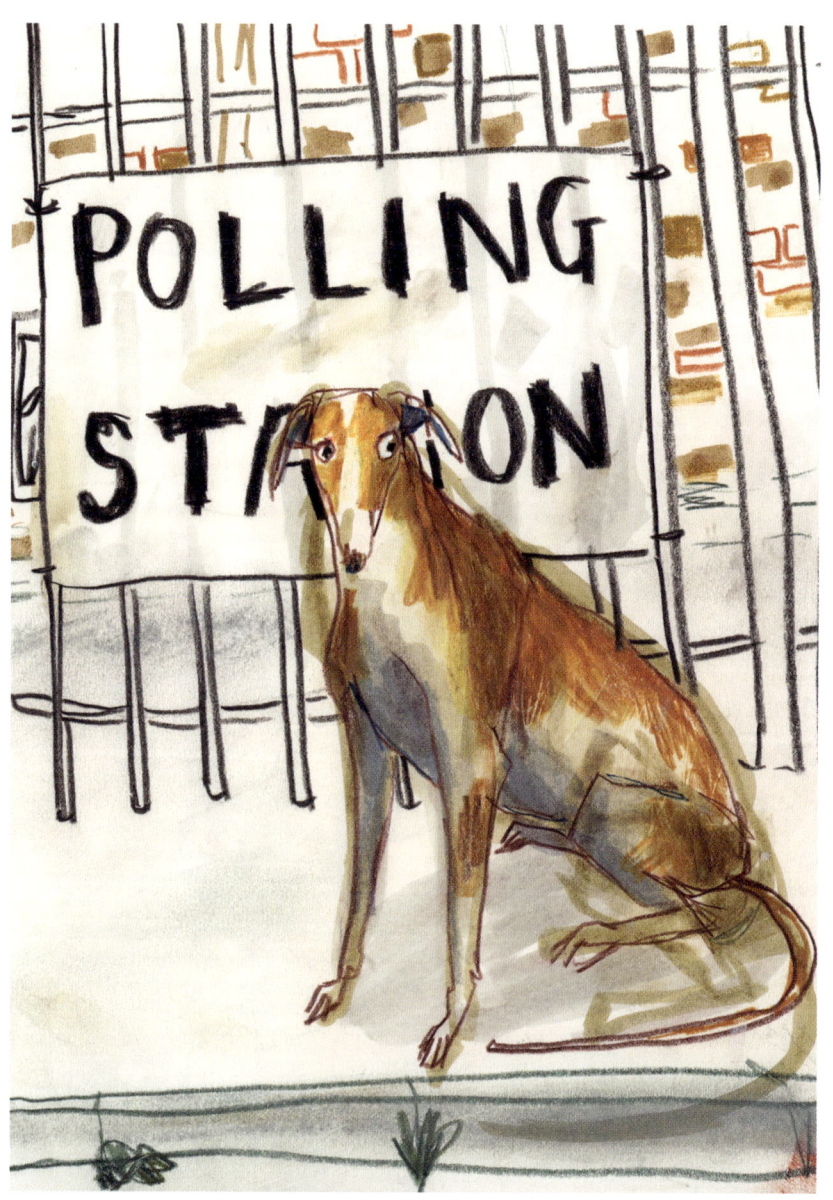

158

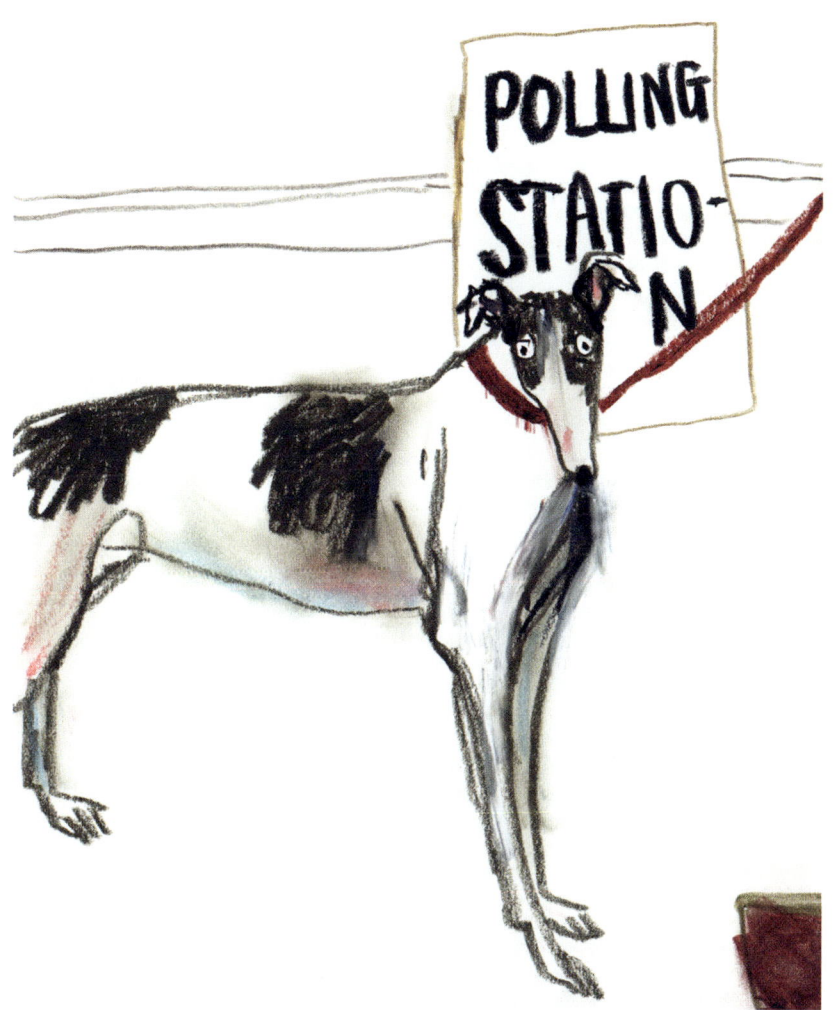

159

Yes, yes I am

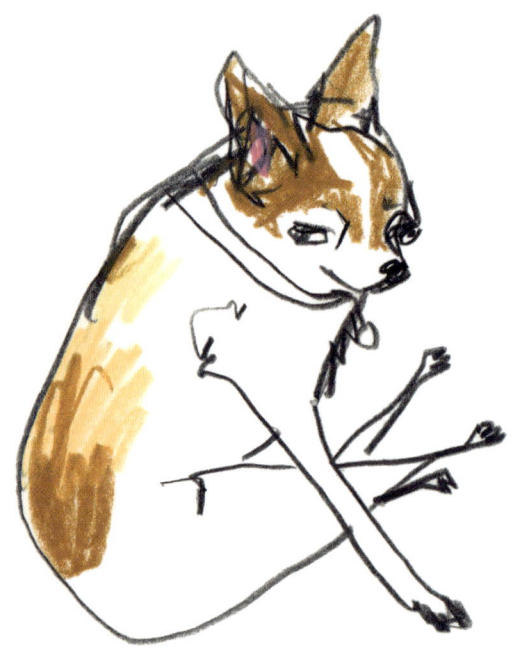

a very good dog

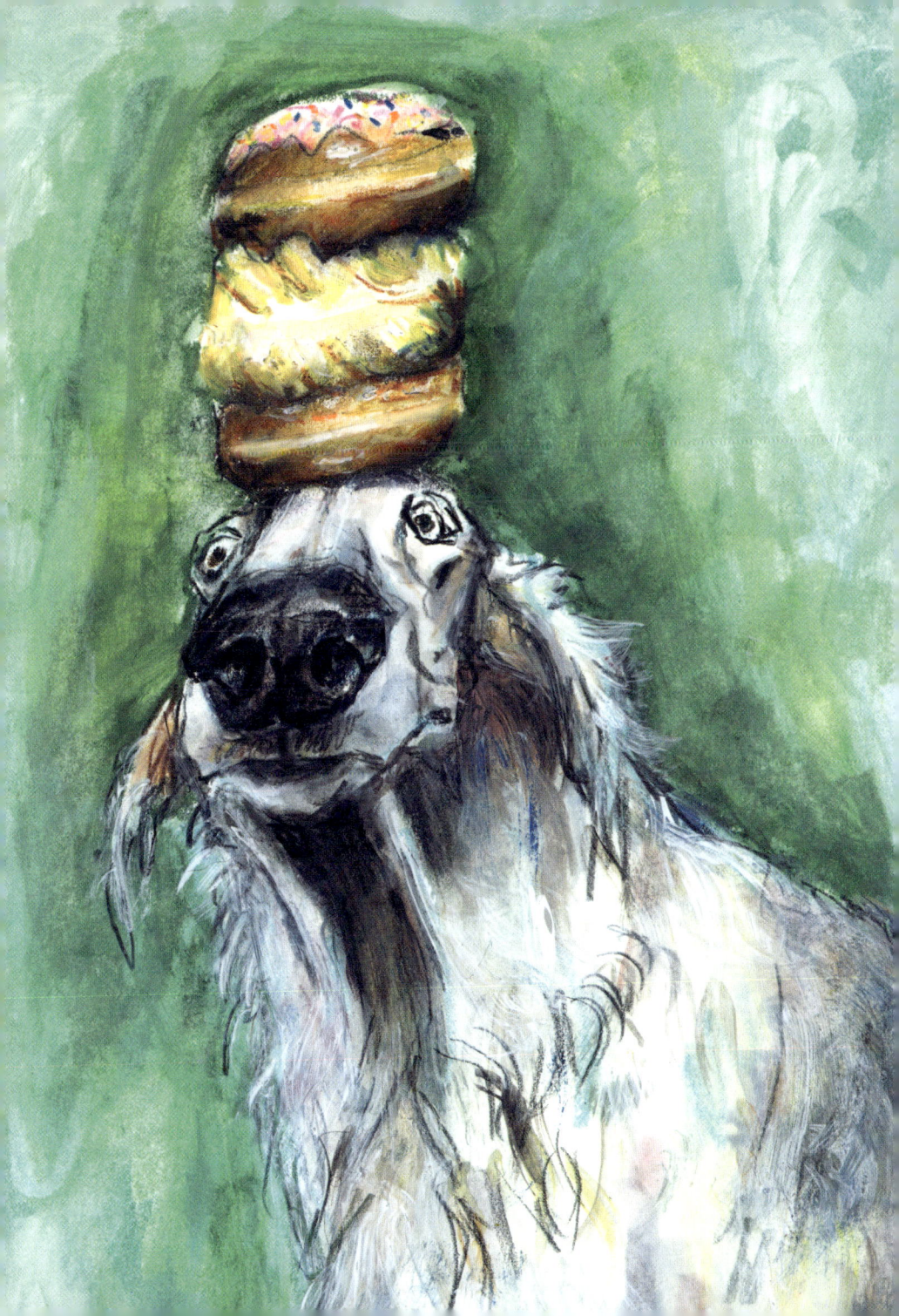

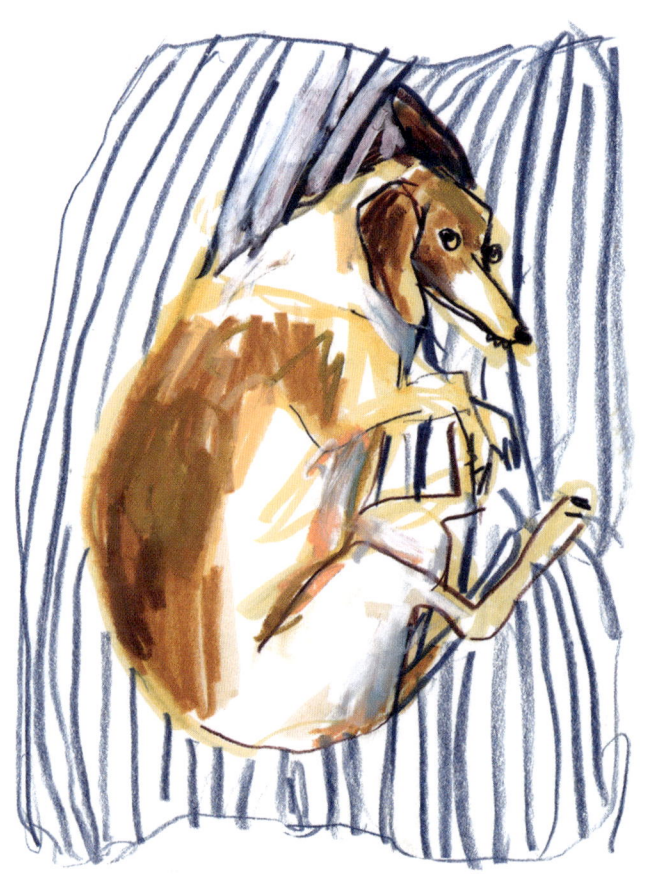

162

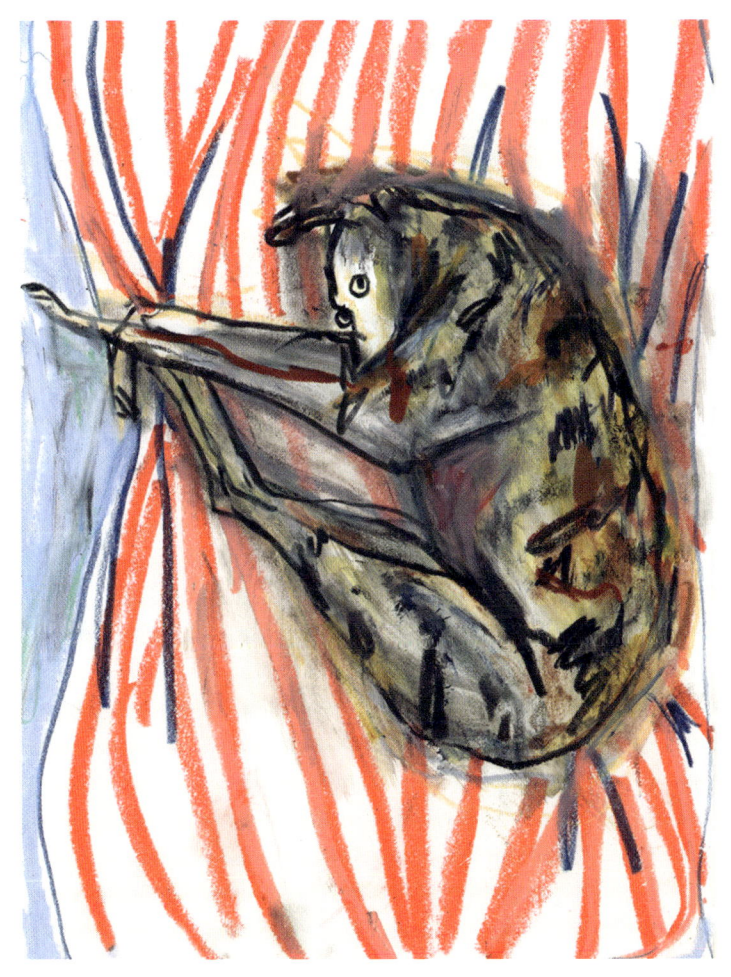

163

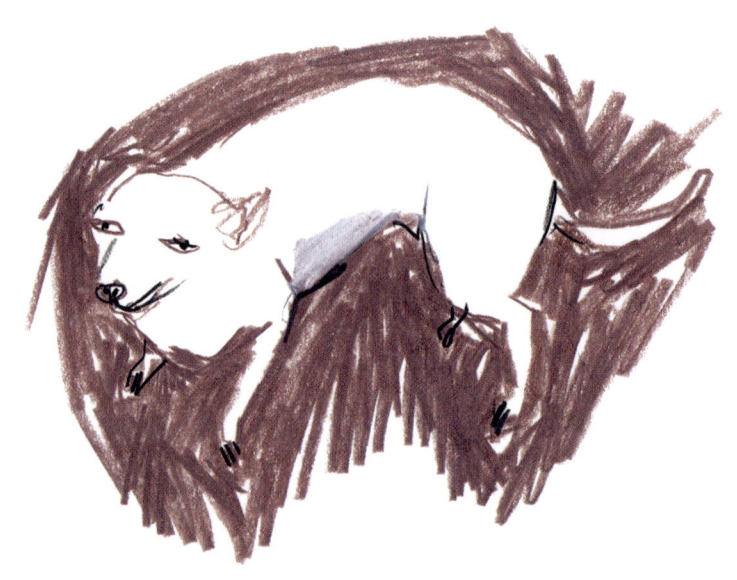

Blep.

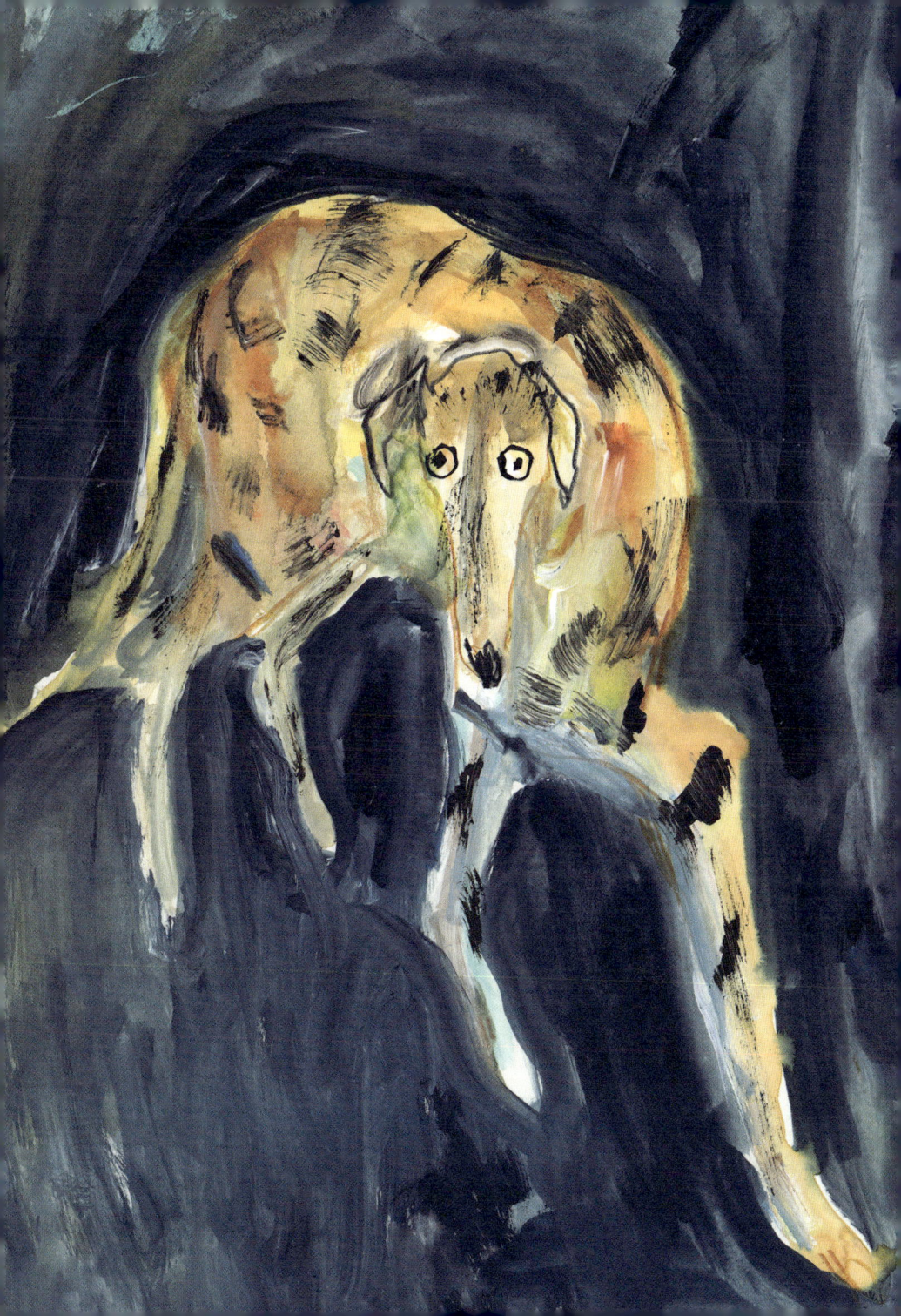

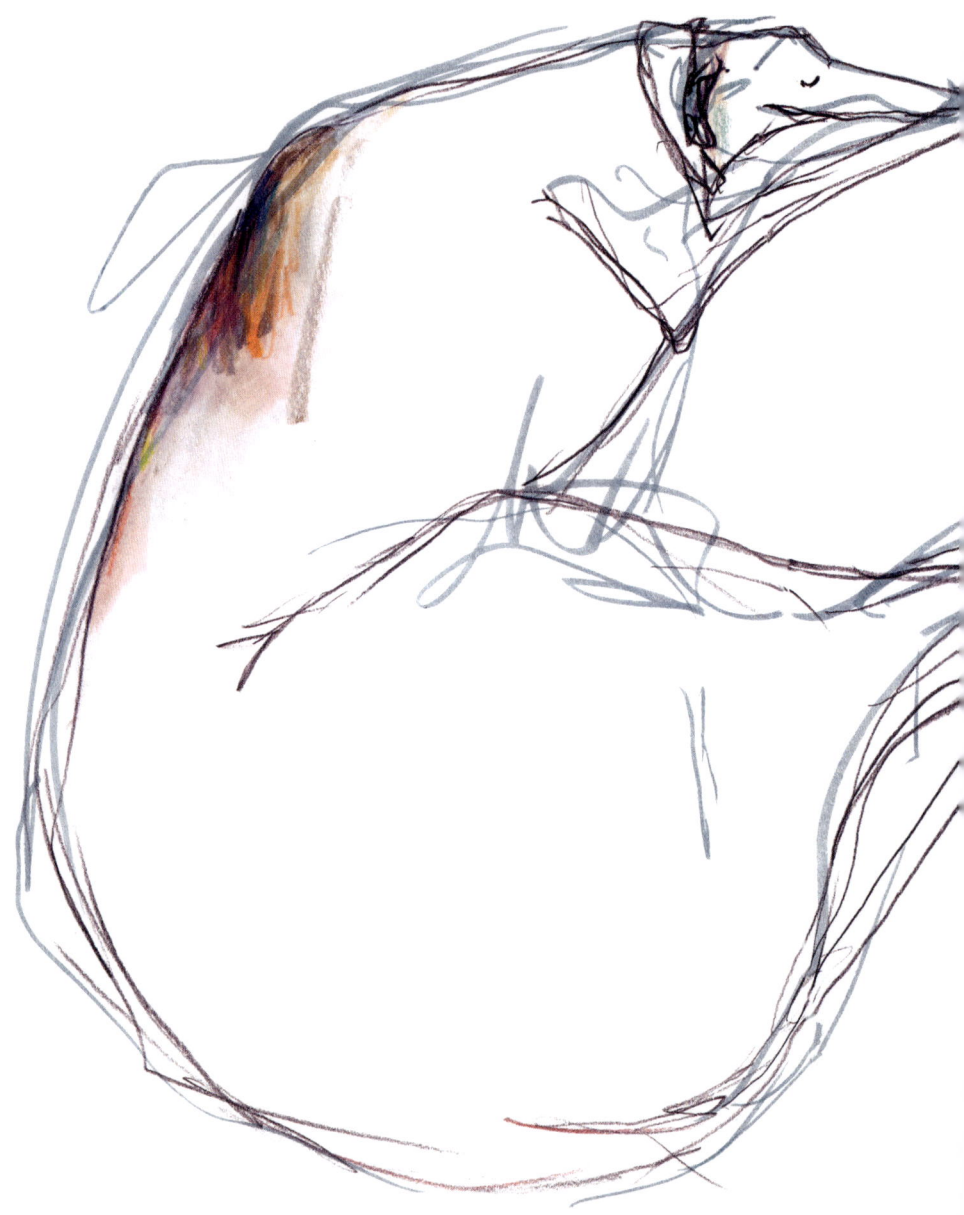

166

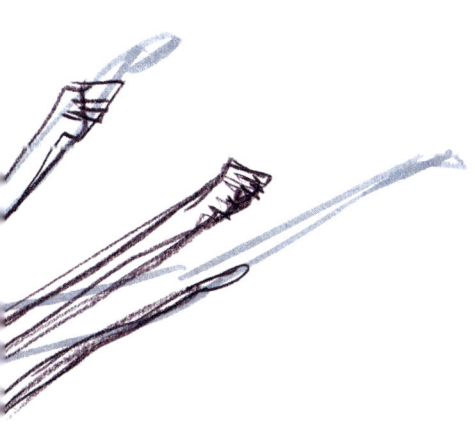

Sleep more

167

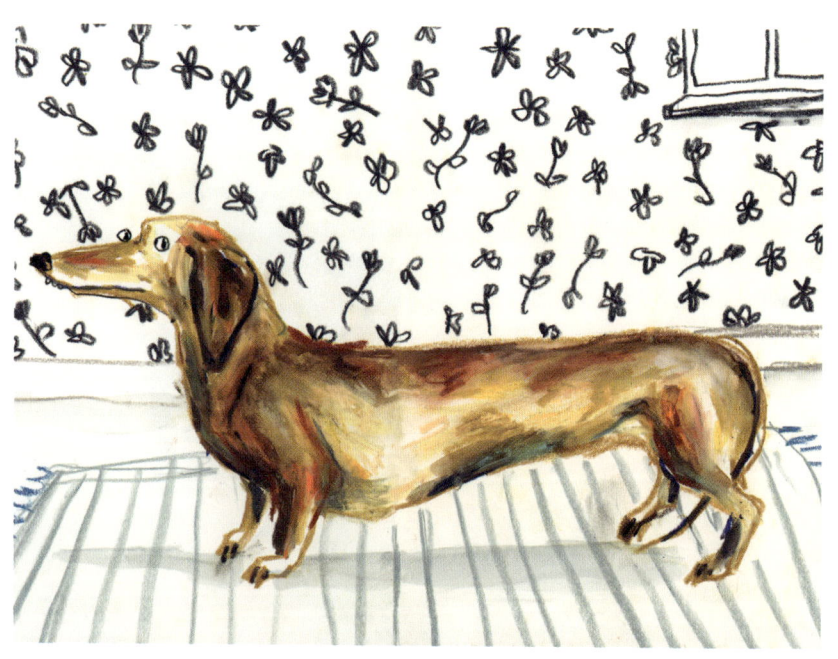

168

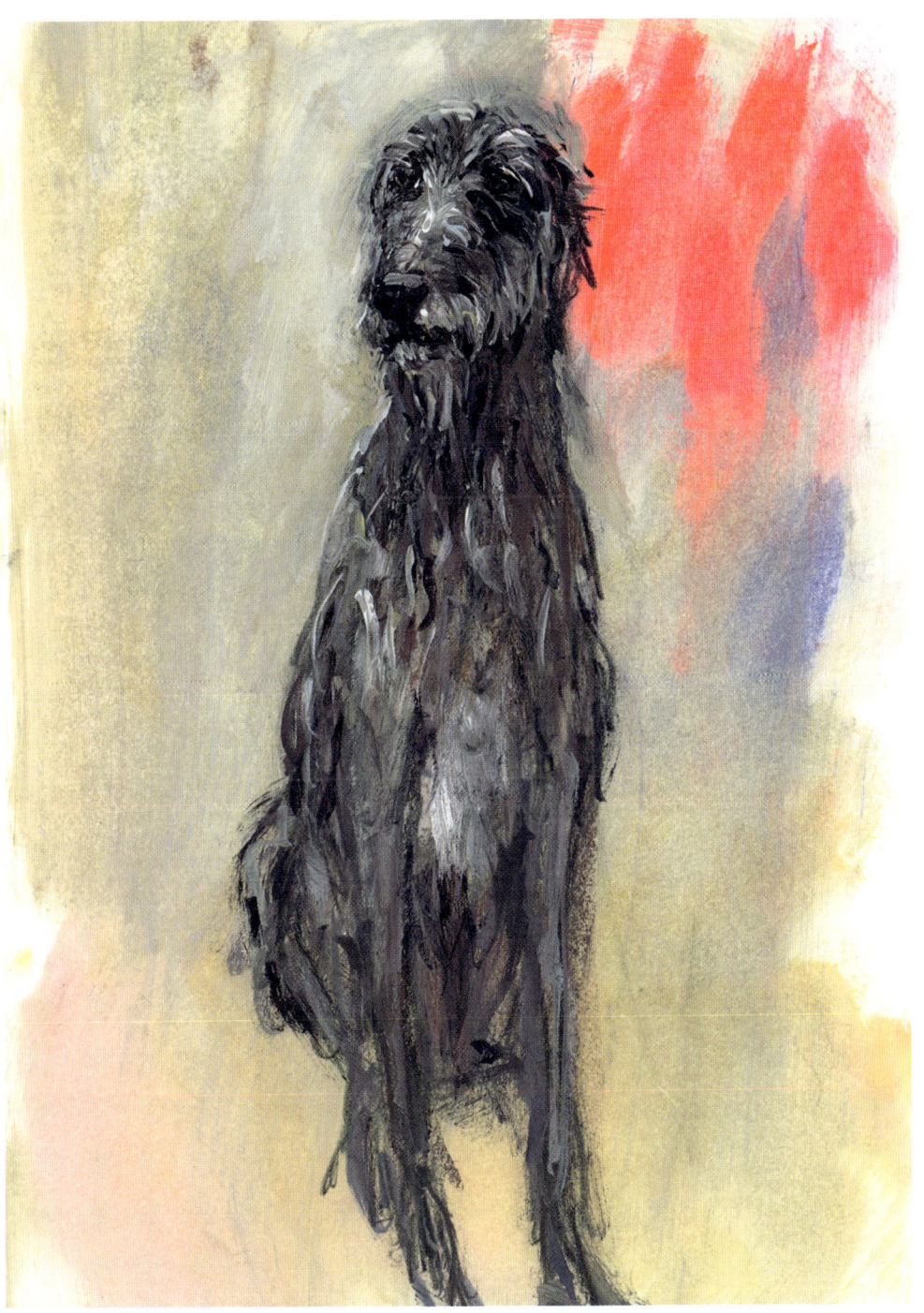

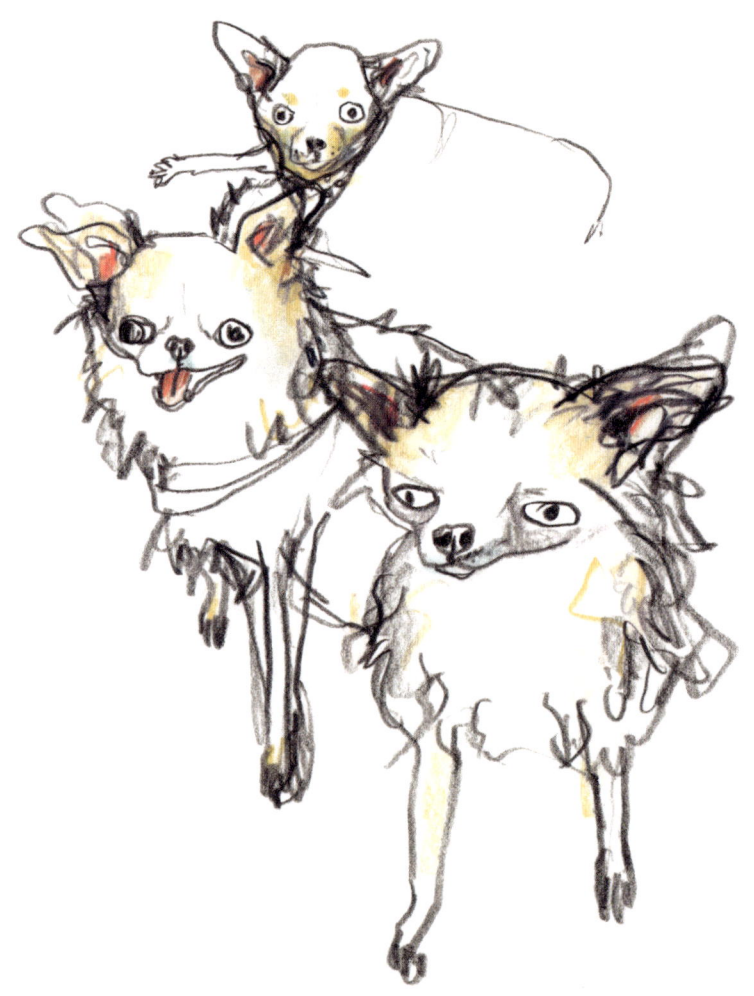

170

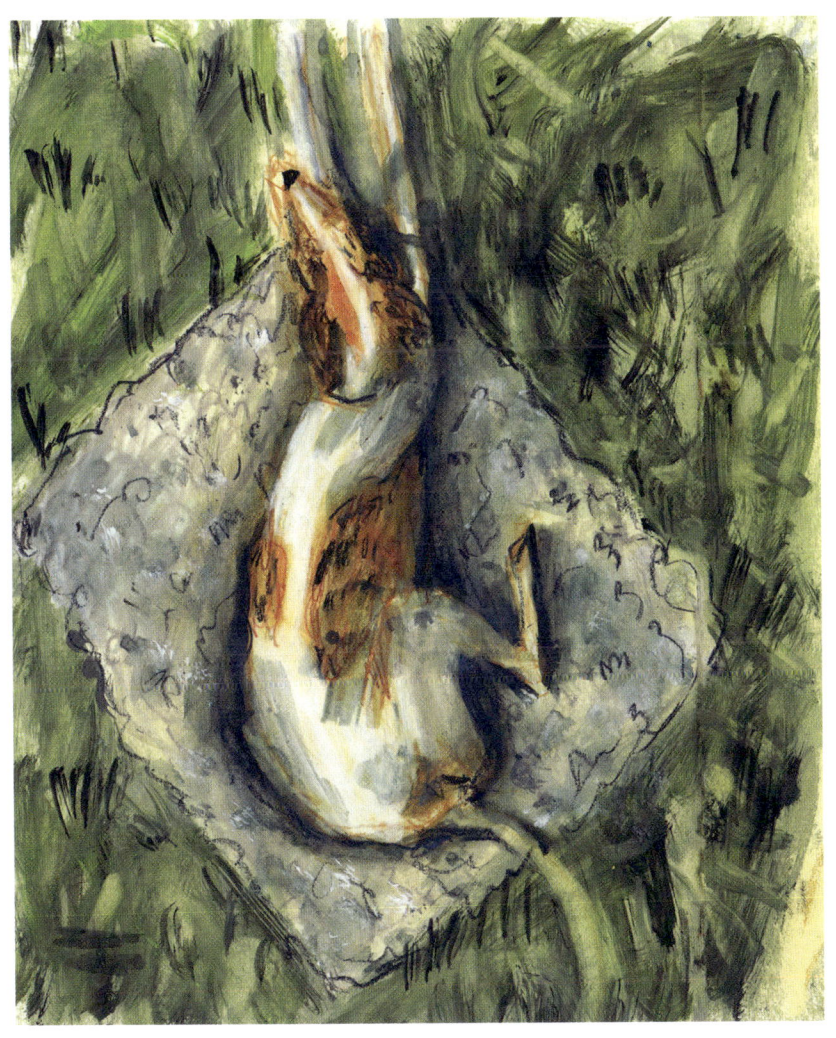

171

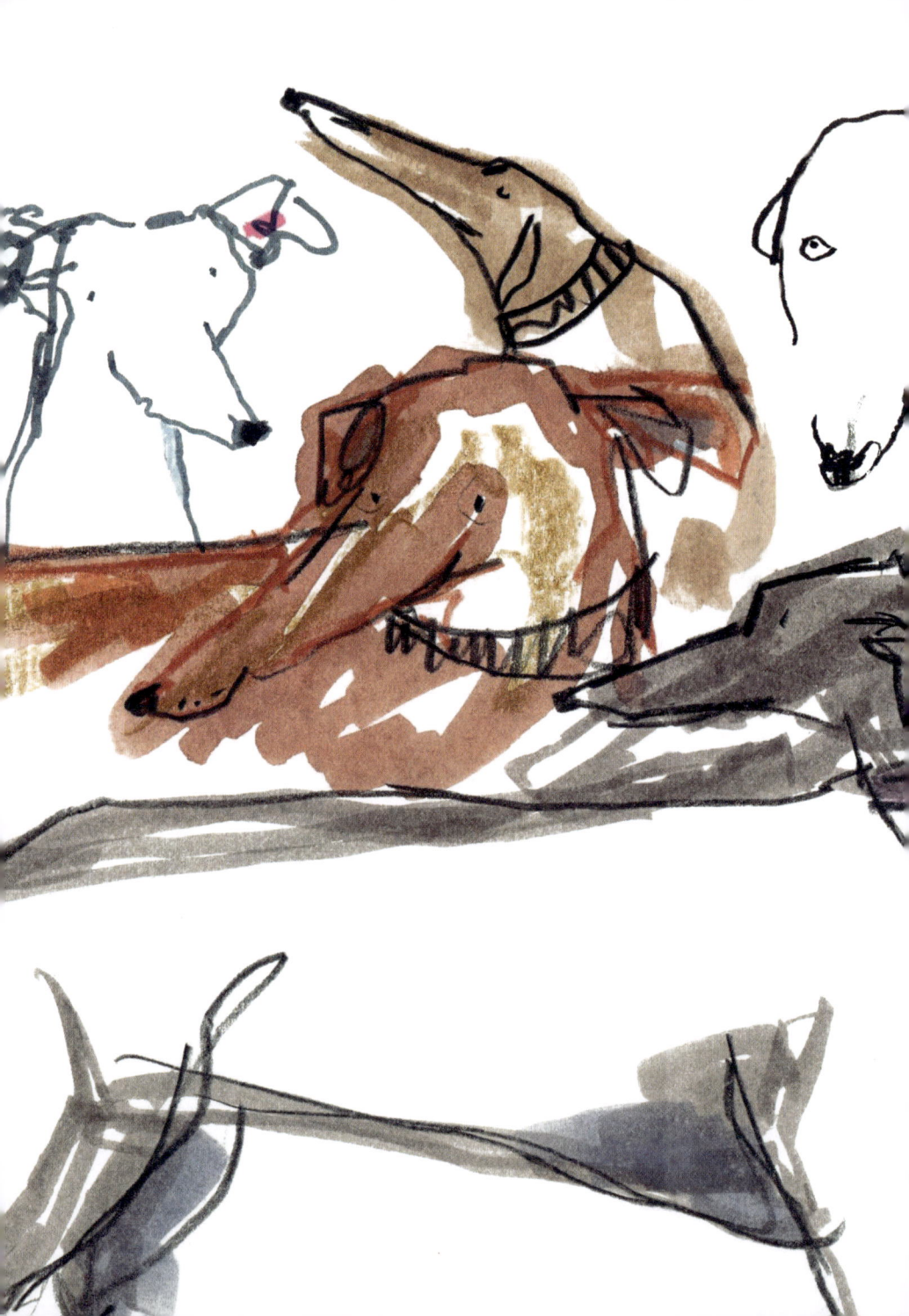

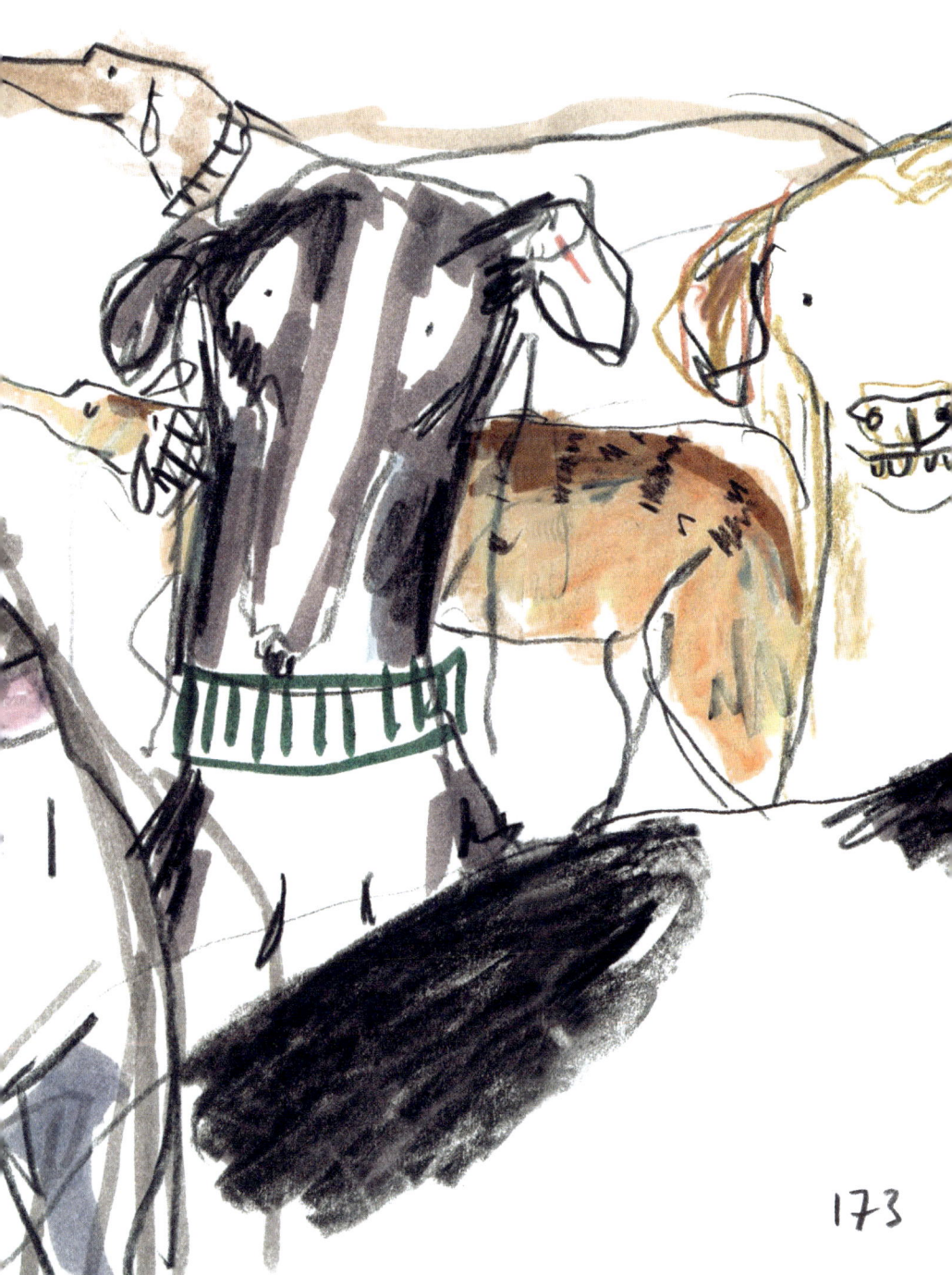

173

ACKNOWLEDGEMENTS

Why am I imagining accepting an Oscar when I say: I want to thank my Mum and Dad and my family for their continued love and support. *checks microphone* Maybe there is just no other way to say it, although I'm much happier writing this from my garden studio in Wiltshire in compost-laden stretchy pants, unkempt hair and a cat sat next to me (really had to try and sneak Sean Connery in here somewhere). From the very beginning, Mum and Dad have been there for me in all of the ways. Thank you Mum for looking at every single drawing I sent you in the very beginning, and patiently giving me advice and feedback. Thank you so much Dad for pointing at my products and being a marketing force to be reckoned with, and a celebrity in your own right.

A huge shout-out to my 'camp family', my close-knit community of neighbours who really are my second family. You've supported me every step of the way, and I love you all so much.

Thank you to my dearest and best friend Emma Carlisle. I'd be lost without her support, her love and her practical advice and patience. She keeps me on track, makes me laugh, and knows me better than I know myself.

Biggest love to my Breakfast Club drawing family: Frances, Lucy, Sarah, Emma, Emily and Becca. Our time spent together, drawing those Covid-y hours away was so precious and fun, and helped me to make work which brings me joy.

Special mention to my biggest boy, Doughnut. You've taught me so much about dogs, life, communication and patience. You are my world and I love you for being you.

Thank you to the entire team at Frances Lincoln. I really, honestly do not know how you've put up with me, and I am forever grateful to you for trusting me and my process, to produce a book which is truly me.

174

Most importantly, I want to thank you. Yes I'm looking at you, the one who is reading this. This book would not have been possible without you. You, who have supported me on this journey so far. You, the wonderful people who have shared your dogs, their lives and their journeys with me. You, who have bought something from my little business, or shared something I've made online, or enjoyed something I've drawn and let me know. You are the people who warm my heart daily, and make me want to carry on drawing.

I really wanted to reach out to every single person whose dog might be in this book, but this mammoth task really was too much for me. But I want you to know how very grateful I am, even if I have not been able to contact you directly. There are a few of you (you know who you are) whose dogs I have come back to draw time and time again. You hold a special place in my heart, and in this book.

Please, please make sure you Tell Your Dog I Love Them.

Harriet x

ABOUT Harriet

Harriet Lowther, owner and creator of Made by Harriet, is a Wiltshire-based artist and illustrator, whose subjects range from animals to plants and interiors. Her preferred subject, and what she is most well-known for, is her dogs.

Harriet creates quirky, expressive illustrated drawings using a tonne of mixed media, including in gouache, acrylic, pen and ink, crayon and water-based brush pens. Harriet enjoys experimenting with pattern, text, colour and different mediums, whilst turning some of her drawings into products for her online shop. Working out of a roomy and chaotic garden studio, she not only produces original drawings, but also homewares, ceramic pieces and prints of her work.

Quarto

First published in 2025 by Frances Lincoln,
an imprint of The Quarto Group.
One Triptych Place, London, SE1 9SH,
United Kingdom
T (0)20 7700 9000
www.Quarto.com

EEA Representation, WTS Tax d.o.o., Žanova ulica 3, 4000 Kranj, Slovenia

Text and Illustrations Copyright © 2025 Harriet Lowther
Design Copyright © 2025 Quarto Publishing Plc

A catalogue record for this book is available from the British Library.

ISBN 978-1-8360-0420-2
Ebook ISBN 978-1-8360-0421-9

10 9 8 7 6 5 4 3 2 1

Design by Sarah Pyke

Publisher: Philip Cooper
Editor: Katerina Menhennet
Senior Designer: Isabel Eeles
Production Controller: Rohana Yusof

Printed in China

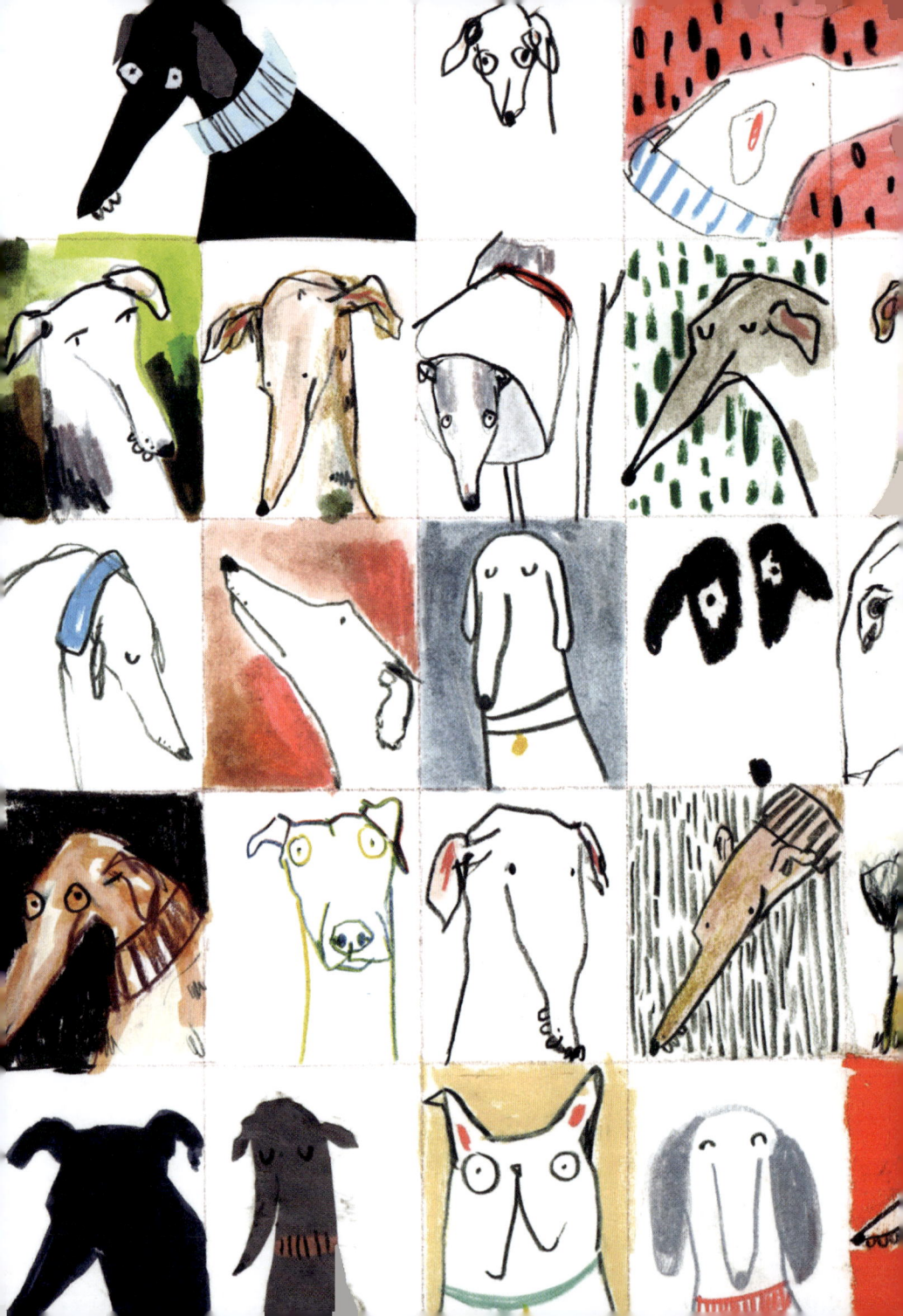